AN ILLINI PLACE

AN ILLINI PLACE

Building the University of Illinois Campus

LEX TATE and JOHN FRANCH

Foreword by

STANLEY O. IKENBERRY

UNIVERSITY OF ILLINOIS PRESS
Urbana, Chicago, and Springfield

Manufactured in the United States of America
C 5 4 3 2 1
∞ This book is printed on acid-free paper.

Cataloging-in-Publication Data available
from the Library of Congress
ISBN 970-0-252-04111-2 (cloth: alk)
ISBN 970-0-252-09981-6 (ebook)

Dedicated to all who plan, design, build, care for, and walk this Illini Place.

We shape our buildings, and afterwards our buildings shape us.

—Winston Churchill, House of Commons,
London, October 28, 1943

Contents

Foreword

The Urbana-Champaign campus of the University of Illinois is among the most beautiful and expansive of any university campus in America. It is an inspiring place with stories to tell. For generations students and faculty have walked the broad expanses of green and entered imposing architectural structures, many of which were created long ago. They come here to learn, to search, to discover. They carry out research; they create, grow, perform, and mature. They engage in debate and contest ideas. They share and collaborate. They forge lifelong bonds; and some even fall in love.

This is the day-to-day life and work that takes place on the campus of a great university. When one walks across this vast campus today, the design and architecture appear more or less coherent. The Illini Union and Foellinger Auditorium anchor a grand quad at the core of what has become a vast enterprise. The campus stretches from the Beckman Institute at the north to the agricultural farms at the south, evolving for more than a century and a half, offering a home for students and faculty members from a vast array of disciplines. What happens here changes lives of those who go on to change the world.

The creation of the University of Illinois in 1867 signaled the emergence of a new kind of campus that would define the American research university as we know it today. The Morrill Act passed by the United States Congress in 1862 was signed by Illinois's own President Lincoln. The act offered incentives—federal grants of land or the proceeds from the sale of such lands—to be used to create universities in each state, "to teach such branches of learning as are related to agriculture and the mechanic arts, in such manner as the legislatures of the States may respectively prescribe, in order to promote the liberal and practical education of the industrial classes in the several pursuits and professions in life."

The consequences were profound: who would go to college, what would be taught, the role of research and public service—all were altered as a result of the Morrill Act. The introduction of science, engineering, and agriculture as part of the curriculum paved the way for expansion of the curriculum that ultimately included the many other disciplines and professions. College was no longer for the few—for those preparing for the ministry, or sons of the wealthy. Under the Morrill or "Land Grant" Act universities were created to welcome the children of farmers and shopkeepers who studied alongside those from big cities like Chicago.

These new institutions—arguably born in Illinois in the mid-nineteenth century—grew to form a national network of high-quality university campuses that today defines the unique character of much of American higher education—Minnesota, UC-Berkeley, Cornell, Illinois, Ohio State, Michigan State, Penn State, and countless others from coast to coast. If one were to point to a single event that shaped the origin and character of the University of Illinois, it would be the founding impetus provided by Mr. Lincoln and the Morrill Act.

Two University of Illinois presidents stand out as especially critical in the early years of the campus. The first "regent" or president was John Milton Gregory, who provided the strength of leadership, vision, and continuity (with his thirteen years at the helm) to ensure the fledging university would survive. It was President Edmund James, however, president of the university for sixteen years shortly after the turn of the twentieth century, whose leadership defined the commitment to excellence, academic vision and ambition, and scale and breadth of reach we know today. Very early in its history, Illinois was known as a great university, and that solid foundation survives today.

Events of each era shaped the development of the campus. Two world wars and the Great Depression stymied growth. On the other hand, returning World War II veterans, the baby boom, elevated aspirations for college attendance, new federal initiatives to fund research—these and other developments shaped the environment for campus expansion and development over the years.

Illinois governors, legislators, and benefactors played a major role in shaping the development of the university campus, its facilities, and positions of academic leadership. Jim Thompson and Jim Edgar, along with legislative leaders of the era, including Stan Weaver, were a powerful force for good during my tenure. Private philanthropy also came to play a formidable role; among the most notable during my tenure were Arnold Beckman and his wife, Mabel. Son of a blacksmith from Cullom, Arnold was a chemistry student on the Urbana-Champaign campus who went on to complete his doctorate at Caltech. His storied career has been chronicled elsewhere, but his passion for Illinois and his gift of $40 million in the 1980s transformed science and technology at the University of Illinois.

While every university campus has some variety in its architectural style, the Urbana-Champaign campus during the 1950s, 1960s, and 1970s had no unifying theme or character. Inevitably, there are mistakes born of inconsistent planning and shortsighted decisions, but Illinois had vastly more than its share. The magnitude of the Beckman gift in the 1980s forced a complete rethinking of the architectural character (in the Georgian tradition) and the campus layout, beginning on the north campus and the renaissance of the engineering campus moving on to a profound re-visioning of the central and south areas of the campus.

Ultimately, universities—their plans and facilities and the priorities and commitments that underlie them—reflect the values, aspirations, and choices made by the society of which they are a part. The University of Illinois is a great university because those who went before were determined to make it so. In the absence of that aspiration and foresight, universities like Illinois and their scholars and students would not exist, nor would their inventions and creativity.

Ours and every generation owes a debt to those who went before. *An Illini Place* enables us to grasp a sense of how it all began, the obstacles that were overcome, the opportunities that were seized, the people who made it happen, and the vision and values that sustained it.

May this history be a fitting prelude to the years that lie ahead.

Stanley O. Ikenberry
June 2016

Acknowledgments

Significant anniversaries demand significant celebrations. And so it is with the sesquicentennial of the founding of the Illinois Industrial University in 1867 in one building set on ten acres, with a Baptist minister regent and a board of trustees asked to chart a future on the boggy prairie of central Illinois.

This book looks only at the "place" of the Urbana-Champaign campus: its midwestern grid pattern of city and campus streets crossing a narrow spine of green spaces—quadrangles—running miles north to south from University Avenue; its massive classroom and research structures; its subtle and restrained landscaping.

Retired University of Illinois architect Roland Kehe proposed in 2005 that a book about campus planning be written. It would be a successor to the Tilton and O'Donnell book begun in 1919, provided to the trustees as manuscript in 1920, and finally published by the University Press in 1930. The 2005 proposal morphed into a more general, popular look at the campus from 1867 to today and is part of the celebration of the 150th anniversary of the university's charter. Kehe's second contribution was successfully approaching a vice president, a chancellor, and an executive director for financial support for research, writing, and photography, and a production subsidy for what would become *An Illini Place*. Finally, Kehe assembled a tiny think tank of University of Illinois affiliates to guide the early development of the basic structure or skeleton of the book on which hangs stories of campus growth and change for 150 years. For all this we acknowledge with gratitude Roland Kehe.

Thanks also to the book committee who assisted the authors in the formative stages: Stanley O. Ikenberry, the university's longest-serving president; architecture professor James Warfield; landscape architect and planning professor John A. Jakle; and campus historic preservation architect David Garner. Planner Alice Novak located and analyzed most of the campus plans.

If the intellectual heart of the campus is the library, the heart of this book is library research in the form of archival documents and photographs; books and contemporaneous newspaper and magazine accounts; interviews and informal conversations. The University Archives, until recently hidden in the basement of the Main Library, yielded thousands of documents that helped the authors uncover the past and recreate episodes and elements to bring life to history.

Other library departments assisted in countless ways. Special thanks are due University Archivist William J. Maher and helpful archives and library staff, including Roxanne Frey, Joanne Kaczmarek, Lisa Renee Kemplin, Christopher Prom, Jeffrey Schrader, Linda Stepp, Ellen Swain, and Bryan Whitledge. This book focuses on buildings and spaces at the Urbana-Champaign campus. Many architects, planners, engineers, and academic and other administrators helped clarify and interpret the what, how, and why of the physical campus. Thanks to Craig Bazzani, Clifford Carey, Ted L. Christy, Tony Graziano, J. Fred Green, William J. Hall, James Lev, Walter Lewis, Donald Molnar, Eugene Pitcher, Terry W. Ruprecht, Sasaki Associates (M. Perry Chapman, Stuart Dawson, Joseph Hibbard), John Severns, Melvyn Skvarla, and Joseph Vitosky.

Thanks also to data and information providers, fact checkers, draft readers, and helpers along the way: Brenda Ankenbrand, Daniel Audette, Trish Barker, Chris Beuoy, Division of Intercollegiate Athletics (Kent Brown, Marla Glasser, and John Lock), Thomas Eakman, Vanessa Faurie and the Alumni Association, Roxanne Frey, Beth Leitz of Facilities and Services, University Foundation (Edward Ewald, Donald Kojich and John Fundator), Illini Media Co. (Lil Levant), J. Michael Lillich, Lawrence Mann, the *News-Gazette* (especially John Foreman), Rebecca Salzman, and Marie Wilson.

For financing: B. Joseph White and Stephen Rugg in the president and vice president's offices; Urbana-Champaign Chancellor Richard H. Herman; and Sidney Micek and Bazzani at the University Foundation.

Photographers: Facilities and Services (Seth Gunnerson, J. Todd Hearn, Chei-Wei Liang and Steve Thompson); L. Brian Stauffer of the campus News Bureau, Darrell Hoemann, who rescued us at the tenth and eleventh hours; and Karyl Wackerlin, who joined this adventure on day 1; and Michael Holtz, who provided the magnificent photographs of Allerton Park and Retreat Center for chapter 8.

Writer Maureen Holtz, who has written extensively about Allerton, contributed the text for the chapter 8 section on Allerton Park and Retreat Center.

The endgame was challenging; the manuscript had thousands of moving parts—words, images, captions, credits, photos, notes—that needed untangling, wrangling, and refining. Special thanks to J. Michael Lillich and John Fundator for their critical help in 2015-16.

The University Press was patient, professional, and helpful on the long journey to *An Illini Place*. Thanks to former director and acquisitions editor Willis "Bill" Regier, editor and director Laurie C. Matheson, production assistant Julianne Laut, production editor Jennifer Clark, copyeditor Julie Gay, and designer Jennifer S. Holzner.

Thousands of bits of information and tens of thousands of words make up this book. The authors gratefully credit all who contributed in the countless ways they did. Errors of fact and interpretation fall on the authors, both of whom, as students and employees, walked the Illini Place.

Invitation to the Companion Web Site

http://www.press.uillinois.edu/books/tate_franch/illini_place/

A companion Web site for *An Illini Place*, created by the University of Illinois Press, offers a rich array of photos and new text content, including short stories about ten men key to the campus's physical development—planners, architects, and presidents—and inventories of campus plans and buildings, current and long gone. Teasers throughout the book text point to some of this extra content on the site. We invite you to visit to take full advantage of this expanded resource.

AN ILLINI PLACE

CHAPTER 1

Prairie to Petascale

An Overview

On the southwestern edge of the Urbana-Champaign campus of the University of Illinois, a two-story glass foyer glows blue against the dark night of Oak Street and St. Mary's Road. The rear of the simple modern rectangular building is unbroken brick veneer and backs onto the campus mail and recycling centers and is a stone's throw from the South Neil Street commercial corridor.

Inside, two-foot-diameter pipes circulate chilled water around the massive electrical system that services the resident supercomputer; the data center machine room, with its below-floor vast array of cables, is efficiently water and air cooled. This is the house where Blue Waters lives.

The building is the National Petascale Computing Facility (NPCF), an eighty-eight-thousand-square-foot structure designed by Gensler, an international architecture and engineering firm. Its $72.5 million cost was picked up by the state; grants exceeding $200 million through 2016 support both the equipment and users of Blue Waters from across the globe.

Day and night, in the boundary-less reaches of cyberspace, researchers run powerful calculations to mimic tornadoes and earthquakes, to study proteins, and to simulate the evolution of the cosmos. Big questions require big data. Blue Waters, a product of Cray Inc., after IBM dropped out in 2011, at its peak can make more than thirteen quadrillion calculations per second. That's thirteen followed by fifteen zeroes.

The building and program belong to the National Center for Supercomputing Applications, which began in 1986 with a little Cray computer wired into one floor of a campus building on Springfield Avenue.

NCSA, including Blue Waters, exemplifies the extraordinary strength of the campus to actualize big ideas in computer science, engineering, and genomics; to gather resources in the form of state, national, and private money; to create functional, durable, and sometimes beautiful work spaces—teaching and research buildings—and to locate these spaces according to a plan. In this case, NPCF is one block from the northernmost edge of the campus's Research Park, itself a product of clever partnerships.

NPCF represents the leading edge of a campus that was born 150 years ago into poverty in a single building between the towns of Champaign and Urbana. Once the thick blanket of tall prairie grasses and flowers linking the two towns was broken and its treasure—rich soil, called loess—a gift of the glaciers—that anchors the region's extraordinary production agriculture—was uncovered, the logic of picking this place for a new kind of American university was obvious.

By 1818, fifty years before the first students set foot on campus, Illinois was a state with an important toehold on a great lake where a great city would arise, but the center portion of the state came to be called the Grand Prairie.

The Grand Prairie was dotted with groves of trees, streams, and ponds but mostly it was rich, swampy earth covered in grasses and flowers. In Big Grove, about four miles northeast of what is now downtown Urbana, a squatter became a permanent settler in 1822 and filed a claim for land. Champaign County was created from the larger Vermilion County to the east in 1833. Railroads linked cities and villages. The U.S. Congress approved, and a lanky, adopted Illinoisan, Abraham Lincoln, in 1862 signed into law the means to help states create new public universities focused primarily on agriculture and engineering.

The Illinois land-grant university in 1867, then called Illinois Industrial University, settled in a secondhand building on the Grand Prairie with John Milton Gregory its first regent. Gregory boldly led IIU from 1867 to 1880, determined the school would exceed its charter and reach well beyond agriculture, engineering, and military science, the core of the federal land-grant act.

Gregory's grave—the only one on the campus itself—is marked with a granite boulder that tumbled south from the Canadian Shield, was shuffled around by repeated cycles of glaciers moving forward and melting back, and was uncovered when Lincoln Hall was excavated. The modest grave marker observes that Gregory's monument is all around—a twenty-first-century university whose prairie roots profoundly shaped both its sense of place and view that the horizon was limitless.

Isabel Bevier visited the campus before joining the faculty in 1900 and remarked on the openness of the space where the adolescent University of Illinois was growing. "I thought I had never seen so flat and so muddy a place: no trees, no hills, no boundaries of any kind. This lack of boundaries, physical and mental . . . opened up a whole new world to me."

Three decades later, U of I architect T. E. O'Donnell called the prairie the University's heritage, "a great sweep of open [space] which fairly invited growth and development and a natural fertility of soil which in time has grown our beautiful campus setting."

That campus's first (and only) building, disparaged as "The Elephant," was nearly 2.5 miles northeast from where Blue Waters is housed today and illustrates several thrusts that have driven campus growth and development since 1867, namely that the campus has grown from north to south, that the campus was planned, and that the planning was purposeful and event driven.

These three thrusts—or themes—are woven through *An Illini Place* and can help make sense of a campus with hundreds of buildings erected over fifteen decades on hundreds of acres. Chapters 2 through 6 present key features of planning, building, and landscaping the campus chronologically from 1867 to 2015. Each is set in the context of the economic climate and ambition of leaders of the time.

The goal of *An Illini Place* is to try to answer one question: Why does the campus look as it does?

Even the earliest U of I campus could be seen by some as growing randomly, but it was not. Its first map in 1871 sectioned the campus into four parts, creating a rudimentary plan. Soon the siting of a major new building, University Hall, shifted the campus south. And this southward push, clearly evident on nearly ninety campus plans since that first one, is obvious.

Campus growth, then, is seen as inexorable, relentless, uneven, and mostly from north to south. Here's an example:

The first board of trustees, months before the campus even opened to students, bought nearly forty acres of land that stretched a half-mile south of its first and only building. That land purchase bridged and consolidated holdings from its original charter, including 405 acres south of Mount Hope Cemetery. In following decades, the U of I farms and horticulture tracts were pushed from what is now the south end of the Quad to the Village of Savoy. The campus today extends north to south some seven miles, occupying about 4,550 acres, on which sit 320 major buildings (of 647 total), excluding farm, temporary, and off-campus properties, such as Allerton Park.

Related to this relentless growth is land acquisition. The campus routinely buys land before it needs it, and then holds it, typically through deals with the University of Illinois Foundation, which was established in 1935. This practice shows both ambition and foresight. An example: the campus had longtime designs on an older residential and light-business neighborhood to the east of the northern portion of the engineering campus. It was intended for college expansion, including a possible research park that would play to the extraordinary strengths and ambitions of engineering at the university.

So the U of I Foundation quietly bought up properties as they came available, held them as landlord, paid taxes, and waited. The 1985 Arnold and Mabel Beckman gift of $40 million, matched with $10 million in state money, meant the campus could build a massive research center with U of I Foundation land and other parcels acquired through eminent domain condemnation. Done well, land banking can hedge against both inflation and speculation, though both certainly occur near the campus episodically.

As the campus moved south, it centered its building program on a meridian, a north-south spine running from University Avenue on the north to Pennsylvania Avenue on the south. If one stands at the highest level of the Beckman Institute and looks south, this spine—punctuated by buildings oriented perpendicular to the meridian—is obvious. Along the spine are the north or Beckman Quad, with an egregiously off-center Grainger Library; the Bardeen Quad, opening south from Springfield Avenue to the Illini Union; the (main) Quad, bracketed north and south by the Illini Union and Foellinger Auditorium; and the South Quad, linked on the north by the Undergraduate Library and terminating in the Stock Pavilion on Pennsylvania Avenue. Along the spine are malls or open spaces with sidewalks, artwork, and landscaping.

Not so successful as the campus's strong north-south orientation are efforts to create and sustain a strong east-west spine on the old Military Axis, near long-gone cavalry and military parade grounds south of the Armory. This east-west axis shows up decade after decade in campus plans and as academic exercises by urban planning and architectural landscaping students, but it did not develop as an organizing feature. A large plot of open land on the axis between Fourth and Sixth Streets and between the Business Instructional Facility and the Art and Design Building is ripe for development, an example of necessary infill. Trustees have approved a $48 million interdisciplinary Design Center, which will form a western terminus on the east-west axis.

That planners took up the east-west axis on the campus decade after decade demonstrates yet another theme of *An Illini Place*: U of I planning is repetitive and reiterative. The campus has created more than eighty plans. Some are full master plans, with vast data on projected enrollment, shifts in curriculum, and the impact of cars. Some are "snapshots" or maps or bird's-eye views of the layout of the campus at a specific moment. Some are minor adjustments from the previous year's or a previous decade's effort, tinkering around the edges.

One plan literally was revised from one day to the next in early December 1944. Some plans are major disruptors, some are fanciful, and some are special-interest plans, such as a retail-district or athletics-facilities plan. The latest planning exercise is coincident to the university's sesquicentennial and is an "in-fill" plan that acknowledges the campus will not keep expanding but will instead become more dense. SmithGroupJJR of Chicago was hired to do the plan for about $1 million.

Planning was an outgrowth of architecture and landscaping. Its earliest practitioners set out to build within a specific environment and be sympathetic to it; they wanted a good setting for their well-designed buildings.

M. Perry Chapman, a longtime planner with Sasaki Associates, said the nation's early campuses, private Eastern Seaboard schools and, later, the great public universities of the Midwest, such as the University of Illinois, "were open to the natural environment around them, and they blended that environment into the campus itself." These campus settings were "bountiful, expansive, in many ways sublime."

These deeply American campuses turned their back on the density and rules of the Old World. "The soul of the new American campus was the land," Chapman wrote in his 2006 book, *American Places: In Search of the Twenty-First Century Campus.* "Buildings were set in the landscape; they enclosed the landscape only as campuses filled out and attained urban character from the nineteenth century on."

Architect and planner Roger K. Lewis says college plans should reflect and nurture a college's history, complement its missions in teaching/research, recognize limits on space, preserve and renovate historic or significant buildings and natural features, and enforce site and design standards, with a dash of vision. A radio and *Washington Post* commentator, Lewis notes the major—and welcome—shift away from plans done "behind closed doors" to a more inclusive exercise. The U of I's plans from the late 1980s forward reflect that trend.

But whether the plan is the first, the thirty-fifth, or the seventy-eighth, two additional things are clear: leadership matters, and competing interests must be resolved. Embedded in the place of the Urbana-Champaign campus are key figures, from presidents to architects, from members of the board of trustees to outside consultants, from a hit-and-run designer to inside and long-term staffers who shaped how the campus looks today. The best physical elements of the campus and the worst are proof of the essential importance of leadership as arbiters of the look of the place. In periods of turmoil or inattentive leadership, the place suffers. Except for a brief introduction in this book, the stories of "Leading Men"—ten central figures in the physical development of the campus—can be read on the companion Web site.

Regardless of the quality of campus and university leadership, it is also clear that planning rarely occurs in a vacuum. The most important plans at Urbana-Champaign were spurred by events, such as the siting of the Auditorium, the siting of the Armory, the surge of World War II veterans jamming themselves into colleges thanks to the G.I. Bill (often with wives and kids), the tsunami of the baby boom roaring into college (after they had stretched housing and the common schools to the limit), and the selection of a site for the Beckman Institute for Advanced Science and Technology. Each of those events set off a wave of planning.

Part of planning is deciding where new buildings should go. A necessary corollary is what a new building should look like—that is, choosing a suitable style of architecture for new construction. Or not. Beginning in the 1920s, the campus began to erect Georgian Revival buildings, many by architect Charles Platt. This style, which is elegant and constrained, features red brick, green slate pitched roofs, dormers and flat chimneys, set-in windows, and horizontal courses of limestone.

Elements and echoes of the Platt style resonate throughout some newer U of I buildings even today, creating a familial look. In the same way that biological families across generations share a "look"—Aunt Emma's curly hair, Grandpa's pointed nose, sister Peg's olive skin—so does the Urbana-Champaign campus have a "look" that ties the place together.

Sometimes, of course, there are outliers, such as the stunning new Electrical and Computer Engineering Building, the Krannert Center for the Performing Arts, or the Assembly Hall, that become signature buildings.

But many buildings are adaptable over time, and needs change as well, leading to a reuse or repurposing of buildings. This often reflects the rise in importance or growth of a discipline or activity. Take present-day Altgeld Hall at the southeast corner of Wright and Green Streets. At its opening in 1896 (cost: $160,000) and until 1926 it was the University Library; from 1926 to 1940 it was the Law Building, and from 1940 to now it has housed the Math Department. Or take Harker Hall, which opened in 1878 (cost: $40,000) as the Chemistry Laboratory, was remodeled to house the law school, was remodeled again to house the Entomology Department, and, after a major interior gutting and renovation and exterior restoration in 1993, became the headquarters of the U of I Foundation.

This reuse and repurposing is possible for two reasons: high construction standards that assume a major building is good for one hundred years, and then, like Lincoln Hall, that it can be refurbished and modernized to last another hundred years. This also means few U of I buildings are demolished. Since 1901 the campus has razed only a dozen permanent buildings, excluding the ongoing "Six Pack" dormitory teardowns, which are being replaced, one by one, by new residence halls.

And while "planning" connotes serious deliberation before the result issues from a year's worth of work, it's also true that there's always room for oddball or quirky ideas to find their way into plans but fortunately not come to fruition. A lake on the Quad with a small walking bridge and the potential to ice skate in winter. A high-rise classroom-office building to replace the Auditorium, which would be torn down. Creating parking below Green Street between the Illini Union's front lawn and the engineering campus à la Chicago's Lower Wacker Drive. Or the perennial notion to buy the cemetery on the south campus, dig up and move the dead, and construct academic buildings or, alternatively, lay a north-south street linking Pennsylvania and Florida Avenues. Such ideas are the product of wild imagination meeting perceived necessity or desire. Sometimes slow-moving processes and bureaucracy, lack of money, and disruptive changes in leadership pay off.

While the National Petascale Computer Facility pushes boundaries in both computing and the geographic footprint of the campus, a national sustainability movement has rolled across American colleges the last twenty years and shows little sign of abating.

The national movement is a "big plan" to reduce greenhouse gases, support research and entrepreneurial activities in energy-use reduction, optimize space utilization, promote efficient transportation and best land use, conserve and reuse water, and handle solid waste. Universities are the perfect hothouse to think through the issues, create hypothetical and experimental models, do real work, organize change in a small setting, hypothesize scalability, and disseminate results.

The movement at Urbana-Champaign is driven primarily by cost and resource allocation, not dewy-eyed idealism. A dollar saved on heating or cooling (like the campus's new solar farm), on heavy recycling instead of transporting and landfilling garbage, on conserving water, on providing efficient campus transit for forty-five thousand students and twenty thousand faculty and staff, theoretically is a dollar available for teaching or library materials or yet another computer station.

The campus signed onto a national "climate commitment" in 2008, joined the U.S. Green Building Council and has earned kudos for a variety of environmental actions. In 2015 it updated its 2010 Illinois Climate Action Plan, advancing to 2035 its goal of being carbon neutral. Notably, new campus construction must be LEED certified, which means meeting stringent requirements for ventilation, temperature and lighting controls, construction materials, and the like. LEED (Leadership in Energy and Environmental Design) is voluntary and market responsive.

The newest major campus building is Electrical and Computer Engineering (ECE), which opened in 2014 just south of the west wing of the Beckman Institute (and blocking its view). It is the first campus building that aims for platinum LEED certification with a "net-zero" energy design, meaning it supplies its own energy using photovoltaic cells, a beam system to heat and cool classrooms, and the most advanced LED lighting available.

At its opening, ECE professor Philip Krein said the new building far exceeds any other new construction in the United States, citing the U.S. Department of Energy that there are only eight net-zero energy buildings in the country, the largest of which is a mere fourteen thousand square feet. "To achieve this in a building nearly 20 times that size reflects the University's sincere commitment to sustainable design while capturing the spirit of a department that's always pushing the limits of technological innovation," Krein said.

It is clear that the U of I's future is a complex stew of old practices (conservation/recycle) in a milieu that is energy intensive. Student laptops, tablets, and phones; computer stations or mobile connections for all employees; specialty research areas, such as clean rooms; residence halls and sports/recreation venues; and so-called smart classrooms: they all require energy and water. Simply put: New practices of energy use are key to a sustainable future, which is the only future.

❖ ❖ ❖ ❖

An Illini Place tells the story of campus growth and development from a planning and building perspective (chapters 2 through 6). But it also reveals a slice of student life in chapter 7, gives a nod to alumni and other friends who helped underwrite campus art galleries, athletic venues, and research centers in chapter 8 (with more on the companion Web site WWW), and lays out (in chapter 9) more than two dozen iconic spaces, places, and manufactured landmarks—such as the *Alma Mater* grouping—that tie generations of students, alumni, and locals to the Illini Place.

The notion of "place" has currency as many Americans live their lives away from home and family, employees telecommute, and reality becomes virtual.

The University of Illinois is one of nearly twenty-five hundred U.S. four-year colleges and universities, each with its own physical history, distinctive groupings of buildings, and random or familial architecture that evokes a unique sense of place.

Urban colleges buy and build tentacles into their surrounding neighborhoods and face obstacles and often resistance to further growth. Rural Big Ten universities may sprawl to the horizon, their growth unimpeded by mountains, deserts, or raging rivers native to the West. But whatever the geography, universities connect their people with the place.

Gerhard Casper, Stanford University president from 1992 to 2000, wrote in a campus guidebook that he asked some friends what they "associated with the architecture" of their own colleges and universities. "They responded," he said, "by talking about how *their* college represented the 'quintessential' college to them: the architecture created community; the architecture connected them to history and tradition; commons, quads, and plazas constituted public fora; eighteenth-century buildings with their simple lines were recalled but also the beauty of recent, modern additions were praised; even the attribute 'majestic' was invoked; quirky, unusual, and bizarre architecture figured in the recollections; much emphasis was placed on natural surroundings."

Our residential colleges, overrun with eighteen- to twenty-four-year-olds, are viewed through the lovely lens of youth, the excitement of fumbling toward intellectual and social adulthood, the memory of walking and thinking big thoughts of the future. The place of our college experience is indelibly imprinted on us. It might be the great California Missions courtyard of Stanford University; the combination of Greek Revival and beaux arts that center the Pentacrest at the University of Iowa; the native stone walls and red-tile roofs of the University of Colorado at Boulder that nestle against the front range of the Rockies; the University of Michigan Diag, crisscrossing the original forty-acre core of the 1837 Ann Arbor campus, or the serenity and sweet scent of the University of Illinois Quad on a late spring night.

CHAPTER 2

In the Beginning

Pre-1919

Trouble with both producing and getting campus endorsement of decorative terra cotta panels above the second-story windows of the new building delayed its dedication for more than a year. But on a sparklingly clear day in February 1913 Lincoln Hall was dedicated, and the university's dynamic president, Edmund Janes James (1904-1920), was thrilled.

"You ought to come out and see our building," James boasted to a friend. "It is really the finest monument thus far erected to Abraham Lincoln in the country." The important distinction—"thus far"—was critical because the Lincoln Memorial in Washington, D.C.—designed by Henry Bacon, who studied in 1884 at the U of I—would "soon throw us into the shade," James said.

Lincoln Hall was the twenty-seventh major building on the still-young campus, which had grown from some fifty students in March 1868 to more than four thousand by the time of the dedication. In that span, there had been about thirty campus plans, most of which were simple drawings showing where things stood, literally. Only a few of the early plans made an impact, in particular the Blackall Plan of 1905, which laid out where Lincoln Hall itself would be located.

The massive Renaissance revival structure, updated and restored to its original stature in 2010-12 at a cost of $65 million, merited its name. The U.S. president's life and words are celebrated on the exterior in a series of detailed terra cotta panels that wrap the building; the interior contains both a bronze bust of the sixteenth president and a tablet with the 272 words of the Gettysburg Address. Writing to President William Howard Taft in 1911, Edmund James said that, because Lincoln signed the Morrill Act into law in 1862, "we . . . look upon him as in a certain sense the founder of the institution."

The Morrill Act gave federal land to the states (not necessarily within their own boundaries), based on their population, to be used—sold—to underwrite the cost of building and endowing a new kind of university: public and practical. The act specifically said these new colleges should focus "to teach such branches of learning as are related to agriculture and the mechanic arts." The zealous Illinois educator Jonathan Baldwin Turner—whose fierce terra cotta image stares out from the southern façade of Lincoln Hall along with nine other Civil War–era national leaders—had crusaded for these practical schools for decades.

FIGURE 2.1. Workers at Lincoln Hall construction. A granite boulder, uncovered in the excavation of the lower level, today marks the grave of Regent Gregory south of Altgeld Hall. (Image dated 1910. Photo courtesy of the University of Illinois Archives 0001879.)

He and others, however, were unhappy when the board of trustees of the fledgling Illinois Industrial University, which the Illinois legislature had set up under the provisions of the Morrill Act, picked John Milton Gregory as the school's first regent (president). A former Michigan superintendent of public instruction and the then-president of Kalamazoo College, the bespectacled, bearded, and frail forty-seven-year-old Gregory was also a Baptist minister. "O Lord, how long, how long," Turner reportedly exclaimed when he heard the news of Gregory's appointment. "An ex-superintendent of public instruction and a Baptist preacher! Could anything be worse?" Turner and like-minded education reformers feared Gregory would too broadly interpret the land-grant act to include the classics and liberal arts. He did.

FIGURE 2.2. Aerial view from University Hall looking northeast, showing Engineering Hall, Physics, and other early buildings. The Illini Union replaced University Hall in 1940. (Image ca. 1917. Photo courtesy of the University of Illinois Archives 0003577.)

When Gregory took charge in the spring of 1867, the one-building campus was located between the two prairie towns of Champaign and Urbana, thanks to the political machinations of State Representative Clark Robinson Griggs, a master lobbyist and Champaign County booster. Griggs wined and dined Illinois lawmakers and engaged in legislative horsetrading en route to landing the plum university for Champaign-Urbana. Champaign County's bid worth $285,000—a single five-story building (nicknamed "The Elephant" and already ramshackle), some land, promises of trees and freight—beat out Bloomington-Normal, Lincoln, and Jacksonville, all of whose bids were worth more. The grossly inadequate Elephant would serve as the main university building for several years. The ten acres of bleak, nearly featureless prairie surrounding it constituted the main campus in these early years; later, Illinois Field would be located here and, much later, the Beckman Institute. The university also owned a 160-acre tract about a half-mile south of the main campus and another 405 acres south of Mount Hope Cemetery.

These unconnected checkerboards of land—nearly one thousand acres—did not include what ultimately would become the university's central campus—the area that includes the Quad. But showing foresight, the board of trustees quickly consolidated its property holdings and acquired this strip of 36.6 acres stretching for one mile south of the ten-acre Elephant tract. This historic land purchase was approved November 26, 1867, and the university launched itself on a course of continuous southward expansion that continues today.

Gregory, who would serve until 1880, had a well-developed aesthetic sense. Important for the story of the University of Illinois is that he also was a graduate of Union College in Schenectady, New York—the first college in America "to follow a coherent architectural plan," according to U of I historian Winton Solberg. From the start Gregory showed concern for the appearance of the campus. He asked trustee John Van Osdel, a prominent Chicago architect, to design a new entrance for the Elephant. With massive stone steps and Grecian columns, Van Osdel's portico dramatically improved the look of the university's only building. These and other renovations made the Elephant respectable by the time students first arrived in March 1868. Gregory tried to hire the services of the nation's foremost landscape architect—Frederick Law Olmsted, the designer of New York City's Central Park. Olmsted advised that the area directly around the Elephant be laid out and landscaped and that further work should wait until the campus developed a fifty-year plan for building needs. The wait would be long.

FIGURE 2.3. John Milton Gregory, charter president of the Illinois Industrial University from 1867 to 1880, laid groundwork for the state's land-grant school to move beyond agriculture and engineering. (Image dated 1875. Photo courtesy of the University of Illinois Archives 0003579.)

In 1870, three years after the university was chartered and two years after it opened, trustees divided the university grounds into four sections: the Campus, thirteen acres in the immediate vicinity of "the Elephant"; the Horticultural Grounds, 130 acres, including an arboretum and orchards; the Experimental Farm, seventy acres; and the Stock Farm, four hundred acres south of Mount Hope Cemetery. Published

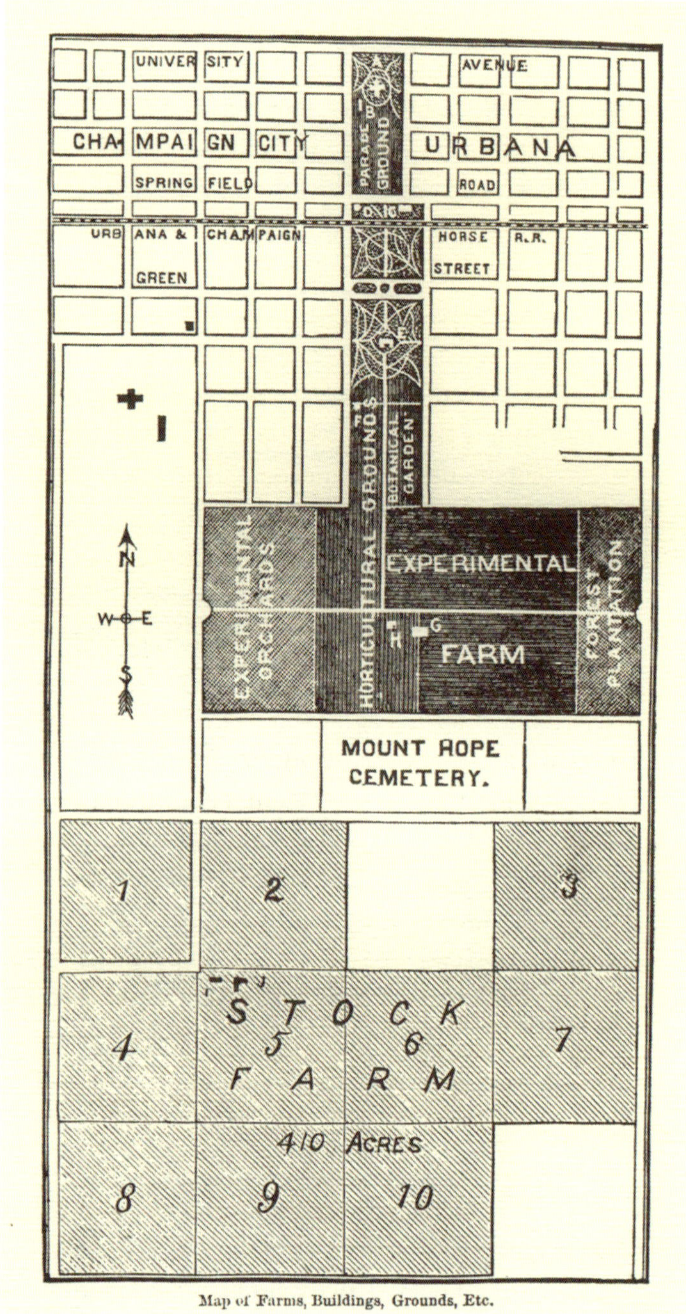

FIGURE 2.4. The first campus plan/map by Harald Hansen in 1871 sites University Hall in the middle of informal garden landscaping, common at that time. Green Street and Springfield Avenue bisect the grounds, and Burrill Avenue forms a north-south axis. (Photo from F&A, courtesy of the University of Illinois Archives.)

in 1871, the first map of campus illustrates the land division. Already, at this early date, the general shape of the main body of the future campus can be discerned as an upside-down T: a pronounced and narrow north-south axis anchored on the south by a broader east-west axis.

It quickly became evident that a single building, especially a shoddily constructed one like the Elephant, could not meet the needs of the university and that thirteen acres provided insufficient land for a campus. So the trustees requested and the Illinois legislature appropriated money for two buildings: a mechanical hall and a new main hall. The decision where to locate the latter was key; the future of the campus's physical development was at stake. Several trustees wanted the new building—the future University Hall—to be north of Springfield Avenue on land to be purchased east of the Elephant tract.

But Gregory boldly called for a location far south of the present campus, south even of distant Green Street, on a ridge smack dab in the middle of the horticultural "garden." Gregory's motion carried, but five trustees voted no. This decision forever shifted the university's center of gravity southward. Unlike his many critics, who feared the University Hall site was "so far south that the University would never grow up to it," Gregory had great faith in the future. He was the first of several presidents ambitious for the U of I.

University Hall formed, in effect, the nucleus of a brand new campus, with the Elephant tract—the former hub—relegated to the northern margin. Indeed, only a small slice of this tract is featured in the university's first plan of grounds, drawn up by architecture instructor Harald Hansen. Probably influenced by the naturalistic designs of Olmsted and others, Hansen's plan showed University Hall in a park densely planted with shrubs and trees and crossed by numerous curving walkways. To the immediate north, Green Street was given a boulevard treatment and widened into a double street. For the area north of Green up to Springfield Avenue, Hansen planned an arboretum: this is ironic because the future site of the engineering campus would long be one of the least green spaces at the university.

Hansen made a real contribution to the university landscape and plan—both the arboretum and the verdant park surrounding University Hall actually materialized—but the greatest beautifier of the barren early campus was professor of botany Thomas J. Burrill—the University of Illinois's own Johnny Appleseed. In 1869 Burrill began developing the Forestry on the eastern fringe of the university's grounds, and a few years later planted elm and ash trees on either side of the roadway delineating the campus's north-south axis. This path would be named Burrill Avenue in the botanist's honor and later came to be known as the Boardwalk, and still later as the Broadwalk. Now nameless, Burrill Avenue lives on as the long sidewalk edging the interior west side of the Quad. In 1911 James White, the long-time—and sometimes long-suffering—university supervising architect made clear what he thought of the school's early architecture when he credited Burrill for planting the trees "which give to the campus more distinction than do all the buildings."

White was perhaps unfair in his assessment. The early architects included White's own mentor, Nathan Clifford Ricker, who for decades was the guiding spirit of the school's College of Architecture and a noted architect in his own right. In a twenty-year period from the 1870s until the 1890s Ricker designed five iconic campus buildings: the future Harker Hall, the future Kenney Gym Annex, the Natural History Building, the future Aeronautical Engineering Lab B (also called the Metal Shop), and the future Altgeld Hall. All of the surviving Ricker buildings are listed on the National Register of Historic Places. James White himself collaborated with Ricker on Altgeld Hall.

No definite plan determined the locations of the various Ricker-designed buildings in that laissez-faire era. During that period, "the only plan apparent for the campus development was to line up the buildings along Green street," White wrote. Indeed, Harker Hall, the Natural History Building, Engineering Hall, and Altgeld Hall were all located near Green Street. The Kenney Gym Annex ended up on Springfield Avenue—a site apparently chosen by Selim Peabody, Gregory's successor, who lacked Gregory's aesthetic sensibilities.

Over time, a rudimentary kind of planning began to replace the helter-skelter early approach to campus development. In 1892 the faculty conducted the first real study of the university's building needs, following Frederick Law Olmsted's advice of twenty-five years earlier. Engineering Hall was the result. Site selection for this building provoked serious debate among the trustees; the final choice north on Green Street permanently fixed the location of the College of Engineering and spelled the eventual end for the beautiful arboretum, which graced many early postcards.

The sleepy campus came to life when the hard-charging Andrew Sloan Draper, Cleveland's former superintendent of schools, became university president in 1894. A master politician, Draper knew his way around the legislature and wrangled record amounts of state money for the university. State appropriations mushroomed from $594,000 in 1895 to $1.8 million in 1903-4, the last year of Draper's presidency. More money meant more buildings, and, indeed, between 1894 and 1904 the number of buildings on campus jumped from six to twenty-seven. They were sorely needed. Enrollment ballooned during Draper's tenure, more than tripling from 810 students in 1894-95 to 2,674 in 1903-4.

But where should all these new buildings go? The Library (Altgeld Hall) and the Observatory—two prizes from Draper's first foray into the Illinois legislature—seem to be the first university structures "located from study of plans of existing buildings and improvements." Though certainly a good start, it was a far cry from a comprehensive plan for campus development. And now, with the construction of Altgeld Hall, such a plan had become critical. Marking the end of an era, Altgeld Hall completed the U-shaped grouping of major buildings south of Green Street. Any new buildings would have to be sited somewhere else.

FIGURE 2.5. Edmund Janes James, president, 1904-1920. (Image dated ca. 1915. Photo courtesy of the University of Illinois Archives 0003578.)

At this key point a real campus plan would have helped, but instead Draper winged it. Acting as the autocrat he tended to be (historian Solberg's assessment), Draper unilaterally decided the new Agriculture Building (Davenport Hall) should be placed south and east of University Hall. The decision turned out to be inspired. The location of Davenport Hall—the first piece of the puzzle—would determine where other buildings would be constructed on the central campus, beginning with the Chemistry Laboratory (Noyes Laboratory) in 1902. Davenport Hall also delineated the east boundary of what would become the university's most sacred space, the Quad.

Already by 1903 university officials were talking about a quadrangle on the central campus. In a September 11, 1903, interview with the *Urbana Daily Courier*, Eugene Davenport, the powerful College of Agriculture dean, spoke of a plan contemplating "a change from a long campus, with a drive straight through it and with wandering rows of buildings on either side, to a spacious quadrangle." It was hoped that this plan would "provide the university with a campus rarely equaled, not only for beauty, but for that space which is so seldom obtainable." Proving that this wasn't just some pie-in-the-sky idea of Davenport's, Draper himself referred to an "enlarged University quadrangle" in the very same month of the *Courier* interview.

But it would be Clarence Blackall, a Boston architect and graduate of the class of 1877, who would develop the university's first true campus plan. Blackall had remained close to the university, and in 1903 he began working on a scheme to improve the Green Street gateway to campus. He quickly realized that issue should be solved in the larger context of a comprehensive campus plan. Blackall recommended to Draper that the University employ eminent landscape architect John C. Olmsted—nephew of the planner of Central Park—for the project. But Draper didn't. The president's stormy tenure (1894-1904) was coming to an end and, indeed, he lacked faith in the future of the school.

Enter Edmund Janes James, Draper's successor as president. James, who might be the university's greatest president, had no doubt about the university's future. "This is destined to be one of the greatest universities of the world," he declared. Short in stature but long in ambition, the forty-nine-year-old James—a German university-trained political economist who left the presidency at Northwestern University to come to Illinois—excelled as an administrator and promoter. By the time he retired in 1920, James had led the transformation of a modest school on the prairie into a world-class university.

In his first year at Illinois, James confronted where to locate a planned auditorium. In a decisive break from previous ad hoc ways, he recommended a commission be appointed to adopt a design for the auditorium and suggest a site. (See chapter 9 for a fuller description.)

In short, the commission led to a comprehensive campus plan with Blackall as the lead. After six months of hard mental labor, Blackall had completed his task by December 1905. "I do not know of a university in the country that would have as good an arrangement as this would be," Blackall told James.

Preservation planner Alice Edwards Novak calls the Blackall Plan of 1905 "perhaps THE most significant plan" among the campus's eighty-plus known Illinois plans. "Blackall for the first time identifies the Quadrangle, not by name, but by form," Novak said. "In addition to the Quad being clearly defined, so, too, is a South Quad/expansion, although it is also not identified as such by name. The engineering campus, which had already been developed rather densely compared to the remainder of campus, is given some sense of design, through a formal symmetrical placement of suggested new buildings to the west of Burrill."

Blackall envisioned a major north-south axis for the campus, approximately midway between Burrill and Mathews Avenues. The auditorium was situated toward the bottom of this axis, where it formed the southern boundary of the main quadrangle. Buildings were grouped by college or department, with the sciences on the east side of the Quad and the liberal and fine arts on the west. For the area south of the auditorium, Blackall proposed a secondary quadrangle with schools of commerce and education, and a natural history museum as well. University Hall and Harker Hall had no place in Blackall's ambitious conception: their removal would have left a blank canvas of uninterrupted grounds from Green Street south to the proposed site of the Auditorium. The Observatory, too, would have been razed. Both survive as important buildings today.

Blackall unveiled this "first true campus plan" to the board of trustees on January 30, 1906. Impressed by Blackall's "radical" scheme, the trustees appropriated $250 for Blackall to get "expert advice" on his plan. Blackall hired the same John C. Olmsted whom President Draper declined to employ three years earlier. Olmsted endorsed Blackall's plan, both settling the location of the auditorium and forever fixing the campus's north-south axis—the campus meridian—as a line running through the center of the auditorium.

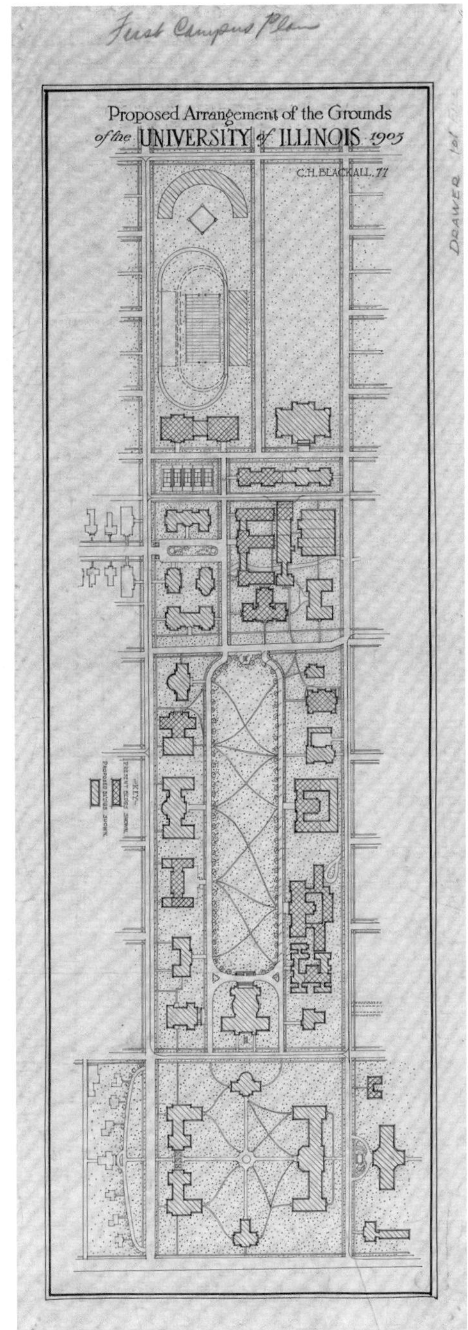

FIGURE 2.6. Clarence H. Blackall Plan, 1905, also called Blackall-Olmsted, was the campus's first formal master plan. It showed specific locations for future buildings and sited the proposed auditorium as the south terminus of a vast open space south of University Hall that is today the Main Quad. (Photo courtesy of the University of Illinois Archives.)

FIGURE 2.7. Students dressed as corn maidens at the 1908 May Fete. (Photo courtesy of University of Illinois Archives 0003749.)

The Blackall Plan of 1905 both organized a chaotic main campus and decisively laid out the lines of future university growth. The scheme quickly demonstrated its value, with Blackall's "road map" soon determining the locations of two important structures: the Physics Building (now Materials Science and Engineering Building) and Lincoln Hall. At last, the days of arbitrary building site selection were over.

State architect W. Carbys Zimmerman had located Lincoln Hall in conformity with the Blackall Plan, but he had his own firm ideas on how the future campus should look. In December 1908, Zimmerman drew up a campus plan—one of three he would prepare—materially different from Blackall's. In this plan, the state architect took the bold if puzzling step of bisecting Blackall's Quad by locating a large structure between Noyes Laboratory and the future Henry Administration Building. Zimmerman's scheme was a non-starter: James White, the newly appointed university supervising architect, couldn't stomach the plan's "sacrifice of the [Quad's] magnificent mall."

Naming workaholic White as supervising architect was a watershed moment in the history of Illinois campus planning. For twenty-five years, he would be "the master hand" guiding university development. As countless others, White had been impressed by the harmony and order of the neoclassical White City at the 1893 Columbian Exposition. The Chicago World's Fair had inspired a generation of urban planners, and now White hoped to do for the university what Daniel H. Burnham and his army of celebrity architects had done for the White City. "The designing of the [University] buildings . . . must be dominated by a single mind, until the essential features of the plan and the spirit of the style are so firmly fixed that the introduction of an unharmonious element would not be tolerated," White said in 1911.

Planning was fashionable in the Progressive Era, and in April 1909 the board of trustees appointed a Campus Plan Commission to select the sites for future buildings, including a planned Armory. The commission members were all architects: Clarence Blackall, W. C. Zimmerman, and Daniel H. Burnham himself, perhaps America's foremost urban planner who once famously said, "Make no little plans; they have no magic to stir men's blood."

White had not been named to the commission, but that didn't stop him from developing a campus plan of his own that served as a working map for the commission. In December 1909 he and Archie Hubbard offered their vision of the future university. This scheme—the first to be drawn up by university staff members—contemplated "some radical changes," in White's words: University Hall, Harker Hall, and the Observatory were to be razed, and Davenport Hall was repositioned north directly across from the English Building.

They also proposed locating a dormitory group west of Wright Street on the south campus and a military/athletic complex east of Mathews Avenue. Hewing to recommendations of a 1908 study, they suggested the congested College of Engineering expand to the west of Wright and to the east of Mathews. The plan was highly rational and symmetrical and embodied the following principles: buildings were grouped together by college; college groups were connected by Burrill Avenue; new buildings were arranged around new quadrangles; and recreational space was set aside for each college.

In the summer of 1910 White and Professor Frederick Mann, an architect, joined the near-dormant commission and sparked action. Even with White on board, the commission didn't produce a single plan until the following June, when the ubiquitous Blackall filled the void. Blackall's ambitious 1911 plan envisioned a much larger future campus with an enrollment of between twenty thousand and twenty-five thousand students (barely fifty-two hundred in 1911). This vision (some might say hallucination) meant the university should buy an enormous amount of land, much to be used for a proposed expansion of the College of Engineering. "If you do not want it all it can easily be rented, but if this land had been acquired twenty-five years ago it is easy to see how much better off the University would be today," Blackall wrote to White.

In this 1911 plan, Blackall saw Healey Street as the gateway to the campus instead of Green Street, which predated the university itself and is shown clearly on the 1871 campus map. This new Healey Street corridor would house an administration building, fine arts buildings, a chapel, and the president's house. In his 1905 plan Blackall had shown the Quad extending all the way to Green Street, but now he positioned a building just south of Green to balance the Auditorium on the other side of the mall. South of the Auditorium, he drew in an elaborate second campus, with the Natural Sciences to the east, the Graduate School to the west, and Agriculture to

FIGURE 2.8. Skeleton view of construction of the Armory through steel frame vault. (Image dated ca. 1913. Photo courtesy of University of Illinois Archives 0003928.)

the south. Again, reinforcing the idea of academic clusters and moving ag farther south.

But Blackall's 1911 scheme didn't site the new Armory. White, on the other hand, addressed the issue head-on and bravely—or foolishly—when he suggested the Armory go east of Mathews Avenue in the College of Agriculture's experimental plots. Howls of protest emanated from Agriculture Dean Davenport, sending White back to the planning board.

That fall he unveiled a promising plan, which mollified Davenport with its placement of the Armory west of Wright Street. In a further example of competing powerful interests, poor White ran afoul of Athletic Director George Huff, who wanted more student recreational space. That December White returned with a "hasty study" that penetrated into uncharted territory: Acquire an enormous tract of land extending west of Fourth Street all the way to the Illinois Central tracks and north to Green. Much of this land was to be reserved for athletics, allaying Huff's concerns.

In the meantime, Blackall returned to his drawing board and developed a plan that built on White's most recent

FIGURE 2.9. Botany Greenhouse, south of Altgeld Hall, viewed from northeast. (Image ca. 1980. Courtesy of the University of Illinois Archives 0003708.)

schemes. He drew the Armory west of Wright at the southern terminus of Sixth Street and oriented it north-south. He filled the vast land acquisitions contemplated in White's December 1911 plan with an enormous drill field extending east-west (edged with buildings on the south) and a graduate school group and an athletic field oriented north-south along the east side of the Illinois Central tracks.

On January 24, 1912, the Campus Plan Commission met to consider Blackall's newest scheme. Daniel H. Burnham—the member whose opinion carried the greatest weight—generally approved but had serious reservations about the Armory location. He thought of the overall campus layout in terms of a cathedral, with the long north-south axis as the nave and the shorter east-west axis—the bottom of the upside-down T—as the transept. He wanted this east-west axis to have a long uninterrupted vista, but Blackall had positioned the Armory in a way that would block the view.

For architects of that generation and beyond, the word of D. H. Burnham—the mastermind of the White City and the great Chicago plan of 1909—was sacred. Blackall scrambled to revise his scheme to satisfy this giant among planners. Completed in just more than a week, Blackall's new plan reoriented the Armory in an east-west direction and moved it to the terminus of Fifth Street, its ultimate location. Perhaps more important, the building was moved farther north in deference to "the development of the long vista east and west which was so strongly urged by Mr. Burnham." Blackall's February 2, 1912, plan also settled the locations of the Stock Judging Pavilion and the horticultural greenhouses, and, for the first of several times, proposed that the university extend southward into Mount Hope Cemetery. (See chapter 9.) "In many ways, this particular plan seems to set the tone for the Platt series of plans—the formal South Quad, the east/west axis and Military Parade Ground, the massive buildings anchoring the corners of the South Quad, and the expansion into the cemetery," Novak said in a plan analysis.

James White endorsed Blackall's site selection proposals, and on March 8, 1912, he offered a summing up, "a restatement of the fundamental ideas in the plans immediately preceding." This restatement guided the discussion, and the Campus Plan Commission approved the locations of the Armory at the terminus of Fifth Street; the Stock Pavilion on the campus meridian due south of the Auditorium; and the greenhouses east of Mathews. Having met its goals, the commission disbanded after three years of service. If one graded the individual members by their participation and thoughtfulness, Blackall and White deserve an A+, Burnham a B, Mann (who finally submitted a plan of his own at almost the last possible minute) a C+, and the otherwise-occupied Zimmerman an F. (After his 1908 plan to bisect what would become the main Quad, Zimmerman's credibility plummeted.)

The Campus Plan Commission had inspired an orgy of planning, the intensity of which wouldn't be repeated until the 1985-2007 era. Still, White did develop two significant plans in the years immediately following the commission's end: a 1913 scheme (complete with a South Quad clock tower) that decided locations for the new library and a women's dormitory (the future Busey Hall) and a 1914 blueprint for the future growth of the university. White went all out on this 1914 plan when he called for the acquisition of all of the land south of Armory Avenue and west of Lincoln Avenue, an ambitious case of land-banking writ large. "This is truly a plan/map for substantial campus expansion, rather than the more tightly focused previous plans for building and grounds placement," Novak says.

World War I and the resulting economic uncertainty brought the university's first era of campus planning to a close. In step with the nation, the University of Illinois would charge into the Roaring Twenties. During this tumultuous decade of jazz and gin, flappers and football, Charles Platt would give Illinois a signature architectural style and a plan for the ages.

❖ ❖ ❖ ❖

Terra cotta panels rim the second story of Lincoln Hall, which was dedicated in 1913, and commemorate the sixteenth U.S. president's life and times. Some feature Abraham Lincoln associates and contemporaries, and others show quotations from his speeches and writings. Read about Lincoln Hall's terra cotta panels on the companion Web site (sidebar 2.1) www.

As the Civil War loomed, the United States was both cash and population poor. The nation's agricultural and industrial sectors needed a kick start that only a more broadly educated populace could provide. Read **"What's a Land Grant"** for the basics of how the federal land-grant law paved the way for public universities, such as the U of I, Kansas State, Massachusetts, Wyoming, and New Hampshire (thirty-seven are so-called 1862 colleges), simultaneously to extend personal opportunity and answer national interests. See the companion Web site (sidebar 2.2) www.

CHAPTER 3

Growth and Transformation

1920-1933

On a cool, wet Sunday in September 1919, hundreds of prospective students—many of them World War I veterans—left Champaign-Urbana after trudging through the rain-soaked streets in a fruitless search for lodging. Those who did find rooms were seen the next morning patiently waiting in a double line that stretched from the registrar's office in University Hall north across tree-lined Green Street to the murky Boneyard Creek. This enrollment boom would surge through the university—now a half-century old—and ignite a drastic rethinking of the "place" of campus.

University officials had anticipated higher enrollment that fall but didn't expect so many to show up. At 7,102, enrollment surpassed 1918's by more than two thousand and was some one thousand higher than the school record, with continued upward pressure predicted. Clearly, the campus would need new buildings to accommodate new students.

The task of expanding the university fell to fifty-eight-year-old President David Kinley (1919-1930), a Scotsman who took over from the ailing President James, whose official sixteen-year term would end the next year. Kinley, a Yale-trained economist, was a natural fit: he had loyally and competently served the university for more than a quarter-century, including as dean of the Graduate School. He excelled as an administrator but was seen as cold, humorless, and brusque, inspiring admiration rather than affection.

"Another man from the East and I think they had better kept him there," the legendary naturalist Stephen Forbes, then the U of I College of Science dean, reportedly said of Kinley shortly after they first met in 1893. Kinley also had a volcanic temper. A botany professor said the U of I president once was so angry during a meeting with a student that he kicked a wastebasket around his office.

Yet he was a hard worker who got things done. He was interested in the physical plant—the place of the university—and campus planning. Frank W. Scott, an influential alumnus, lamented what he believed was Kinley's neglect of academics in favor of "architecture, construction, and landscape gardening." But the times called for a CEO who was a planner and builder. And once again, the man met the moment.

Late in 1919 Kinley surveyed the campus and found that at least fourteen new buildings and twelve additions were urgently needed. This sheer scale of development demanded

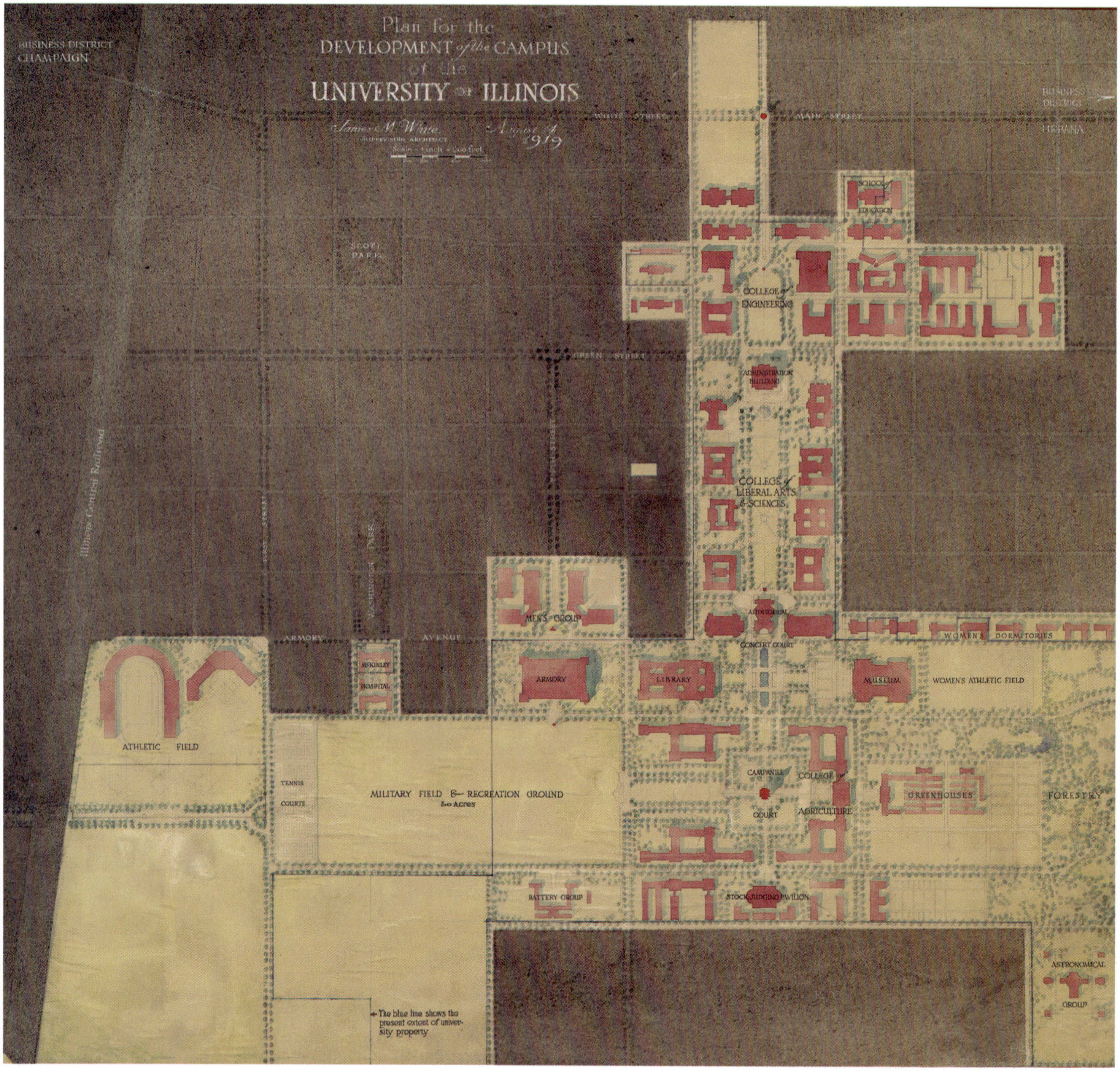

FIGURE 3.1. White (and Tilton) Plan, 1919, presented 1920. This ambitious plan included new ideas, such as terminating the east-west campus axis, making Green Street a boulevard, and siting a "men's group" of buildings north of the Armory. The Military Grounds and recreation areas are enlarged. (Image courtesy of University of Illinois Archives.)

significant planning, and the board of trustees created a Campus Plan Commission to help. Unlike its architects-only predecessor of the previous decade, this group was a mixture of trustees and academics. Not a single architect. The commission's driver was its chairwoman, Margaret Day Blake, a Chicago society woman and social reformer.

Like her husband—a *Chicago Tribune* editorial writer—Blake had strong opinions on many things. But her views on architecture and planning brought her into conflict with James White, the veteran university supervising architect. White believed Blake dismissed him as parochial; according to White, Blake thought that "a Chicago architect must have more wisdom than one practicing in a smaller community." Blake had a powerful ally: board president Robert Franklin Carr, class of 1893 and a chemical company executive.

In January 1920 White presented his latest campus plan to the board. It was primarily the work of Leon Deming Tilton. This scheme, largely an elaboration of previous plans, was both conservative and familiar. It attempted to address the growing automobile traffic problem with more roads, proposed a concert court south of the Auditorium, and an Engineering Quad. It was vintage White—rational, sensible, and sane—but it didn't win over trustees who wanted a more comprehensive plan.

So Carr hired the fabled Chicago firm of Holabird and Roche to guide the commission. Founded in 1880, Holabird and Roche designed innovative "Chicago School" skyscrapers, such as the Marquette Building, and ornate hotels, such as the Palmer House. A 1915 conversation between Robert Franklin Carr and William Holabird, the firm's founder, launched the relationship. "We have such an interest in the State University and its success that we would be willing to assist in making the exterior of a building," Holabird told Carr. Not long after this meeting, Holabird and Roche was hired to design the University's new Education Building (now University High School). But the firm had larger ambitions.

That was obvious as early as January 1916 when Holabird and Roche panned the campus layout. "It is evident to anyone that the buildings as a group have lacked so far the benefit of a general plan of development," the architects said. (One can only wonder what White or Blackall thought of that assessment.) The firm urged creation of a plan to harmonize the campus, one featuring "low buildings" with "well-studied and appropriate detail" and "a simple and uniform color scheme." They advised the trustees to settle on a suitable architectural style for the buildings and suggested the Woman's Building (the English Building) as an ideal model.

Four years after this trial run, Holabird and Roche finally got its shot at reshaping the U of I campus. James White did not welcome the news, as he explained in a letter to President James. "I am opposed to the whole proposition," White wrote, "because the Board have already located all of the buildings which can be built within the next five years, and we haven't very many thousand dollars to spend on that sort of work at this time. I should like to have Holabird and Roche in a consulting relation to us, but I feel that they are not the best people to make such a study of the campus development, providing the trustees want one made."

Despite White's reservations, Holabird and Roche forged ahead. Early in the process, the firm proposed that the board of trustees adopt the Georgian style of architecture for all future campus buildings, with the future Horticulture Field Laboratory pegged to kick things off in that style. White had no problem with the suggestion. "I can't feel that it makes much difference whether the new group south of the Auditorium be Gothic, Renaissance, or Georgian, so long as they are all good examples of the same style," he said.

White, though, was less sanguine when it came to Holabird and Roche's campus plan. He watched bewildered and horrified as the firm's big and bold—and wildly unrealistic—vision for the campus unfolded in the early months of 1920. Based on preliminary drawings of the massive and very long-term plan, White calculated development

FIGURE 3.2. University Hall entrance with portal detail. The building was demolished in 1938, and the Illini Union built in its place in 1939–40. The portal was salvaged and eventually used to create the Hallene Gateway north of the Alice Campbell Alumni Center on the east edge of campus. (Image undated. Photo courtesy of University of Illinois Archives 0003705.)

at "possibly a quarter of a billion dollars and one which we might grow into some time in the next century" some seventy years later. "I confess it is a little too intangible for me," he candidly admitted to James. (A quarter-billion dollars in 1920 is roughly $3 billion in today's money.)

In September 1920 a representative of Holabird and Roche let the trustees take a peek at the monster his firm had created. It was an eyeful. The scheme contemplated an entirely new campus with all academic units shifted south of Armory Avenue, including the entire College of Engineering. Holabird and Roche carried the university's ongoing slow-and-steady southward expansion to the extreme; it extended the main body of the campus through Mount Hope Cemetery all the way down to the prominent ridge on the South Farms.

The trustees didn't endorse this pipe dream, and Holabird and Roche's service as a University of Illinois campus planner came to an inglorious end. (The firm, though, would continue to design campus buildings, including the iconic Memorial Stadium and the less glorious Foreign Languages Building.) "Holabird and Roche have not proved successful," White blandly summed up, "and did not prove helpful on the study of the Campus Plan." He hoped this ill-fated exercise had educated the trustees "with reference to our needs, and the restrictions which must be placed on our development by . . . practical considerations."

Lucky for him, White would be able to contribute the next time trustees went looking for a campus planner, in the fall of 1921. The board, now led by sixty-year-old electrical pioneer William Abbott (the campus power plant later would be named for him), wanted an architect who would be a twofer: someone who would both develop a comprehensive campus plan and design the new Agriculture Building in a style intended to set the architectural look for the entire south campus. Abbott, who would serve for sixteen years, appointed a commission of architects, including White, to find that man.

The panel gave trustees four architects to choose from, "any one of whom we thought would take the lead in the solution of our problem." They were John Russell Pope, who had recently developed a campus plan for Yale University; Delano and Aldrich, which also had a Yale connection, having designed a number of buildings there; McKim, Mead, and White, a renowned firm that had left its mark on many college buildings, including the Woman's Building (the English Building) at the U of I; and Charles Platt, a landscape gardener/architect who had recently branched out into campus planning. All of these architects were safe and sane choices: conservative New York–based professionals well versed in the popular, though increasingly old-fashioned, Beaux-Arts style.

The trustees picked sixty-year-old Charles Adams Platt to do for Illinois what Thomas Jefferson had done for Virginia. "If anyone were to ask me what I had to sell, I should say style," Platt once said. His distinguished silver mane, meticulously sculpted beard and mustache, and immaculate and fashionable attire made the New York aristocrat a walking advertisement for style. Publicly, James White praised the choice of Platt, saying it showed the trustees "fully appreciate the magnitude of our campus problems." Privately, he was more guarded. "I am in hopes that he may prove helpful to us, even though he may do nothing more than choose from among the various schemes that we have worked out," White confided to ex-President James. If he had his way, White and his staff would handle most of the university's architectural work.

But Platt would not merely pick and choose among the plans that White had developed over the years. He visited the campus for three days in late December 1921 and by the following February had produced a campus plan almost as fantastical as Holabird and Roche's 1920 scheme. Platt's February 1922 plan envisioned an enormous cross-shaped campus stretching far to the south, engulfing Mount Hope Cemetery along the way. The campus was shown densely packed with buildings: the area between Armory Avenue and Taft Drive alone had more than twenty structures. It was sterile and uniform, a landscape of big boxes. White was struck by the incredible building density. "I do not think that Mr. Platt has provided any where nearly enough open area in proportion to his proposed building development," he told President Kinley.

Reflecting White's help and sensibilities, in September Platt submitted to the board a new plan that was a model

FIGURE 3.3. Platt Plan, 1927, "Plan for the Development of the Campus" by Charles Platt, consulting architect, and supervising architect James M. White; this plan revised the 1922 plan and generally was followed for decades. It is orderly and contains open spaces. (Photo courtesy of University of Illinois Archives.)

of sobriety and containment. It was significantly less dense. Mount Hope Cemetery was resurrected as a southern barrier, which reduced the overall size of the campus. He preserved Olmsted's north-south axis and laid down a pronounced east-west axis with the long vista Daniel H. Burnham favored. White especially liked Platt's revised treatment of the south campus. "The proposed buildings within this area cover about twenty-five per cent of the ground area," White told Kinley, "but are so distributed as to avoid monotony and to introduce the greatest possible variety into the avenues separating the buildings."

Avenues and walkways were important components of the new plan. Platt called for the extensions of the Quad's east and west (Burrill Avenue) sidewalks south to Maple (Pennsylvania) Avenue. He proposed a major rerouting of traffic circulation around the campus, with Gregory Avenue extended east to connect with an enlarged Sixth Street and Goodwin Avenue. More radically, he also called for the closing of both Wright Street and Mathews Avenue south of the Auditorium.

Platt's famous 1922 campus plan and its many iterations shared elements with the plans of Clarence Blackall, including a formal South Quad with massive buildings anchoring its corners, the perennial east/west axis, and the Military Parade Ground.

But Platt's great innovation was massing or clustering buildings with ornamental gateways and enclosed cozy inner courtyards connecting the clusters, like little neighborhoods. Platt's imposing structures—think Mumford Hall and the Library—had both public and private faces. On the side facing the broad malls—grassy open spaces—they presented a monumental front with uniform high cornice lines. But the view from the courtyards was more human and homey, with lower cornice lines and less detail.

In October 1922 the board of trustees approved "in general" Platt's plan, and Margaret Day Blake dissolved the Campus Plan Commission, which she chaired for three years. She said its work was done and that, thanks to Charles Platt, the school had an architectural style, neo-Georgian or Georgian revival.

Platt had been hired not only to draw up a campus plan but also to design the new Agriculture Building (Mumford Hall), which would be the trendsetter and model of the new architectural style slated for the entire south campus. The new Library originally was supposed to be the exemplar, but Illinois Governor Len Small in 1921 vetoed its appropriation. Platt had quickly settled on Georgian revival for his Illinois work, the same style Holabird and Roche recommended two years before. White, too, favored the choice. On a recent tour of several eastern universities he was especially taken with Harvard's new freshman dormitories, built in "Georgian style of brick and stone."

Though he was confined with pneumonia to a Chicago hospital for several weeks, Platt quickly designed the Agriculture Building. A March 1922 preliminary study shows a structure almost identical to the finished one, suggesting little involvement by James White. Agriculture and Architecture, in fact, are the university's only Platt buildings that don't credit White as co-designer. With a steeply pitched green slate roof, an abundance of chimneys and dormers, and a red-brick exterior trimmed in limestone, the three-story (plus attic) new Agriculture Building would determine the look of the south campus.

David Kinley's bold building program and a cooperative and generous Illinois legislature helped define the south campus beginning in fall 1924. Alumni who returned for Homecoming that year were amazed not only by Red Grange's record-shattering performance against Michigan in the new red brick and limestone stadium—designed by Holabird and Roche—but also by a south campus abuzz with construction. It was a far cry from a serene country campus where cows once outnumbered students.

The new Agriculture Building was surrounded by the steel and concrete skeletons of five major buildings under construction: the McKinley Hospital, the new Library, the

FIGURE 3.4. Greenhouse north of (second) President's House at the corner of Wright and Green Streets where Everitt Lab stands today. (Image ca. 1910. Photo courtesy of University Archives 0003709.)

Commerce Building (David Kinley Hall), the Men's Gymnasium (Huff Hall), and the Dairy Manufactures Building (the Agriculture Bioprocess Laboratory). All were designed by Charles Platt and James White in what was fast becoming the university's signature Georgian style.

By 1926 these five buildings had been completed and more were on the way, most notably the Architecture Building—perhaps Platt's Illinois campus masterpiece. They took care of the need for space Kinley and campus planners understood was desperately needed. The old Library (Altgeld Hall) could comfortably handle only 265 students at a time when a thousand typically wanted in. The Men's Gymnasium (Kenney Gym) hosted classes until ten at night; a new men's gym (Huff Hall) would relieve the overcrowding. Indeed, the 1919 boom in student enrollment was not an aberration: two years later, Illinois would boast the third-largest enrollment of regular full-time students in the country, behind only California and Columbia.

FIGURE 3.5. View from the northwest of the exterior of Women's Residence Hall, later called Busey Hall, on Nevada Street. This was the campus's first residence hall. Men's residence halls wouldn't arrive until after World War II. (Image dated 1918. Photo courtesy of University of Illinois Archives 0003718.)

Illinois also became a national leader in campus planning in the 1920s. "At present we hold the leading position among the universities of this country in campus planning," White told Kinley in fall 1923. New Yorker Charles Platt and midwesterner James White share the credit. White, the in-house supervising architect, had fixed the locations of the Library and the new Agriculture Building well before Platt created his plan, and Platt worked within the boundaries White fixed. White was nationally recognized as a campus planner; the University of Texas at Austin and the University of North Dakota, among other schools, employed him to design their campuses.

Even the student newspaper, the *Daily Illini*, noticed the action. "Illinois is expanding in the right way," the paper editorialized. "New buildings, instead of being strewn indiscriminately, are being built according to a well laid out campus plan. . . . Walks between classes may seem a bit long now, but it is better to sprint a bit than to have a campus spattered out and mixed with business houses and dwellings, as other institutions which have under-estimated their own growth find themselves today."

Platt's plan also considered trees, but was it no substitute for a full-blown landscape design to complement the buildings, walkways, and courts.

"The chief problem in our academic campus is that of the plantings around the buildings," White told President Kinley in fall 1926, about halfway through the building boom. Well aware of the issue, Platt recommended the University hire Italian-born Ferruccio Vitale, a renowned landscape gardener and friend. Platt would earn about $100,000 ($1.4 million in today's money) from his U of I work and already had helped another friend, the artist Barry Faulkner, secure an $8,000 (about $106,000 now) commission from the university to paint four murals for the new Library.

Vitale's reputation as a high-priced landscaper preceded him, so White at first tried to hire him on the cheap as a lecturer. When this failed, the university reluctantly agreed to Vitale's demands of $100 per day for a preliminary campus visit and $3,500 (about $48,000 now) for the preparation of a general campus landscape plan.

"I think it is very fair," Platt said. "He is prompted by the same desire as I was to do the best he can for the University at a minimum rate." Vitale visited the campus several times during fall 1928 and developed a landmark landscaping plan that he presented to the board of trustees the next May.

Vitale tried both to enhance the grandeur and to preserve "the dignity, unity, and effectiveness" of Platt's Campus Plan, which had been revised many times since its 1922 inception. Perhaps most important, the landscape architect

FIGURE 3.6. Hat racks on the underside of seats in the New Gymnasium, now Huff Hall, designed by Charles Platt and James White in the Georgian revival style. With a seating capacity of 4,536, Huff was home to Illini basketball for forty years—and men wore brimmed hats that could be stored under their wooden seats. Huff is now the venue for Illini volleyball, wrestling, and men's and women's gymnastics. A 2014 north wing, which substantially completed the original design, is named for the Khan family, which donated its cost. (Photo by Darrell Hoemann.)

called for the positioning of present and future buildings on broad terraces defined by hedges, posts, walls, urns, and the like, but "free from heavy vine covering or small-scale shrubs and bushes." He had no use for ivy, but he loved trees. He agreed with Charles McKim that "architecture is best enjoyed through trees."

Vitale advised that native trees, such as elms, be planted in single or double rows along the campus's major thoroughfares, and proposed a double line of American hornbeams, fifteen to thirty feet high, to demarcate the University's future boundaries. He also harked back to Clarence Blackall's entrance gateways on Green Street and suggested even more gateways on Sixth Street as well as on Armory, Goodwin, and Mathews Avenues.

Parts of Vitale's landscaping plan were quickly put in place. The campus planted three hundred elms to line

FIGURE 3.7. Southward view of Henry Administration Building anchored by dwarf crab apple trees, short hedges, and tall trees as key elements of the campus landscape plan developed by Ferruccio Vitale. (Photo by Karyl Wackerlin.)

campus walkways (although he warned against this kind of monoculture that risks disease disaster) and twenty-five hundred Japanese yews to mark the new terraces around the buildings. These yew hedges terminated in terra cotta urns, which tied the landscaping to the architecture of the buildings. Twenty stone benches were also purchased and placed at strategic spots on the south campus.

Workmen began to trim ivy that had grown over some campus windows. A *Daily Illini* writer raised an objection, fearful that this ivy trimming would be followed by wholesale ivy removal (which happened decades later). "Perhaps the new south campus buildings look better without ivy," this journalist wrote, "but some of the architecture prevalent on our north campus—well, we've often thought that ivy was a rather convenient plant."

Vitale and his associate, Alfred Geiffert, continued to work on their planting plan as late as 1933. But by then the university had more serious concerns: confronting the Great

Depression. The campus slashed operating expenses, including cutting faculty salaries by ten percent. The university's biennial budget for 1933-35 was less than $8 million—the lowest it had been since 1919. "The university is really in a critical condition," said Harry Woodburn Chase, the school's new president. The liberal-minded Chase would leave the university in 1933 after a short three-year tenure, driven away in part by the clamor (including a legislative hearing and scolding) over the cost of the new President's House, the tenth of Charles Platt's eleven buildings.

Times had changed. David Kinley, Chase's predecessor, had presided over a flush period of record enrollments, record appropriations, and record building. His $10.5 million building program yielded the campus more than a dozen major structures, many of them landmarks then as now. The *Daily Illini* lauded Kinley for solving what it termed was "the chief problem" of his administration—"the erection of a physical plant that would provide adequately for the 10,000 sons and daughters of Illinois who sought education here." Mission accomplished, the sixty-eight-year-old Kinley retired in the summer of 1930 after thirty-seven years of service at the university, and in the nick of time, just before the economy cratered.

James McLaren White, Kinley's right-hand man, remained at his post of supervising architect until his death at age sixty-six in early 1933. Ferruccio Vitale died at age fifty-eight that same month, February, of pneumonia, and Charles Adams Platt would die later that year at age seventy-one. Over the span of little more than six months, all of the university's master planners—giants in the Illini Place—were gone.

FIGURE 3.8. University of Illinois architecture alumnus James McLaren White was a professor and the supervising architect at the U of I for forty-three years beginning in 1890. His planning and design fingerprints are all over the campus. (Image ca. 1905. Photo courtesy of University of Illinois Archives 0002257.)

Illinois Brick

The Urbana-Champaign campus loves its red brick and takes care that its quality and color are true. For nearly a half-century the Western Brick Company in nearby Danville provided a million bricks a year for campus buildings. Later, Streator Brick manufactured a million bricks for the Beckman Institute alone. Read the story of "Illinois Brick" on the companion Web site (sidebar 3.1) www.

Historians of the Campus Plan

A seminal book about the U of I took more than a decade to pull together and captures the first sixty-three years of campus planning, architecture, and growth at Urbana-Champaign, including transcripts of important letters and reports. Leon Deming Tilton wrote the first version; nearly a decade later Thomas Edward O'Donnell updated and polished what became *History of the Growth and Development of the Campus of the University of Illinois*. Read **"Historians of the Campus Plan"** on the companion Web site (sidebar 3.2).

Georgian Revival: Illini Style

Low (but massive) buildings, steep roofs, red brick, lots of limestone, chimneys, and dormers provide the "look" of the Urbana-Champaign campus, thanks to a conservative New Yorker who first brought the campus its signature style in 1922. It's not uniform or identical, but is pervasive even today. Read more about **"Georgian Revival: Illini Style"** on the companion Web site (sidebar 3.3).

All the Presidents' Houses

If timing is everything, it couldn't have been worse when U of I trustees, after about a decade of study, delay, and contention, approved the location, architect, and plans for a new President's House at the edge of campus just as the nation sunk into the Great Depression. The sixteen-room mansion at 711 West Florida Avenue is the fourth residence for the U of I's chief executive. Read the history of **"All the Presidents' Houses"** on the companion Web site (sidebar 3.4).

CHAPTER 4

Stability and Transition

1934-1954

A bitterly cold wind swept across Mount Hope Cemetery as the body of James McLaren White was laid to rest February 8, 1933. Admirers, including U of I president Harry Chase and his predecessor, David Kinley, turned out on a bright, zero-degree day to pay respect to the longtime campus supervising architect. Two of the men carrying White's casket to the grave would help guide the course of university development for decades: Charles Stewart Havens and Ernest L. Stouffer.

White's unexpected death stunned his staff. He seemingly had recovered from surgery and was about to return to work when influenza struck him down. "Prof. White's death just at the time when we had concluded that his long trials were over and that it was but a matter of a few days until he would be with us again has left the men in his organization bewildered," said Stouffer, the assistant supervising architect.

Thirty-seven years old in 1933, Ernie Stouffer had been an architect in Streator, Illinois, before he joined the U of I staff near the end of Kinley's big building program. He had a hand in the designs of the President's House, the Woman's (Freer) Gymnasium, and the Chemistry Annex. He seemed the logical choice to succeed White.

But the Great Depression guaranteed there would be no money for buildings and therefore little need for architectural design. Instead, the time called for someone to keep the university's vast physical plant running, humming, and clicking along, someone hardheaded, hardworking, and hard driving.

In stepped Charles Stewart Havens. Only twenty-eight years old in 1933, the handsome, wavy-haired Havens was mature for his age. He had worked in the supervising architect's office since he was in high school and had vaulted up through the ranks, rising from a messenger to chief clerk. As chief clerk, Havens was in charge of "room assignments and schedules, the issuing of keys, the handling of the public in the front office, and the relaying to the proper parties of all sorts of requests which come in over the telephone." White came to rely on Havens and once even assigned the young man to take his place at a meeting with President Chase. "Mr. Havens is quite thoroly [*sic*] familiar with all of our operations," White assured Chase.

A little more than a week after White's death, the board of trustees named Havens as acting superintendent of buildings and grounds operations. Then in May 1934, the board approved the reorganization of the Supervising Architect's Office into the Physical Plant Department and named Havens as the department's director and Stouffer as the university's assistant supervising architect in charge of construction. Unlike James White, who reported directly to the president, Stouffer reported to the younger Havens. Much later, as Stouffer neared retirement, he called for a new chain of command that would have the university architect report to the executive vice president instead of the physical plant director. But even Stouffer recognized Havens's talents, calling him a man of "remarkable ability and capability."

Stouffer said he was "a builder, not an administrator," though there was little building on the U of I campus in the early 1930s. Havens's annual report for 1932-33 noted that for the first time in thirty-one years, the U of I had not put up a single new building, so there was little demand for Stouffer's skill set then. On the other hand, skilled administrator and manager Havens flourished in this period of scarce money and declining enrollment. He promptly effected what he called "rigid economies." That meant curtailing maintenance, postponing equipment purchases, cutting staff and wages, and eliminating overtime. He also helped secure cheaper gas and electricity rates from Illinois Power and Light Corporation.

He knew this regimen could be pursued only for so long before the university's physical plant would suffer. In 1932-33 the university had many more buildings than in 1925-26, yet it spent about the same on building maintenance. Havens didn't think it made sense to call for new buildings when existing ones couldn't be properly maintained. "Above all," he wrote, "it does not seem logical to add to the present plant when funds are not available to operate and maintain existing structures at a proper standard."

Logical or not, Arthur Cutts Willard (1934-1946), the U of I's new president (following a single year when Arthur Hill Daniels was acting president), wanted new buildings and in particular a new student center. Even legendary Illinois football coach Bob Zuppke had endorsed Willard's 1934 election. "He's all right," Zup said. "He came here the same year I did." That year was 1913, and in the intervening period Willard, a native of Washington, D.C., had served as head of the Mechanical Engineering Department, acting dean of the College of Engineering, and director of the Engineering Experiment Station. In the 1920s Willard, a heating engineer, gained international recognition for his work on the ventilation system of New York City's Holland Tunnel.

Fifty-five years old in 1934, the tall, sad-faced Willard had a reputation as a hard worker and the best-dressed man on campus. He recognized his limitations and wisely delegated his authority, including to secretaries who wrote many of his letters. "I don't think Mr. Willard ever dictated a letter in his life," said Betsy Ross, Willard's niece, who acted as official hostess in the President's House. "He said his secretaries could write a better letter than he could. That's what they were trained for."

Willard also encouraged dissent among his subordinates; Havens became one of the few persons willing to openly engage Willard in argument. The president's management style attracted some criticism. Later on, a consultant's report would characterize the university under Willard as lacking "driving administrative leadership."

Times were tough when Willard took office in 1934. Enrollment was in decline and there was no end to this trend in sight; the university budget stood at only $8 million—the smallest since 1921. No help could be expected from Springfield: the Democratic administration of Governor Henry Horner was paying out $3 million per month in relief to unemployed citizens.

Enter the federal government.

Campaigning in 1932, Franklin Delano Roosevelt had promised to combat the Depression using "bold, persistent experimentation." The New Deal was the result. FDR created an alphabet soup of agencies, including the gargantuan Public Works Administration (PWA). Helmed by the crusty secretary of the interior, Harold Ickes (Ickes's wife had been a U of I trustee in the 1920s), the PWA spent $1 billion over its lifetime constructing bridges, dams, municipal buildings, hospitals, sewage systems, and port facilities. Historian William Leuchtenburg said Ickes was "a builder to rival Cheops," the pharaoh who built the Great Pyramid of Giza. Indeed, Ickes's PWA transformed the public face of America.

The PWA financed the construction of roughly 70 percent of the educational buildings erected in the United States between 1933 and 1939, including those at the University of Illinois. Willard and the board of trustees first received PWA funds in 1935: a $354,724 PWA grant and a $1,091,000 loan from the Reconstruction Finance Corporation for the second unit of the Dentistry, Medicine, and Pharmacy Building in Chicago. This was the first large loan in the university's history, and the newly formed University of Illinois Foundation served as the trustee for the bond issue.

Then Willard again turned to the federal government for aid, this time for a student center. For a generation Illini envisioned a Student Union building to meet students' social and recreational needs. Willard shared this vision, and in the long and hot summer of 1936 he set the wheels in motion; the university applied to the PWA for a partial grant for the estimated $1 million student center. Getting the money would prove difficult.

Governor Horner was a major obstacle. In 1937 he torpedoed university-sponsored legislation to create a commission that could issue bonds for a student center and a men's dormitory. Since the PWA would provide only 45 percent of the total needed for these buildings, the university hoped to use the commission to raise the rest of the money.

FIGURE 4.1. President Arthur Cutts Willard led the campus from 1934 to 1946. During the Great Depression, he relied on the federal government, particularly Franklin Delano Roosevelt's Public Works Administration, for building funds. (Image dated 1933. Photo courtesy of the University of Illinois Archives 0002259. Photo copyrighted by Keith Swanson.)

Horner also axed the university budget by $600,000 that year, which wiped out the school's entire building program. The governor's move prompted a rare public outburst from the normally calm Willard. Speaking to the press, the U of I president warned that the cash-strapped university might have to hike student fees, raise entrance requirements, or eliminate some scholarships. "I am unwilling, as president of the University of Illinois, to see it become a second or third class institution," Willard said.

As this political war waged on, the university, in a public relations gambit, published a thin leaflet that was undated but probably distributed in 1934. "The University of Illinois is a vast laboratory of science and citizenship built for and by the people of Illinois," said the cover. The university, the brochure said, receives six-tenths of 1 percent of the total tax bill paid by Illinoisans, an amount "so small as to be negligible," and a bargain to students, beneficiaries of important research, and the larger society from the civic contributions of its alumni.

Willard's concern about the university's capacity and appropriation was well founded. In fall 1936, university enrollment had ballooned unexpectedly, reaching record levels, and new building space was suddenly needed. Willard pointed out the staggering fact that the university had received from the State of Illinois a paltry $50,000 for building additions in the previous eight years, compared with more than $10 million the school had obtained for buildings in the 1920s.

And then, just like that, the conflict between Horner and Willard came to an end—thanks to a fall of plaster in University Hall, the school's oldest and still most-used classroom building. Just before one o'clock in the afternoon on a drizzly and unseasonably mild day in January 1938, roughly a ton of plaster and metal lathing gave way from the ceiling and crashed onto the floor in Room 315. Fortunately, there were no students in the classroom at the time: the chunk of ceiling, measuring twenty-five feet by twenty feet, fell with enough force to knock the writing arms off many lecture chairs, leaving behind only stumps. Trustees quickly ordered University Hall to be dismantled, and the dilapidated Second Empire structure that had long been the bane of campus planners finally met its end. Willard, a man who wanted to be known as a builder, jokingly referred to himself as a "razer" of buildings.

During a campus visit the following March, Governor Horner indicated his full support for a new building to replace University Hall, and the *Daily Illini* applauded. "Gov. Horner has been the greatest obstacle to a resumption of the University building program," the student newspaper editorialized. "Now that he has changed his mind, the road is clear—at least as far as the replacement of University hall is concerned." True to his word, Horner helped secure a $700,000 appropriation for the new classroom building—the future Gregory Hall.

The demolition of University Hall also opened up a prime spot for the new Illini Union Building at the campus's front door. Since early in 1937 two committees had debated where to put the student center, with one ultimately suggesting a site on the Morrow Plots (see chapter 9) and the other a spot at the northwest corner of Daniel and Wright Streets. The location question was revisited after University Hall was taken down, and in July 1938 a site for the Illini Union finally was chosen. It would be built on "the center axis of the central quadrangle, south of Green Street, between the Natural History Building and the Law Building [Altgeld Hall]." In the meantime, the financing had fallen into place; the U of I would couple a $450,000 PWA grant with a $550,000 loan from the Connecticut Mutual Life Insurance Company through the U of I Foundation.

Willard suddenly had a building program, including Gregory Hall, the first air-conditioned structure on campus, and the Illini Union. New additions to the Library and McKinley Hospital were also going up, and on the south campus a Natural Resources Building was beginning to take shape. This last structure would provide much-needed space for the State Geological and Natural History Surveys, then scattered across campus in several buildings. The project took a long time to get off the ground, with the State of Illinois and the university wrangling over the building's location and over who was responsible for its design. These new buildings soon would be accompanied by two more: Abbott Power Plant, looming on the west edge of campus, and the Men's Residence Hall.

But for all the building underway, there was little new planning going on. In these twenty years, 1934 to 1954, in total there were eight plans/plats. One was a one bird's-eye-view drawing of the campus, three related in-house plot plans associated with the siting of the Illini Union, an often-revised postwar project list, a traffic plan, and a pair of plans prompted by where to put a proposed biological sciences group. There was no grand plan and no proposed invasion of Mount Hope Cemetery.

But the influence of Charles Platt, the master planner, remained strong: all these new structures were designed in the Georgian style he had advocated. The university also continued to adhere largely to Platt and Ferruccio Vitale's Campus Plan. For example, as site selection was discussed for the Natural Resources Building, Havens opposed a location that would obstruct the long east-west mall—and its vista—so favored by Platt and an integral element of his plan.

But Platt had his detractors, people who objected to the Georgian style of architecture, to his plan, or to both. Way back in 1926, an anonymous student, writing in the *Daily Illini*, criticized "the new factory district" then emerging on the south campus. "Every new building that has been built recently has been as devoid of beauty as the proverbial mud fence," the writer complained. "Each follows the same plan: four square walls and a roof, sickly red brick trimmed with dingy white stone. One of such might be excused as adding variety on the campus but such is not the case. The New Ag, Gym, Library and Commerce buildings are all as much alike as sparrows on a fence and about as beautiful."

More recently, in 1934, marble company president Frank L. Davis, class of 1888, told Willard that there was "considerable dissatisfaction among our Architectural graduates concerning the Campus plan and Georgian style of buildings." Davis suggested that the university scrap Platt's plan entirely and "go back to the general principles of the Blackall Plan." Speaking of Clarence Blackall, Davis said that the university's pioneering campus planner—"the one man who first brought national recognition to his architectural Alma Mater"—resigned from the Alumni Association because of his "treatment by his University." Blackall had been excluded from the campus planning discussions of the 1920s.

"We cannot build at present, but it is a good time to plan," Davis told Willard. U of I officials and staff delivered only one plan for campus development in the mid- to late 1930s. The 1937 plan came in two versions, each showing different locations for a proposed biological sciences group. Scheme A put the biology buildings northeast of the Stock Pavilion and had some other interesting features, including a new Auditorium east of Huff Gym, an Illinois Union south of Lincoln Hall, and a journalism building on the southeast corner of Sixth and John Streets (current site of the Swanlund Administration Building). Scheme B situated the biology group west of the Stock Pavilion, the Illinois Union southeast of Smith Memorial Hall, and the journalism building south of Lincoln Hall. Both versions stayed true to the Platt-Vitale plan in their use of building groups, interior courtyards, and wide-open grassy malls.

In December 1940 Otto Schaffer, a professor of landscape architecture, brought the simmering controversy over the Platt-Vitale plan to a boil. Writing to Willard, Schaffer called for the creation of a committee to assess the plan. "If in the light of our present knowledge, the existing Campus Plan fails to meet our present and probable future needs," he said, "it should be reviewed and revised." A zealous proponent of the Platt-Vitale construct, Schaffer hoped that "we may develop our campus in harmony with the spirit in which Messrs. White, Platt, and Vitale conceived it."

Havens signaled his support for a committee "passing on the Vitale plan," and early in 1941 the Advisory Committee on Landscape Planting and Development was formed to do just that. The committee included Schaffer, university architect Ernie Stouffer, agronomist William L. Burlison, and Rexford Newcomb, an expert on architectural history. Very quickly, the committee decided that the Platt-Vitale plan

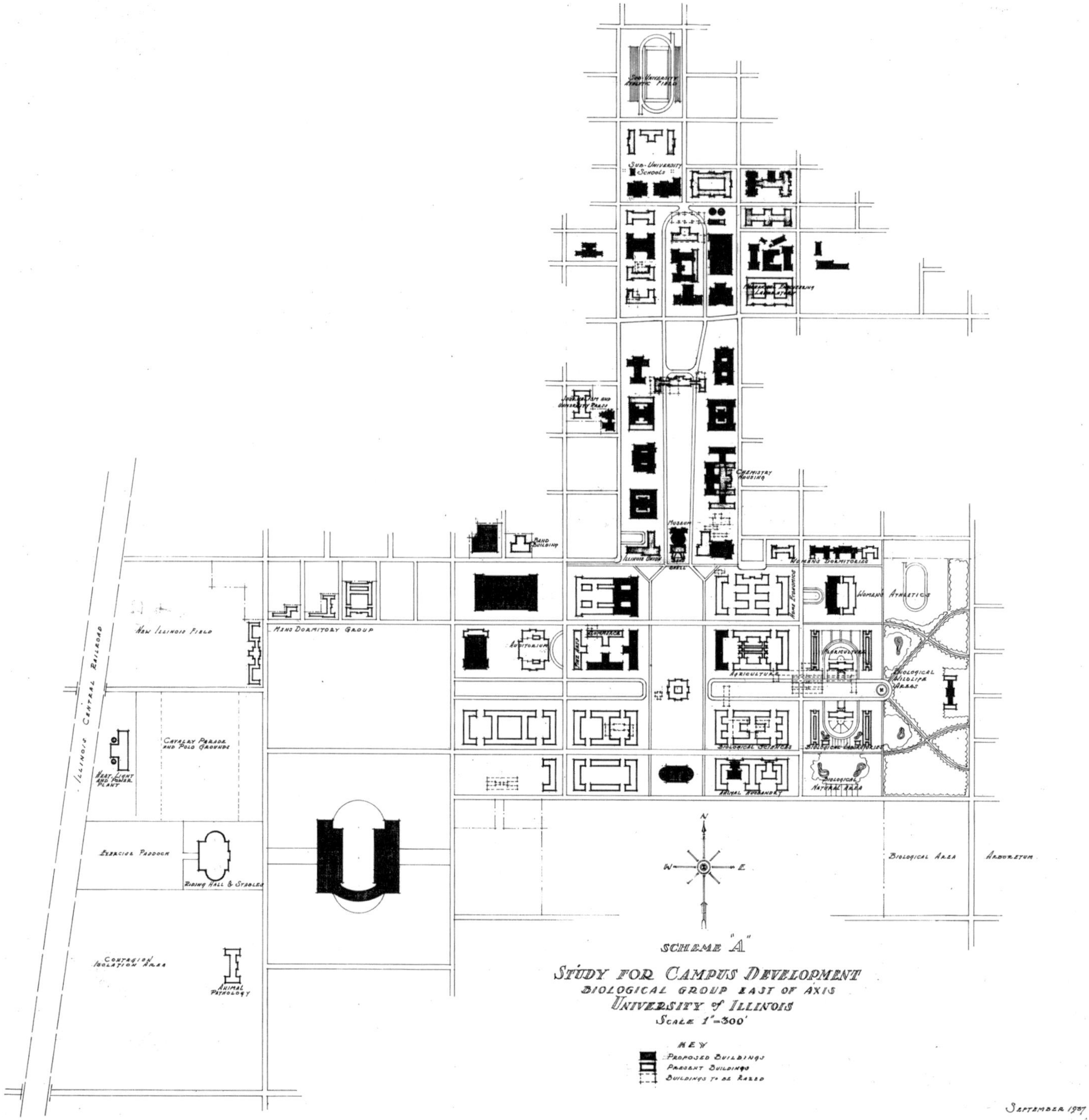

FIGURE 4.2. 1937 Plan, Scheme A. Study for Campus Development, Biological Group. Uncredited but certainly University Architect Ernest L. Stouffer and staff created the plan, which put biology buildings northeast of the Stock Pavilion, a new auditorium east of Huff Gym, and an Illini Union south of Lincoln Hall. (Photo courtesy of University of Illinois Archives.)

should be "essentially retained," but modified slightly. Most notably, the committee members recommended "a reduced extent for the ultimate campus development." In their view, Platt's plan had "envisioned a larger University and greater expansion of building than the facts now justify." Time, of course, would prove them wrong.

The committee met off and on for several years, suggesting several important changes to the Platt-Vitale plan along the way. For example, it advised that Platt's scheme for an Engineering Quad be put on hold because it would have required the "destruction of so many useful buildings." But committee members recognized that such a Quad "would undoubtedly improve the general appearance of the Engineering area." They also called for the opening up of two arterial streets in the campus area "as contrasted with the basic principle indicated on the Vitale Plan of discouraging . . . any through traffic." They proposed connecting Florida (Urbana) and Kirby (Champaign) Avenues via a subway under the Illinois Central tracks (at Neil Street) and an extension of Goodwin Avenue south through Mount Hope Cemetery, once again threatening to disturb the sleep of the dead.

The committee's shortsighted recommendation for a smaller campus can only be understood in the context of the times. With World War II raging overseas, university civilian enrollment was plummeting to its lowest levels since the 1910s, and building construction stopped. There seemed no need for a bigger campus in the short term. But some university officials were thinking longer term. Provost Albert Harno, later dean of law, predicted early in 1943 that the state and federal governments would launch huge building programs after the war in an effort to prevent "an economic nosedive," and he urged the university's Building Program Committee to think big.

The committee did. In summer 1944 it submitted a $32 million building wish list to the board of trustees. Reflecting the high hopes of U of I officials in the final year of the war, a 1944 campus plan showed dozens of new structures, including buildings for electrical engineering, mechanical engineering, chemical engineering, home economics, animal husbandry, and physical education. The scheme was rigidly divided by college, with Engineering north of Green Street, Liberal Arts and Sciences centered on the main Quad, and Agriculture south of Gregory Drive. Smaller areas were set aside for the Library, Law, Veterinary Medicine, the Fine Arts, Commerce, Journalism, Physical Education, and Military Training. A service area was positioned on the fringe of the campus, west of First Street. And this was the first plan to explicitly segregate the campus area into a "Men's Zone" (west of Sixth Street), and a "Women's Zone" (east of Goodwin Avenue).

The Illinois legislature responded well, giving the university a record building appropriation in 1945—more than $16 million. But President Willard would miss out on the action because stratospheric postwar inflation made it difficult for the university to obtain fixed bids in the face of constantly rising costs of labor and material. Skyrocketing inflation took a toll on the university budget. Only a decade before, Gregory Hall had cost $8.20 per square foot to build. By contrast, the Electrical Engineering Building—completed in 1949—cost almost three times as much to build, $22.40 per square foot.

These new buildings were desperately needed. In fall 1946 the university's Urbana campus registered an enrollment of 18,378—by far a school record. A large majority were veterans returning on the G.I. Bill, and 20 percent of them were married. The university responded by erecting temporary "cardboard villages" around the campus: the Illini Village and Stadium Terrace complexes for 595 couples and the barracks-like Parade Ground Units for 1,357 single students. In addition, two entire new university undergraduate branches were opened within the space of a summer—one at Navy Pier in Chicago and the other at Galesburg, "The College Made in a Month."

FIGURE 4.3. The U of I Undergraduate Division at Navy Pier in Chicago helped meet the demand for college World War II veterans using the G.I. Bill. The temporary branch campus of the U of I at Chicago opened in 1946 as a two-year undergraduate program with about thirty-eight hundred students, who called the Navy Pier location a "sideways skyscraper" and "horizontal cathedral of learning." In 1965 the new Chicago Circle Campus opened, and "Harvard on the Rocks" closed. (Image dated 1950. Photo courtesy of University of Illinois Archives 0003717. Photo copyrighted by Al Augustyn.)

The university's new president was forty-eight-year-old George Dinsmore Stoddard, a respected child psychologist and former New York State commissioner of education. The liberal Stoddard had grand plans for the university. He began by filling the school's top administrative spots with some of the best men in the academic world. His ambitions were clear in the record-breaking $104 million appropriation he sought from the legislature in 1947.

Stoddard's request included almost $30 million for buildings. These new structures were ready to go, their plans having been drawn up during the Willard administration. Overwhelmed by "the magnitude of the University's post-war

FIGURE 4.4. Aerial view of the Galesburg Undergraduate Division of the University of Illinois. Driven by an acute need to accommodate World War II veterans using the G.I. Bill to enroll in college, the Galesburg campus enrolled students into 1949 in buildings that comprised the former Mayo General Hospital. (Image dated 1946. Photo courtesy of University of Illinois Archives 0003710.)

construction program," Chuck Havens and Ernie Stouffer had been forced in 1945 to hire outside help in designing these new buildings. They turned mostly to Chicago firms such as Graham, Anderson, Probst and White; Fugard, Burt and Wilkinson; and Skidmore, Owings and Merrill. Following architecture historian Rexford Newcomb's advice to seek "the best talent that the country affords," Havens and Stouffer also tapped two out-of-state architects for this design work. "The University . . . must keep its sights high in this matter," Newcomb warned. "The fine work of White, Platt and others could be seriously marred by wrong steps in our immediate building program."

FIGURE 4.5. Steam tunnel construction near the Observatory with the Women's Gymnasium (later Freer Hall) in the background. Steam heat from a central power plant is efficient and economical for this expansive campus. (Image dated November 2, 1934. Photo courtesy of University of Illinois Archives 0003571.)

When Willard first saw the designs of the Chemical Engineering, Electrical Engineering, and Mechanical Engineering buildings in May 1946 (a bit more than a month before his term ended), he clearly believed they were a step in the wrong direction. The buildings were modular, streamlined, and unornamented—in short, modern. Willard was a fan of old-school and classic architecture. He had endorsed the colonial revival design of the Illini Union because it made the building, in his view, look "old and traditional, even more so than Uni. Hall ever did." Willard couldn't stomach the new designs and suggested they be changed.

Others shared Willard's view, including Leo Bauer, class of 1913. An architect, Bauer had seen sketches of the new buildings in the *Illinois Alumni News* and was outraged by what he called "this sinister departure" from the ideas of Charles Adams Platt. He wrote to the board of trustees. "Under his [Platt's] able guidance and direction," Bauer said, "the Illinois Campus has become one of the most renowned in the land, so distinguished by the elegance and charming simplicity of the Georgian Period. The proposed program is a trend away from those traditions which made of Illinois a center of culture." Bauer urged that the university promptly correct the designs to avoid placing "a blight on the remainder of the Campus structures."

Stoddard, the new president, took this criticism seriously and in response created a committee to advise on architectural design. This Consultative Committee on Architecture had three traditional architects, including Howard L. Cheney, the co-designer of the Illini Union, and one wild card, Eliel Saarinen, the progressive Finnish architect whose entry in the 1922 competition for the design of the Chicago Tribune Tower is one of the most famous—and consequential—failures in the history of architecture. Saarinen's art deco–inspired conception of "a tapered, soaring ziggurat" came in second place in the contest. But according to architecture historian Leland M. Roth, the Saarinen design exerted "a far greater influence on subsequent skyscraper design" than did the winning entry of John Mead Howells and Raymond Hood. Saarinen only reluctantly agreed to serve on Stoddard's committee: he was wary of what he termed the U of I School of Architecture's "stylistic tradition." "And 'stylistic tradition,' imitative in spirit as it is, is an approach to architecture with which I never have been able to cooperate," Saarinen told Stoddard.

It was clear the three traditionalists on the committee strongly favored Georgian architecture. "This style is flexible enough in character to readily adapt itself to special conditions," argued Oak Park landscape architect Chance Hill, "and it is difficult to understand why it is to be abandoned on the fringes of the campus for the so-called 'Contemporary' style whose very name implies that it is fluid, subject to constant change, and the personal whims of individual designers. This procedure has all the elements for adding to a hodgepodge campus over the years."

Demonstrating that he had read Tilton and O'Donnell's important 1930 book on U of I planning (based on a history begun in 1919), Hill feared that the university was "dangerously near to slipping back into the procedure of the old days when various architects were employed from time to time to design buildings for the University with results that are only too well known."

Hill spoke for the traditionalists whose views were firm. On April 19, 1947, the trio sent a telegram to President Stoddard calling for all new buildings to be designed "in Georgian character." Stoddard was astonished. "It had never occurred to me that the Consultative Committee on Architecture would want nothing but the so-called Georgian for these great engineering structures," he wrote. Stoddard had some qualms about modern architecture—the design of the Mechanical Engineering Building, for example, reminded him of "cell blocks I have seen"—but he was open to new ideas. "How to wed the old and the new on this campus in a spirit of transition and without conflict is surely our major problem," he told Eliel Saarinen.

The absolutism of the telegram sealed the fate of the committee, which would meet one more time before beginning to dissolve. It is not surprising that Saarinen was the first to resign. "We are now [in the] midst [of] an intense transition from dormant imitation to creative progressivism," Saarinen declared in his August 1, 1947, resignation letter to President Stoddard, "and . . . the growing generation of architects [is] not going to follow dictatorial stipulation of style whether Georgian or otherwise. They are all going to approach their design problems progressively and organically. And progressive and organic architecture requires entirely another design-pattern in the planning of a University Campus, as required that dwindling echo of imitative styles of yesteryear." Saarinen concluded on a warm note: "In these thoughts of mine, Mr. President, you might find drastic and unyielding tendencies, but after all they spring from an honest endeavor to see the truth in the eye."

The three traditionalists on the consultative committee had hoped to impose Georgian architecture on the entire campus, but, ironically, they opened the door to modernism instead. Stoddard was convinced that "neither duplication and imitation, on the one hand, [nor] 'modernization' on the other" was the answer. Old and new should be wedded somehow, he believed. This marriage of past and present would turn out to be a hallmark of the Stoddard presidency's building program, from the modern-Georgian Lincoln Avenue Residence Hall (1949) and Veterinary Medicine Building (1952) to the even more modern-Georgian Electrical Engineering Building (1949) and Chemical Engineering Building (1950) to the starkly modern Mechanical Engineering Building (1949), Student-Staff Apartments (1950), and Animal Sciences Laboratory (1952).

The consultative committee also paved the way for a reconsideration of Charles Platt's campus plan. Howard Cheney had advised Stoddard to hire an "outstanding firm of site planners and landscape architects to develop a revised Master Plan of the campus." The U of I president didn't immediately do so, and in the meantime the cities of Champaign and Urbana employed J. Robert Swanson—the same man who had served as Eliel Saarinen's representative on the consultative committee—to come up with a master plan for the region. Two months after the Urbana-Champaign master plan was unveiled in October 1949, Stoddard tapped Peoria architect Cecil C. Briggs "to make campus studies, plans and models looking to the future development of the campus at Urbana-Champaign."

FIGURE 4.6. View of Illini Village temporary housing for married veterans returning from World War II and their families. The housing was just east of Mount Hope Cemetery near the southwest corner of Pennsylvania and Lincoln Avenues in Urbana. (Image dated 1946. Photo courtesy of University of Illinois Archives 0003959.)

Briggs, a visiting professor at the time, had given advice on the designs of the Veterinary Medicine Building and the Animal Sciences Laboratory that Stoddard said had led to "very substantial savings without a diminution in building function." In short order the Peorian produced a January 1950 preliminary report with his own views on the university's campus-planning problem. Briggs was careful not to criticize the premises of Platt's twenty-year-old plan and famed buildings but saw fading usefulness and relevance. "It is sufficient to say that the obvious mistake was to allow any future plans to become static," he wrote. "All such plans should be flexible enough to allow changes which take place in functional operation without jeopardizing the architectural quality of the whole scheme." Briggs alluded to the ongoing and heated controversy between the proponents of Georgian and “progressive” architecture, blaming it for certain building designs that were “last minute compromises not entirely satisfactory to either guiding principle.”

Briggs studied and worked hard on his vision of a U of I campus for the booming post–World War II era. By August 1950 he was ready to challenge key premises of Platt’s “landscape campus,” including the use of space as an organizing principle. “The center of everything [under Platt’s scheme] is the ‘open space,’” Briggs said, “and all buildings, important or unimportant, are scattered around the perimeter. This open formal campus space had become a very expensive and rigid ‘park’ while teaching efficiency has dropped with every major expansion.”

He called for a radical rethinking of the campus layout. He recommended that the university’s landscaped areas be dramatically scaled down in size. “Organized and related smaller areas well designed for smaller groups of buildings are more appreciated than a tremendous acreage of distant vistas that are hard to keep up and even more difficult to traverse,” Briggs argued. He wanted to cover over much of this green space with new buildings. “Our recommendation . . . concentrates upon a theory of placing new buildings down the center of the main campus and . . . eventually east and west in the lower cross mall,” Briggs told Stoddard. Beauty took a distant back seat to functionality in Briggs’s technocratic scheme. His other ideas included opening roads for automobile traffic on the east side of the Quad and north of the Library, the latter in a shallow tunnel.

Stoddard found many of Briggs’s ideas to be “stimulating,” but even so he recommended in June 1951 that the Peoria architect’s consultancy be terminated. In a few short years, another professor would be plucked from the academic ranks to do planning and design work for the university. Ambrose Richardson would do more to shape the look of campus—this Illini Place—than anyone since the days of James White and Charles Platt.

In the span of almost twenty years, Richardson would design close to twenty-five campus buildings, each one showing the minimalist, less-is-more, influence of Ludwig Mies van der Rohe. It was a low point for the traditionalists. Trustee Wayne Johnston, the Illinois Central Railroad president and a fan of old-time architecture, once growled at Richardson: “Ambrose, you’ve done more damage to this campus than an atom bomb.”

CHAPTER 5

Building Boom and Bust

1955-1984

On a summer evening in 1953 some of the university's most powerful men gathered in architect Ambrose Richardson's basement to view the architect's model for the new Law School Building. Richardson, tall and poised, was a master salesman. Now, aided by his vivacious wife and a tray of cocktails, he theatrically removed the sheet covering the elaborate eighth-scale model and savored the oohs and aahs that spilled from his guests.

"This is just wonderful," Albert Harno, the Law School dean, was heard to remark. "I'm so thrilled." Then, the bespectacled Harno added, "Now, the only thing I don't understand is what it's going to look like."

The new Law School building looked like a series of boxes—sleek, red-brick, aluminum, and glass boxes. "It was a Miesian type of thing, very cold, sitting on the fringe of this oversized Georgian campus," Richardson told an interviewer years later.

The minimalist architecture of Ludwig Mies van der Rohe had become the go-to design approach for a generation of postwar architects. "He (Mies) had shown us a way that we thought was the sensible and logical way to design," Richardson said. "You do it on a modular, sensible, structural system. No nonsense. This is a good way to do it, and so everything became boxes."

Richardson had a direct connection to Mies van der Rohe. He was a senior at the Armour Institute of Technology (now the Illinois Institute of Technology) when Mies became head of the architecture school there in 1938. Educated in the old Beaux-Arts system, Richardson had had extreme difficulty adjusting to the radical new ideas and methods of Mies. But he succumbed, and his subsequent work as the chief designer in the Chicago office of Skidmore, Owings, and Merrill displayed a pronounced Miesian stamp.

Reduced to a self-described "raving wreck" by the excessive demands of his job, the thirty-four-year-old Richardson left Skidmore, Owings, and Merrill in 1951 to take a teaching position at the U of I, filling the slot vacated by the Peoria architect Cecil Briggs. Richardson's reputation as an SOM alumnus preceded him, and soon university architect Ernie Stouffer came calling, offering him the chance to design the new Law School building.

A year's worth of effort led to the dramatic unveiling in the basement of Richardson's modest home in Champaign. Shortly after that triumph, Richardson packed the model into his station wagon and transported it to the office of president George Stoddard for an encore performance.

Richardson recalled that Stoddard was "delighted to see . . . the contemporary stuff as a change from this eclectic, false-chimney architecture." Writing to physical plant director Charles Havens on July 17, 1953, the U of I president praised Richardson's "very handsome designs and models" and called for the continuation of the architect's work on this "fine project."

Only a week later, the board of trustees fired the controversial Stoddard during a notorious late-night meeting, but the "fine project" and Richardson's work on it continued uninterrupted.

Richardson had a powerful patron in Havens, and the architect flourished during the successive administrations of Lloyd Morey and David Henry. He also enjoyed the strong support of another influential figure: Park Livingston, president of the board of trustees and one of the prime movers in the ouster of Stoddard. "He thought I was some kind of genius," Richardson said of Livingston. "He said, 'The hell with this old architecture! We've found ourselves a way.'" Livingston also liked that Richardson tended to bring in his projects under budget.

Pleased with the law building, Havens and Stouffer next assigned Richardson to design the first three units in the men's residence hall complex, later popularly called "the Six-Pack." The buildings turned out to be major disappointments for Richardson. They were constructed on "a very economical basis and were pretty raw," he admitted. Worse, and unknown to him, large pieces of mechanical equipment were set to be placed on the roof of each building. "They were never shown on the drawings," Richardson recalled. "I wasn't aware of this, and to my horror, when these buildings were almost completed, I saw these things put up, frankly, almost on the edge of the roof, and they're as big as a trailer truck."

The new residence halls were part of a $36 million emergency housing program developed in response to the baby boom. It was a familiar story: how to cope with an expanding enrollment. But the magnitude of the postwar baby boom was extraordinary. In the state of Illinois, 141,056 babies were born in 1945; a year later that figure increased to 177,607; and by 1951, it had jumped to 202,845. Adding to the problem, the number of high school students choosing to go to college mushroomed from only 15 percent in 1940 to 40 percent in 1955. This "avalanche of children," in Richardson's words, threatened to overwhelm an already overcrowded university.

In summer 1954 a faculty committee estimated that enrollment on the Urbana-Champaign campus would reach twenty-three thousand in 1962-63 and a whopping thirty-eight thousand by 1972. (Enrollment on the UIUC campus in the winter session of 1953-54 was only 17,652.) The committee recommended new spaces to address both current overcrowding and the future enrollment surge. It also made a case for the establishment of a four-year U of I campus in the Chicago area, with the argument that half of the university's students and half of the state's population lived in Cook County and its surrounding collar counties.

Acting President Morey was fully on board with the recommendations. He set the wheels in motion for the creation of a Chicago campus and prodded Urbana campus planners to get going on an ambitious building program. Morey wanted university officials to start thinking in the longer term regarding campus planning and development.

"It seems to me that we should begin now to determine what additional facilities are needed at Urbana-Champaign to take care of the enrollment of 23,000 predicted in this schedule," the acting president wrote in March 1955 to Whitney Huntington, chairman of the Building Program Committee.

Planning was critical to Morey's successor, David Dodds Henry, the former executive vice chancellor of New York University. A onetime president of Wayne State University

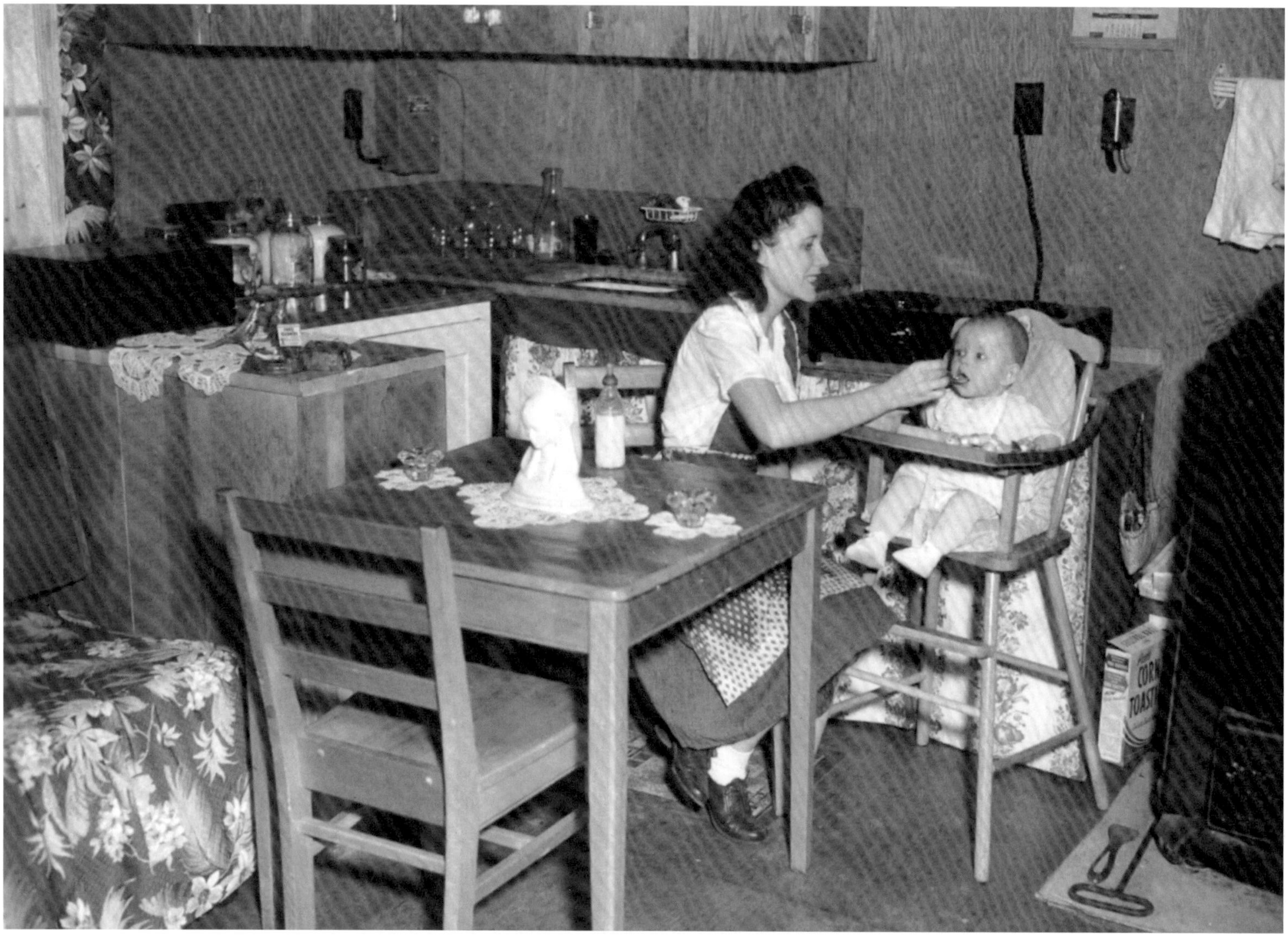

FIGURE 5.1. A woman and child inside a unit of Stadium Terrace, a temporary married-student housing complex built after World War II, primarily for veterans who flooded the campus. The prefabricated houses were lined up northwest of Memorial Stadium. In 1959 Orchard Downs opened as permanent housing for married students. (Image dated March 1946. Photo courtesy of University of Illinois Archives 0002805.)

and the owner of three degrees from Penn State, the forty-nine-year-old Henry—a slight man with a thin mustache and thick glasses—had a reputation as one of the ablest education administrators in the nation. Not long after taking office on September 1, 1955, Henry realized the urgent need for "extensive planning." "Although the University was on [an] even keel, its management in good order, its structure sound and well manned, it was not ready for the changes that I felt were coming," he wrote in his memoirs.

Not only was the university ill-prepared for the tsunami of baby boomers born between 1946 and 1964, it was also more generally was underinvested in good space. "The

Urbana campus had had little, relatively limited capital expenditure in the previous two decades," Henry said. "There was great need for updating facilities." A severe space deficit was already evident: in the years of depression and war, the U of I had received little money for buildings, and even in the booming postwar years, added building space failed to keep pace with the growing enrollment. So, the university purchased sixty-seven former residences and business properties and pressed them into service for classrooms, offices, and laboratories pending a permanent solution. This temporary space equaled the square footage of five buildings the size of Gregory Hall.

The need was obvious, but where would the money come from to finance these new buildings? Even during the administrations of Illinois governors Dwight Green and Adlai Stevenson—the last Illinois governors "without severe budgetary problems," according to journalist Robert Howard—the university never received the capital appropriations it wanted. But the current Illinois governor, William Grant Stratton, was a firm friend of higher education, and he had a plan.

"He was the most far-sighted governor whom I encountered in my years of public service in Michigan, New York, and Illinois," Henry later wrote. Stratton, an authority on Illinois government, concluded that only a $231 million bond issue could take care of the capital requirements of the state's public universities. All of the Illinois university presidents and their boards eagerly endorsed Stratton's idea and launched a public relations campaign to persuade Illinois voters/taxpayers to back the bond issue in a November 1958 referendum.

President Henry said he gave the bond issue "virtually all of my public speaking time, using the on-going plethora of public appearances and accepting special engagements to help further the cause." But the bond issue failed. Undaunted, Governor Stratton arranged for a smaller bond issue to be brought to voters in November 1960, a presidential election year. The universities upped their game for the new campaign, raising $110,000 instead of the paltry $2,305 in 1958, mobilizing an army of four thousand workers, distributing 1.5 million brochures, and obtaining the endorsements of eighty-two statewide organizations. Students got into the act, holding a marathon run from southern Illinois to Chicago. This time, a $195 million bond issue passed.

FIGURE 5.2. President David Dodds Henry, left, with Urbana-Champaign Chancellor Jack Peltason, Chicago Circle Campus Chancellor Norman Parker, and Chancellor of the Medical Center in Chicago, Joseph S. Begando. The chancellor system, begun in 1967, was a new organization for the university. (Image dated July 25, 1967. Photo courtesy of University of Illinois Archives 0003958.)

The university received nearly half of the proceeds from the bond issue—$98 million. Of that, $50 million was earmarked for the building of the Chicago campus, with the remainder going to Urbana-Champaign. The bond issue was a watershed event in the university's history. "In retrospect," Henry asserted, "it can be said that had the bond issue not succeeded, the Chicago development would not have been possible in the time frame that later occurred. The Urbana campus could not have accepted the large enrollments that the new buildings made possible." Some of these new buildings made possible by the bond issue included Commerce West (Wohlers Hall), the Education Building, and Turner Hall.

The university already knew precisely where it would build, thanks to the planning work of Ambrose Richardson, John Severns, Harlan Bareither, and others. In 1956 the Department of Architecture had refused Richardson's request to work half time for the Physical Plant, citing the possible negative effect on faculty "morale." So Richardson resigned from the university and set up his own architectural firm. As Severns put it, the Architecture faculty had forced Richardson to choose between teaching or an active architectural practice. And "Am" responded, "OK, I'll practice." And practice he did: Richardson continued to be the Physical Plant Department's go-to outside person on architectural matters for more than a decade.

In summer 1955, as Lloyd Morey's term as president was ending, Charles Havens assigned Richardson to work on a plan for a campus having an enrollment of twenty-three thousand. During the administration of David Dodds Henry (1955-71), the plan's scope enlarged to cover a ten-year period and a projected enrollment in 1969 of 27,500 undergraduates and six thousand graduate students. Completed in late September 1960, Richardson's groundbreaking *Ten Year Development Plan*, authored by Richardson, Severns, Scheeler & Associates, established "the first thinking on expansion since Platt's 1927 plan," according to preservation planner Alice Novak. "Thus it was this document that set forth much of the modern era of campus . . . as we know it," Novak writes.

The Richardson ten-year plan tipped its hat to previous planners and leaders. "The University of Illinois, in contrast to other similar institutions, is indeed fortunate to be able to reap the benefits of the foresight of the planners and administrators of the past," the report said. "Anticipating growth beyond all normal expectations of the time, they recommended that the University acquire land for expansion years in advance of critical need. They established the great malls with generous spacing around the building groups, and . . . they were able to create, through contrast and careful site planning, a sound campus core of scale appropriate to the desired atmosphere of an institution of learning."

The 1960 plan showed considerable respect for the long history of university planning. Indeed, James White and Charles Platt would have agreed with most of the report's "fundamental planning principles," which, among other things, called for keeping the mall concept, a building density of no greater than 25 percent, the general use of low-rise buildings for academic purposes, the grouping of buildings by college, and banishing vehicular traffic and student housing to the campus's periphery. The plan revived the old idea, once championed by Daniel H. Burnham, of an east-west mall on the South Campus. Only a decade earlier Peoria architect Cecil Briggs had proposed covering the malls with rows of buildings.

The 1960 planners faced a tough task: they had to determine what colleges were most in need of expansion and then decide how best to meet these space needs. For this work, they relied heavily on the calculations of Harlan Bareither, the U of I's "space commander." A Mattoon native and U of I graduate known for "his crisp comments to complicated questions," Bareither pioneered in the study of university space use and allocation. Using early IBM tabulating machines, he helped develop space calculations that took into account, for example, the fact that "it costs more to educate a student in Engineering [with his/her laboratory requirements] than in English." These calculations, of course, relied on estimated enrollments, he said.

Armed with data from Bareither, Richardson and his associates decided which colleges needed new buildings and which didn't. They also advised where to locate these buildings, ever mindful of the existing campus layout. For example, a proposed site for Commerce West on the mall east of David Kinley Hall was deemed "undesirable in view

FIGURE 5.3. Aerial view of campus looking northwest with a focus on the main Quad. The bounds of this image are Peabody Drive to the south, Gregory Street to the east, Interstate 74 to the north, and Neil Street and beyond to the west. (Image ca. 1962. Photo courtesy of University of Illinois Archives 0003589.)

of the importance of keeping the malls as the vital aesthetic elements of the campus."

"This particular open area is one of the best planned areas on the campus, and any building or buildings placed in this location would probably detract from the studied relationship of David Kinley Hall and Mumford Hall directly across the mall," the report said. Most of the planners' site recommendations, including this one, were followed.

Student housing loomed large in the 1960 campus plan. To meet projected 1962 enrollments, the university estimated it needed 4,446 additional housing units for undergraduate men and 2,130 more units for undergraduate women. Richardson and company proposed the construction of three more housing complexes on the periphery of the campus: to the west, the last three units of "the Six-Pack" (Snyder, Scott, and Weston Halls); to the south, the Pennsylvania Avenue Residence Halls; and, to the north to serve the engineering campus, the Illinois Street Residence Halls. President Henry nipped in the bud a proposal that would have cleared the Illini Grove, which had already been reduced on the north in 1925 by McKinley Hospital, to make room for additional dormitory space.

The campus planners of 1960 also sought to push cars to the fringes of the campus and create in the campus core car-free zone—"an attractive island with grass, trees and shrubs, well-planned and carefully situated buildings, and a ban on motor vehicles." Under this ban Mathews Avenue and Wright Street south of Green Street would be closed to car traffic.

The number of automobiles on campus had increased exponentially in the postwar years, a trend exacerbated when the university in 1953 lifted the "no-car rule" in effect since 1926. By 1960, there were on campus some fourteen thousand cars registered by students and faculty/staff but only about thirty-eight hundred parking spaces available in campus lots. Richardson and his staff hoped to win the "bumper battle" by building many parking lots, mostly on the outskirts of the campus. Surface parking lots with a total of 11,051 spaces and parking garages with another 4,690 spaces were recommended. It was a valiant but ultimately futile effort. "You've got to solve the parking problem," John Severns, Richardson's business partner, remembered being told in the late-1950s. "It's still never been solved," he said in 2006.

Ambrose Richardson was well known as a big thinker with a penchant for bold, often far-out, ideas. He famously suggested that enormous, climate-controlled plastic domes be used to cover everything from football fields to entire cities. For the most part, Richardson's 1960 campus plan was safe and sane, but one visionary idea did find its way into the final report. In the late 1950s Richardson had developed what he called the "South Campus Concept." He proposed that an entirely new satellite campus be built on eighty acres south of Mount Hope Cemetery. Able to accommodate eleven thousand students, this branch campus would be restricted to freshmen and sophomores or to students belonging to certain colleges. A big advantage of this scheme was "the fact that some 11,000 students might be separated for the most part from the congestion of the main campus," he said. "Such a separation would imply equal relief in terms of parking, traffic and building space now overcrowded."

University officials considered Richardson's radical "South Campus Concept." The university was running out of room on the main campus, and land acquisition to the east or west would have been out of reach because the neighborhoods were fully developed with private houses, churches, and businesses. The scheme attracted some heavyweight supporters. Provost Gordon Ray, the university's second-highest-ranking official, said the concept had merit: "Facilities could be provided less expensively in such a location than in the area east and west of the present central campus." University architect Ernie Stouffer also endorsed the plan, telling a *Daily Illini* reporter, "In the future, we will be building mostly on the other side of the cemetery."

Debate over the "South Campus Concept" reached the highest levels. At a May 1958 meeting on the third floor of the Administration Building, Physical Plant director Charles Havens and Norman Parker, chairman of the Building Program Committee, discussed Richardson's plan with President Henry. The result: defer and delay. "It was agreed . . . that on the basis of present studies, it appeared that the south campus development could, if necessary, be delayed through the 10-year period," a memo of the meeting said. As is often the case, delay meant death. Richardson's concept did make it into the final version of his campus plan, but by then it was largely a nonstarter. Henry later commended the Building Program Committee for its action—or rather inaction—on the "South Campus Concept." "That decision was not easy," he wrote in his memoirs, "but it was made wisely."

Looking back on the *Ten Year Development Plan* from the vantage point of late 1963, Havens gave it a mild thumbs-up. "In general, the plan has proved adequate for the projects anticipated in 1958, as well as for projects not then contemplated," Havens wrote. Campus development had largely followed along the lines set by Richardson's scheme, though a few unanticipated buildings such as the future Krannert Center for the Performing Arts had since cropped up, complicating the picture.

But Havens found fault with some of the assumptions of the plan. Enrollments proved to be even higher than projected, the ratio of graduate students to undergraduates exceeded expectations, and students were carrying heavier academic loads than even five years earlier. The Physical Plant director also believed that some of the scheme's fundamental planning principles had to be abandoned, such as limiting building density to 25 percent and requiring that buildings for academic and housing purposes be low-rise. Havens recognized as well the failure of the ten-year plan to provide for enough research space. Thanks to a flood of federal grants, scientific research was flourishing at the university, but the supply of laboratory and other experimental space had failed to keep up with the demand.

Havens wanted to carry on campus planning studies for the 1965-75 period, but he ran into a brick wall: Provost Lyle Lanier. In the university's organization chart, the only officials Havens had to report to were the president, the comptroller, and the provost, so Lanier's opinion mattered. The provost was a skeptic when it came to Richardson's ten-year plan, and he didn't see the need for yet another extended exercise in long-range planning, especially when future enrollment figures were so uncertain. Besides, Lanier asked, what would be the faculty role in the planning process? To the provost, Havens seemed to be working "on the general assumptions that physical plant planning can proceed in virtual isolation from educational planning—since there is no indication that departmental officers and faculty members would be involved in the analyses of what kinds of facilities would be needed during that decade." Excluding faculty would cause dissensions, Lanier said, and weaken the validity of the plan.

At times Havens was under siege in the 1950s and 1960s. His time as the Physical Plant ruler was ending. Increasingly, outside actors demanded a say in campus planning and development, and sometimes they got their way. As in the past, the issue of building design—the chronic controversy between Georgian and modern architecture—turned out to be one flashpoint. This time the proponent of Georgian architecture was none other than the university president, David Henry. Arrayed against him were most of the architecture faculty and Allen Weller, the influential dean of the College of Fine and Applied Arts.

The battle that would seal the fate of Georgian architecture on campus for the near future centered on the new Education Building. In spring 1959 the campus Building Program Committee approved a site for this structure in the open space between the Architecture and Natural Resources buildings. The committee did so "on the assumption that anything constructed in this area should be of Georgian design" similar to that of Architecture and Natural Resources and Henry strongly agreed. "By no means an advocate or an expert on Georgian architecture, my position is simply that we should have something that is authentically harmonious in a situation where the proposed building is so close to prototypes of a specific style," the president wrote to Havens.

Later, a majority of the Advisory Committee on the Selection of Architectural and Engineering Services advised that only architects "experienced with and sympathetic to"

FIGURE 5.4. Completed in 1964, the Education Building was designed by U of I architecture professor A. Richard Williams. The Education Building is on the South campus and is architecturally modernist, breaking the grip of Georgian revival. (Photo by Karyl Wackerlin.)

the Georgian style should be employed on this project. Two members of the committee dissented: Alan Laing, chairman of the Architecture Department, and Nathan Newmark, head of the Civil Engineering Department. The pair objected to Georgian architecture on two grounds: one based on cost and the other on philosophy. A structure built in this style, they argued, would cost some 15 percent more than one having "good contemporary architecture." As for philosophy, contemporary architectural thought had as its core belief the notion that design should express its time. "We feel," Laing and Newmark asserted in a letter to Henry, "that the continued use of Georgian architecture on the proposed site will mark the University of Illinois as a university which is still living in the 1920's architecturally."

Bewildered, Henry agreed to reopen the question of architectural design. "One of the problems, of course," he wrote to Laing and Newmark, "is how to get an informed view when most people have made up their minds as to whether all new construction should be strictly contemporary or whether it is possible to get harmony with older styles." The president thought that public opinion should have a role in the final decision. "A problem of this kind is not one exclusively for the experts to decide," he said.

Henry hit upon the brilliant idea of staging a throwdown between the traditionalists and the modernists. Two designs—one Georgian and one modern—would be submitted to the members of the board of trustees Buildings and Grounds Committee, and they would choose the winner. FAA's Dean Weller objected to this procedure, saying that it was "a dangerous policy to submit alternate stylistic designs to a body of laymen." Henry stuck to his guns. "Presumably the Board should consider the professional advice which differs in substance from the professional view held by those who believe that no more Georgian architecture should be constructed," the president replied.

Weller tapped young professor A. Richard Williams to champion the modernist cause, while two staff members in the university architect's office were assigned to represent the Georgian side. The ensuing "battle of styles" was waged before the Buildings and Grounds Committee in the fall of 1960, and, by all accounts, Williams wowed the committee members with a dazzling presentation. Henry later praised Williams for making his contribution "with imagination, skill and understanding."

In late December 1960 the Buildings and Grounds Committee picked Williams's low-slung, colonnaded contemporary design for the new Education Building. The decision opened wide the door for modern architecture: no neo-Georgian building—with the notable exception of Commerce West—would be constructed again on the campus until the 1980s. "Along with other new master planning proposals across the campus, most involving a much more positive role for landscape architecture, particularly in prairie grove character, the yoke of Neo-Georgian conformity was broken," Williams later said.

University planners gave more attention to landscape architecture during the Henry administration. The guiding force behind this renewed focus was Robert S. Chamberlin, the Physical Plant Department's longtime superintendent of operations. A university employee since 1938, the energetic Chamberlin had been the point man in handling the elm catastrophe of the 1950s, perhaps the single most devastating blow dealt to the beauty of the campus. Struck by the one-two punch of phloem necrosis—a viral ailment—and Dutch elm disease, the university's elms began to die off in 1949. Within a decade they were almost all gone, leaving the campus a barren wasteland dotted with more than a thousand stumps. A staggering 90 percent of the trees on campus—some eighteen hundred trees in total—had been American elms.

Ambrose Richardson's 1960 campus plan described the loss of the elms as "the single biggest problem facing the University in terms of appearance" and had urged the development of a major landscaping program. Some tree replanting had already been done. In fall 1956, for example, Chamberlin had overseen the transplant to the deforested Quad of thirty-three ten-to-twelve-year-old thornless honey locusts (moraine locusts), uprooted from their homes near Illini Village, Stadium Terrace, and the Parade Grounds. The landscaping program expanded in the early 1960s, and soon row after row of young trees began popping up along campus thoroughfares and malls: different varieties of trees such as red oak, sweet gum, sugar maple, and European linden. Chamberlin had said no to monoculture.

To aid this beautification, Chamberlin helped secure the appointment of the world-renowned landscape architect Hideo Sasaki as a program consultant. A U of I graduate and Harvard professor, Sasaki had formed a consulting firm in 1957—Sasaki and Associates—that in a few years had become the toast of the architectural world for "the excellence and scope of its planning work." Chamberlin, recently named

FIGURE 5.5. Landscape architect and U of I alumnus Hideo Sasaki founded Sasaki and Associates, an interdisciplinary planning and design firm in Watertown, Massachusetts, near Boston that created a series of important campus plans from 1986 to 2007. (Photo courtesy of Sasaki Foundation.)

university landscape architect, hoped that Sasaki would offer "a critical opinion, from a philosophical and broad view, on projected plans for the entire campus."

Sasaki's assessment of the campus landscape was blunt. He had no use for "fussy"—his favorite epithet—details and wanted the university to get back to the basics, to the landscaping principles established by Charles Platt and Ferruccio Vitale thirty years earlier. As had Platt and Vitale, Sasaki called for "simplicity, unity, massive scale, and strength in all plantings." Chamberlin saw merit in Sasaki's advice, but he wondered whether this 1920s approach was suited to modern forms of architecture.

"Since the planting format of trees, hedges and crabapples so appropriate to the South Campus [Platt development] assumes a rather uniform architectural design in style, setback and consistent spatial relationship," Chamberlin wrote, "it is difficult to see how these principles can be applied as literally as expressed by Mr. Sasaki to the contemporary design of the more recent past and the future."

Setting reservations aside, Chamberlin continued to employ Sasaki throughout much of the 1960s. Sasaki's influence still can be seen all over the university: in the mounds in front of the Fine and Applied Arts Building, in the benches on the Quad, in the brick-paved sidewalks, in the landscaping (now remnants) of "the Six-Pack" courtyards, and especially in the "long sweep of lawn, the massing of trees in large groups, the strong lines created by hedges and allees of trees" that so define the campus. The efforts of Chamberlin and Sasaki did much to restore the lost beauty of the campus. Writing to Chamberlin in 1965, Sasaki predicted that, after a few years, "the young trees will begin to give shape and coherence to the campus as the elms did before their destruction by the Dutch Elm disease."

"The Illini campus, without doubt, will again be one of the most attractive in the country," he said.

The honey locusts, the maples, and the oaks were giving a new look to the campus. But it was the forest of new buildings that really transformed the campus in the 1960s. The building boom ushered in by the 1960 bond issue continued in several bursts until the end of the Henry administration in 1971. This decade witnessed the construction of some twenty major buildings, including the Assembly Hall (1963), Morrill Hall (1963), the Education Building (1964), Commerce West (1964), Turner Hall (1964), the Materials Research Lab (1966), the Newmark Civil Engineering Lab

FIGURE 5.6. Aerial view of the Assembly Hall under construction. Opened in 1963, it unquestionably is one of the campus's most architecturally noteworthy buildings. Architect was Max Abramovitz. The building, renamed the State Farm Center in 2013, cost $8.35 million. A $170 million renovation was undertaken in the spring of 2014, with State Farm Insurance committing $60 million over thirty years for naming rights. Alumni, friends, and student fees are paying the rest, which could reach $285 million with debt service. (Image dated 1962. Courtesy of the University of Illinois Archives 0003936. Photo copyright by Curt Beamer, *Champaign News-Gazette*.)

(1967), the Psychology Building (1969), the Undergraduate Library (1969), the Intramural Physical Education Building (1971), the Foreign Languages Building (1971), and numerous residence halls.

Looking back on his long presidency, Henry expressed pride in his accomplishments as a builder. The value of the university's physical plant had ballooned during this period, going from $128,145,805 in 1955 to $625,837,223 in 1971. Henry answered critics who said he had been too much of a builder and not enough of an educator. "The emphasis upon building, it must be stressed, was in effect an emphasis upon educational opportunity and upon quality instruction, quality faculty, and quality research," Henry wrote in his memoirs. "Buildings are for people. To maintain a distinguished University without adequate facilities for its people is not possible."

By the late 1960s the boom years were coming to an end, and campus development ground to a halt, literally. In early 1969 the newly elected governor, Richard Ogilvie, imposed

FIGURE 5.7. Architect Max Abramovitz and Ernest L. Stouffer at the Assembly Hall under construction. Abramovitz was a U of I alumnus who also designed the Krannert Center for the Performing Arts and the United Nations headquarters in New York City. (Image dated July 13, 1961. Courtesy of the University of Illinois Archives 0005066. Copyright *Champaign News-Gazette*.)

a freeze on campus construction after surveying the state's sorry finances. During his four years in office, Ogilvie continued to take a hard line against university capital spending. Adding to the university's woes, the combative Illinois Board of Higher Education—created in the early 1960s to coordinate the state's universities—often sided with the governor on budgetary matters. By 1971 there were four new state universities—Chicago State, Governors State, Northeastern Illinois, and Sangamon State—as well as many new junior colleges competing with the University of Illinois and the other five state schools for a share of a diminishing pot of state money. In 1948 a whopping 78 percent of the state's tax dollars devoted to higher education went to the U of I; by 1968, that figure had fallen to 49 percent.

The *Provisional Long-Range Campus Planning Report, 1971-1980* well reflected the era's lowered expectations. The product of a request from the IBHE, the report was a far cry from the optimistic, far-reaching Richardson plan of 1960. "It's boring, even noticeably so for a plan," preservation planner Alice Novak notes. The dull, subdued tone made sense because this 1970 plan was based on projections showing a leveling off of undergraduate enrollment during the decade. Though suggesting some possible sites for future campus development, the report offered "more a statement of policy than a physical outline of activity" and largely preserved the status quo. The 1970 plan did have one novel aspect: it proposed the demolition of several university buildings, including two iconic ones: the Auditorium and Harker Hall. (Both were born again, thanks to private support. See chapter 9.)

In fall of 1971 David Dodds Henry retired as U of I president after a productive, sometimes stormy, sixteen years in office. He had served the longest of any university chief executive: Edmund James also had sixteen years to his credit, but he had been on sick leave during his last year. Henry termed the last few years of his tenure "the most strenuous, with the struggles with the Board of Higher Education, the student unrest, and the growing financial limitations on the University's growth and development." But he said that the tenor of the times had not influenced his decision to retire: he simply made up his mind to leave office at the conventional age of sixty-five.

Some of the biggest builders responsible for the Illini Place exited the stage with Henry: Robert Chamberlin, Ambrose Richardson, and Charles Havens, who had a combined 105 years of service to the university. It was a changing of the guard that matched in importance the one that had occurred in 1933 with the deaths of James White, Ferruccio Vitale, and Charles Platt. Chamberlin, head of the Division of Campus Development, took early retirement, leaving behind a greener, healthier, and better-designed campus landscape. With little to no university work left for him to do, Richardson moved on to South Bend, where he became the chairman of Notre Dame's Department of Architecture. For better or for worse, he had modernized the look of the campus, dragging it kicking and screaming into the space age, and his ten-year plan had paved the way for the explosive development of the 1960s.

The U of I's Physical Plant master since 1933, Charles Stewart Havens retired in 1971 at age sixty-six. In his prime, Havens was, according to John Severns, "the most powerful person on the campus." Severns found him to be hard-nosed and as straight as an arrow. Once decided, Havens expected no deviation from the plan.

In the 1960s, the Physical Plant director devoted much of his time to the Chicago Circle campus: his work in getting the Chicago campus up and running in less than two years was widely regarded as "an educational and construction miracle." In 1967 Chicago Circle became one of the university's three campuses, along with Urbana-Champaign and the Medical Center, each headed by a chancellor. Soon after, the vast Physical Plant empire that Havens had spent decades building was carved in two: into departments of Plant and Services, and Planning and Construction. Havens served his last years at the university as the director of Physical Plant Planning and Construction. Clearly Havens's old job had become too much for one person to handle, just as in 1933 the vast responsibilities of supervising architect James White were divided between Havens and Ernie Stouffer.

As for Stouffer, the other heir to the legacy of James White, he had retired in 1965 after thirty-five years of service at the university. During his final years as university architect, Stouffer had been a persistent thorn in the side of Havens. In 1961, for example, Stouffer balked at having to approve payments to Ambrose Richardson's firm because his office had no effective authority over that firm's planning efforts. Later, in a letter to Provost Lyle Lanier, the university architect accused Richardson's firm of "perhaps illegally operating independently of the Architectural Division

FIGURE 5.8. President John Corbally, right, with Chancellor Jack Peltason near the Krannert Center for the Performing Arts. (Image dated 1975. Photo courtesy of the University of Illinois Archives 0003157.)

[Stouffer's office]." In the same letter, Stouffer called for a new chain of command that would have had the university architect report directly to the executive vice president (Lanier) instead of to the Physical Plant director (Havens). Shortly before his retirement in early 1965, Stouffer told a *Daily Illini* reporter that his happiest years had occurred way back in the 1920s when he was an architect in Streator—an unvarnished commentary on his time at the university.

In one of his last official letters to President Henry, Havens painted a bleak picture for the future of campus development in the 1970s. The mood was hostile in Springfield, with lawmakers implying that state universities were "building monuments" and with Governor Ogilvie holding up the release of university capital funds. Delay meant there was little campus construction occurring.

And there wasn't likely to be much in the way of future construction either, given projections showing an enrollment drop after 1982 to roughly the 1976 level. "As a result," Havens wrote, "it is unlikely that the planning and construction activities of this office [the Physical Plant Planning and Construction Department] will reach the levels of recent years within the foreseeable future." He predicted that the campus planners would take a back seat to the bean counters and numbers crunchers during the 1970s. "I anticipate that in this decade the emphasis will be on cost analysis and justification," Havens said.

Into this grim environment strode president John "Jack" Corbally in September 1971. Morale was down, budgets were down, and even enrollments were down. Between 1959 and 1970, the university's Urbana-Champaign campus had experienced record enrollments for twelve years in a row, jumping from 20,219 to 34,018 students. This remarkable streak came to an end in the fall of 1971, when enrollment unexpectedly dropped more than sixteen hundred students.

The tall, sturdy, forty-six-year-old Corbally, the former president and chancellor of Syracuse University, brought with him a sense of humor the university would need in the dispiriting years that followed. His tumultuous first year in office set the tone for his tenure at Illinois. A battle was waged against Governor Ogilvie and his budget cuts—and lost. A battle was waged against the Illinois Board of Higher Education and its controversial executive director James B. Holderman—"probably the most hated man on the Urbana-Champaign campus," according to the *Daily Illini*—and lost. The university was fighting for its very financial survival, Corbally declared in January 1972. "Our task is to run as fast and as hard as we can to stand still—to avoid losing ground," he said.

Trapped in "a rapidly-closing vise of falling enrollment, stringent budgets, and declining support from the state and federal governments," Corbally hoped to achieve cost savings through administrative reform and reorganization. As Havens had predicted, the bean counters and numbers crunchers came to the fore, with the elimination of waste and duplication as their goal. The Department of Plant and Services, for example, was dissolved, and its responsibilities were scattered among three different administrative units; Haven's Office of Physical Plant Planning and Development was reorganized and renamed the Office for Capital Programs. The twenty-something Ronald Brady, Corbally's vice president for university planning and allocation, spearheaded these reform efforts. A figure who had an "all-pervading" influence in the Corbally administration, Brady was "widely feared and disliked by lower-level administrators who mutter

FIGURE 5.9. The Taft House, now at 1401 South Maryland Avenue, is transported down Sixth Street from its original location on John Street where the Swanlund Administration Building stands. Lorado Taft, sculptor of the Alma Mater, lived in the house as a youth. His father, John Carlos Taft, was a U of I professor of geology who built the house in 1873. The U of I paid $80,000 in 1949 for the Taft House. (Image dated November 1981. Photo courtesy of University of Illinois Archives 0001854.)

FIGURE 5.10. Stanley O. Ikenberry was U of I president from 1979 to 1995 and for nine months for during 2009-10. He is the longest-serving and one of the most productive U of I leaders. Responding to what he called a "facility crisis," Ikenberry led extensive campus planning and building booms, combining federal, state, and private money. (Photo courtesy of University Office for University Relations.)

darkly about the 'General Motors mentality' that has taken over the president's office," *Daily Illini* columnist Jim Gehring claimed.

Administrative reform wasn't enough for Corbally. Like most university presidents, Corbally wanted to build, and Brady, the whiz kid from Ohio State, showed him the way forward. Over the years, the university had sought state money for various College of Agriculture and College of Veterinary Medicine building projects without success. Brady trumpeted the idea of packaging all of these projects into one program dubbed Food for Century III. As one journalist put it, the university was betting on the hope that "the way to the state's purse strings is through its stomach."

The bet paid off, and in 1977 the university received some $10 million from the legislature—the first installment in what would ultimately be a $70-million-plus program. Crucially, Food for Century III had early support from all seventeen of the state's agriculture organizations, along with the Illinois Board of Higher Education and the newly elected Governor Jim Thompson. You don't say no to farmers in Illinois, and that's how the program was marketed.

Corbally wouldn't be around to reap the benefits of the Food for Century III program. Feeling "an increasing sense of repetitiousness in the tasks of my position," and citing "waning enthusiasm" he retired from the U of I presidency in the fall of 1979.

Only three academic buildings had been constructed on the Urbana campus during Corbally's tenure: the Music Building (1972), the Medical Sciences Building (1975), and the Speech and Hearing Sciences Building (1977). The first new structures made possible by Food for Century III wouldn't come online until the early 1980s during the administration of Corbally's successor, Stanley O. Ikenberry: the Veterinary Medicine Basic Sciences Building (1982) and the Agricultural Engineering Sciences Building (1983).

At age forty-four, Stanley Ikenberry, Penn State's former senior vice president, was the youngest-ever U of I president. Energetic, optimistic, and charismatic, Ikenberry gained from his father—the longtime head of a small West Virginia college—an appreciation for campus design and development. "The president is in a unique position, I think, to both observe . . . and have an impact on the physical character of the campus," Ikenberry said.

He pedaled his bicycle around the university and at first was impressed with the "big and beautiful" campus. But, over the years, he saw some things that bothered him. Little things, like the "garish" blue and orange Illinois Field fence, and big things, like the lack of "a discernible architectural style" on the campus. "I think that many people referred to the Urbana-Champaign campus as being a hodgepodge of architecture at that time," Ikenberry recalled in an interview. There were "old Georgian buildings combined with a roughly equal number of fifties and sixties architecture," and "we hadn't figured out what to do next."

Ikenberry's first years, though, were preoccupied with the merger of the Medical Center and Chicago Circle campuses to create the University of Illinois at Chicago. But, even then, the new president had to attend to building matters. For example, the designs of the Veterinary Medicine Basic Sciences Building, the UIC Pavilion, and the Agricultural Engineering Sciences Building caused Ikenberry no little heartburn. Ikenberry believed that all three structures were, aesthetically, "less than they should have been." In the back of his mind, he thought, "We can't let this happen again."

And then there was the case of Maybelle Swanlund. The 1932 U of I graduate sent a "very stern" letter to Ikenberry during his first months in office demanding that he send her plans for the administration building she intended to finance. Confused, the new president discovered that the "problem had been sitting around" since the Corbally administration. "I could understand why she was annoyed," Ikenberry said. But Ikenberry didn't want a new administration building. The university was in dire financial straits, and the "last thing I wanted to do . . . was to turn around and say to the faculty . . . that I had good news for them, that I wanted to build a palace for the new president." Ikenberry and Ron Brady traveled to California in an attempt to interest Swanlund in other projects, but she "wouldn't bite on anything." So the university got the Swanlund Administration Building developed for the Urbana-Champaign chancellor and vice chancellors.

The Swanlund incident suggested a possible path forward for the university in terms of future funding: persistent gaps in state and federal funding could be filled by private philanthropy. Indeed, the U of I Foundation's "Campaign for Illinois," launched during the Corbally administration, was proving to be a rousing success and ultimately would raise some $132 million against a $100 million goal from private donors. One of the biggest contributors to the campaign was the scientific instrument manufacturer Arnold Orville Beckman, inventor of the pH meter, a founding father of Silicon Valley, and U of I graduate. Almost immediately, the billionaire Beckman appeared on Ikenberry's radar screen.

Eminent Domain

As early as 1914 the campus employed eminent domain to assemble land for expansion as the U of I grew well beyond its original borders. Agriculture, student services, the performing arts, and big science all laid claim to private land by invoking the law to seize property if voluntary sale weren't possible. Read about "Eminent Domain" on the companion Web site (sidebar 5.1).

The University Golf Courses

When a new cattle barn shortened the third hole to a mere 135 yards, early U of I duffers knew their rough 1899 campus golf course, built on a pasture south of the Natural History Building, would yield completely to agriculture. New campus golf courses opened in 1906, 1950, and 1965. Read about "The University Golf Courses" on the companion Web site (sidebar 5.2).

CHAPTER 6

Plans, Partners, and Big Ideas

1985-2015

On a cool and overcast Saturday morning in the autumn of 1985, scientist-inventor-entrepreneur Arnold Orville Beckman stood at the front of the slightly shabby law school auditorium at the University of Illinois to accept thanks for his $40 million gift to the Urbana-Champaign campus. Nearby stood his wife of sixty years and partner in philanthropy, Mabel S. Meinzer Beckman.

The son of a blacksmith from small-town Cullom, about sixty-five miles north of Champaign-Urbana, Beckman earned bachelor's and master's degrees from the U of I in 1922 and 1923 and a doctorate from the California Institute of Technology in 1928. He met his wife in New York—he was a Marine based at the Brooklyn Navy Yard, and she was serving the 1918 Thanksgiving dinner at a local YMCA—and the couple lived and worked the rest of their lives in California.

In their later years, together they were determined to give away a half-billion-dollar fortune made over a lifetime of invention and hard work. "I don't know whether my payoff in philanthropy is to help humanity or prevent the IRS from getting it," Beckman told *Business Week* in March 1986.

U of I President Stanley O. Ikenberry (1979-95; 2009-10) had made the formal announcement of the Beckman gift, believed to be the largest single donation to a public university from a private individual to that date, October 5, 1985. Then-Governor James R. Thompson, a Republican known as "Big Jim" during his record fourteen-year term as Illinois's chief executive officer not only for his six-foot, six-inch frame, but for his gregarious and outsized personality, committed a $10 million match from the State of Illinois. Ikenberry successfully lobbied the four state legislative leaders to deliver on the governor's promise.

The gift (and match) to establish the interdisciplinary Beckman Institute for Advanced Science and Technology, astonishing in its own right, was, however, profoundly important to the University of Illinois for another reason: it ignited a surge of campus planning theretofore unseen in more than half a century.

Finding the right location for the new institute, programmed for about 330,000 square feet, provided the perfect opportunity to look closely at the north, or engineering, campus, which would host the new building and several others already in the works.

Within six months, warp speed by academic measure, Sasaki Associates Inc. of Watertown, Massachusetts, had prepared a sixty-six-page North Campus Master Plan, and Ikenberry and Chancellor Thomas E. Everhart (1984-87) had moved the plan to approval by the University Board of Trustees on April 10, 1986. It was, as Urbana planner Alice Novak put it, "a more complex plan for a more complex time."

Beckman had jumped onto Ikenberry's radar screen early in his presidency with a generous $5 million commitment to the Campus Research Board—and the requirement of a dollar-for-dollar match. "Arnold was not only a wonderful philanthropist, but the toughest businessman," who brought a "pure business perspective" to his purposeful giving, Ikenberry recalled in a 2008 interview.

In fact, the match of private dollars and state/federal money became emblematic of major gifts then as today. Donors challenged the university to secure government funding and would match at the rate of 1:1, 1:2, or 1:3. The Beckman gift was 4:1, $40 million from the donor and $10 million from the state, a ratio not seen since. (More recently, forty, fifty, or several hundreds of donors will contribute to projects, such as the ACES Library, the Alice Campbell Alumni Center, and the giant energy-efficient ECE Building [Electrical and Computer Engineering] that overflows the last empty space of the Beckman Quad.) For a couple of years, the ECE Web site updated every day its "Buy a Bit" campaign that yielded more than $90 million. Of that, $47.5 million is state funds, the rest in private money ranging from $10 million from the Grainger Foundation to several hundred gifts less than $1,000.

Arnold Beckman regularly visited the campus en route to or from board meetings of SmithKlineBeckman, the corporation formed from the 1982 merger of Beckman Instruments, the source of Beckman's wealth, and SmithKline, a pharmaceutical company. According to Theodore Brown's 2009 book *Bridging Divides: The Origins of the Beckman Institute at Illinois*, the Beckman campus visits included time with interesting and productive faculty members, including Beckman Fellows and others working under Beckman Research Awards. Brown was at that time campus vice chancellor for research and dean of the Graduate College; he became the founding director of the Beckman Institute (1987-93) and spearheaded the proposal that led to the Beckman gift.

The executive director of the University of Illinois Foundation, Lewis Barron, had told Ikenberry that the Beckmans wanted to liquidate their substantial estate and give it away during their lifetime.

Earlier, in 1983, Barron had urged campus officials to employ a strategy common among private universities in approaching major donors for new facilities. He called for "sweeping, imaginative new projects that would move the campus to the forefront in promising research areas, and which were of such a scope and character that the state would almost certainly not provide funding for them," Brown wrote of Barron's idea.

Brown took leadership of the elaborate effort, and throughout 1984 a select group of faculty developed the proposal, which first went to the Beckmans that fall. A supplement—making the case that the Urbana-Champaign campus was a proven winner in interdisciplinary research—went in summer 1985.

The "ask" was $50 million, nearly twice as much as Ikenberry had first calculated. "It was hard for me to conceptually put my arms around that," Ikenberry said in 2008. The "big idea" was born.

Facility Crisis

But the Beckman Institute did not develop in isolation. Independent of the prospect of a huge gift was the stark reality of what Ikenberry termed a facility crisis. While the campus's student enrollment had not increased dramatically, the size

FIGURE 6.1. The Beckman Institute tower medallion. (Photo by Karyl Wackerlin.)

of the campus's research program in dollars, faculty, and engaged students had expanded materially. "So the research expansion was causing a crisis in precisely the area in which the Urbana campus has a long-standing position of strength: science and technology," he said.

This concern for facilities was joined with the Beckman opportunity. A less imaginative outcome would have been to build a long-needed chemistry and life sciences facility, which finally was constructed in 1996 in the central campus, but that would be a "non-starter" with Beckman himself, as he had solicited proposals from schools other than Illinois. Those other schools included big-science and engineering competitor Caltech, where Beckman had earned his doctorate and served on the board of trustees for two decades.

Both Arnold and Mabel Beckman read and critiqued the proposals, and as the weeks rolled by, Ikenberry said he despaired that a gift would materialize.

On one visit to California—and one more lunch with the Beckmans at the Pacific Club in Newport Beach—Ikenberry said he wondered to himself when it would all end. "Mabel must have sensed that I was sagging a little bit or getting discouraged . . . I must have had the 'wrong' look on my face, but she came up and put her arm around me and said, 'Stan: Don't worry. I've read all the proposals that have come in and Illinois is best."

Illinois also was first. Late that summer Ikenberry learned the U of I would receive $40 million contingent on a $10 million state match. Barron whispered the good news in Ikenberry's ear during a break in a regular board of trustees meeting in the second-floor General Lounge of the Illini Union.

"And I was just weak," Ikenberry recalled. "The difficult part was I couldn't tell anybody," not the Board of Trustees or campus officials until he had lined up the state match, which he did in short order.

Campus Planning

Earlier in his presidency, Ikenberry keyed in on how all three campuses looked: Urbana-Champaign, the Medical Center in Chicago, and Chicago Circle. The latter two would be consolidated in 1982 to form UIC, the University of Illinois at Chicago. Ikenberry brought no special talent or insight to the physical campuses, but said he looked for "the theme" of the campuses, how they acquired land, how they were planned, how buildings would fit the plan and, important as well, how the buildings would look at ground level. He rode his bike on the Urbana-Champaign campus for both a modicum of fresh air and to make observations. "I believed it was management by riding around," he said.

There had not been a formal campus plan since the "Provisional Long-Range Campus Planning Report, 1971-1980," a 1970 in-house effort by staff of the U of I's Division of Planning and Construction, and its 1960 predecessor, the "University of Illinois Ten-Year Development Plan, 1959-1969," which was driven substantially by the incoming tide of baby boomers; undersized, makeshift, and temporary buildings, especially student housing; and the never-resolved (and perhaps irresolvable) issues of traffic and parking. The campus was mature—nearly 120 years old—and, at its edges, uneven and in need of a facelift.

The 1986 Sasaki north campus plan enabled the U of I to site the massive Beckman Institute as the campus's northernmost terminus in a new and more refined space. Historic Illinois Field, which once housed not only baseball but also football and track at the corner of University Avenue and Wright Street (and ranging all the way south to Springfield Avenue), had already been bumped out and moved to a new baseball diamond and ancillary buildings east of Fourth Street and just south of Florida Avenue.

The 1986 plan also made way for several other research buildings on the engineering campus, reasserted an architectural and landscape style, established pedestrian-friendly open spaces (two quads), and tied the north campus to the central campus from which it had seemed to be physically and psychically estranged for decades. "North of Green Street" was more than a geographic designation.

The North Campus Master Plan was first in an ambitious series of plans that, within five years, examined literally every acre of the Urbana-Champaign campus; explored ways to cluster and site new buildings and public spaces; called out land use and transportation principles; and drew fresh-eyed attention to the place, its history, and its aspirations.

"Master plans, as other visionary schemes, are subject to the tugs and pushes of changing requirements and resources," wrote Ikenberry and Everhart in their foreword to the 1986 North Campus Master Plan. "This plan, as its predecessors, is not a blueprint but a dream toward which we will work. [It] boldly reaches for the future while honoring our past."

Roland Kehe was campus architect from 1982 to 2003, the high-energy planning and building era. He said in a 2009 interview and later email exchange that the Sasaki engagement was exemplary. "Working with Sasaki on the master plans and especially the North Campus plan was a lesson that more master planners and architects should learn from," he said. First, they were listeners and asked good questions. Second, they learned organically about the campus: no preconceived notions of what the campus was looking for or even what they thought the campus was looking for. And third, "they respected the history of the planning that had preceded them and especially the strengths of the Blackall plan that had set the stage for the north-south axis and the open spaces."

Cascade of Plans

In quick succession, Sasaki, other outside firms, and campus staff prepared fourteen additional plans that under Ikenberry (1979-95) and his successor, James J. Stukel (1995-2005), the board of trustees reviewed and/or approved. The plans also looked at retail in near-campus neighborhoods, parking, athletics, and a proposed research park.

Then, as suddenly as it started, the orgy of planning stopped in March 2007 after Sasaki and U of I staff combined and updated the north, south, central, and south farms master plans into one. The omnibus plan recognized new buildings and other developments that had occurred since the mid- and late 1980s. Also, by then, another president, B. Joseph White, and Urbana-Champaign chancellor, Richard H. Herman, were in charge.

In 2015—fully thirty years from the announcement of the Beckman gift (and a revolving door of leaders)—the campus proposed a fresh look at its all-campus master plan and hired a new firm, SmithGroupJJR, to consolidate previous plans and, once again, examine the present and peer into the future with fresh eyes. SmithGroup is an international firm with about eleven hundred staffers in a dozen offices, including Chicago. Sasaki Associates was interviewed.

The plan was expected to be done in the sesquicentennial year and would not only integrate master plan strategic and academic goals from other campus sources but also include other plans for the Research Park, campus bicycles, parking, and the like.

The 1985-2007 plans and updates represent contemporary thinking and contain depth lacking in earlier U of I plans, especially those of the first half of the century. This clearly reflects trends in the practice and discipline of planning, which was a natural outgrowth of architecture; the significant growth of the campus (hundreds of buildings versus a handful when the 1905 Blackall and 1922 Platt plans were developed, for example); and the ability of the institution to quantify and track its own physical plant through sophisticated computer-based information management.

But it also is clear that the long-term and repeated engagement of Sasaki gave continuity and brought efficiency to planning efforts in the 1980s and 1990s; knowledge and trust developed over two decades allowed for honest assessment and advice. Sasaki planner Joseph Hibbard, for example, aged into his profession with the U of I (his alma mater) as a major, ongoing client. That longevity positively informed the plans. And the campus was better for it.

"The campus today is far more beautiful than when I first came to the campus in 1981," retired campus architect Kehe said. "This is in part due to a series of events and an understanding of who we are as a campus community." The planning exercises brought forth a vision of controlled growth and adherence—mostly—to the plan, especially during Ikenberry's presidency.

"What was especially enlightening during my time as campus architect was that, with rare exceptions, everyone—administration, faculty and staff—bought into the planning process, the master plans and supported them. The landscaping is maturing and [complements] the buildings it supports."

Context of the Directional Plans

The timing of the directional Sasaki campus plans—north, south, central, and south farms—was fortuitous, and the mood was optimistic. Student enrollment had climbed, topping the thirty-six-thousand mark in 1985 for the first time. (Enrollment was barely twenty-seven thousand in 1964, the first year of baby boom enrollment, and about forty-four thousand in fall 2015.) State operating support in the campus budget rose steadily from $188 million in FY 1985 to a high of $327 million in 2002 before sliding backward and then stalling out completely in fiscal 2016, with only $47 million appropriated. The budget for fiscal year 2017 showed $119 million in state support, down nearly two-thirds from its high, not adjusted for inflation. But in the late-1980s, when the early Sasaki plans were created, the state was spending freely and the U of I was on the march.

The campus's aggressive move into encouraging and promoting high-level entrepreneurial research—after two decades of nonstop talk—coincided with a state political and economic climate open to significant brick-and-mortar investments and partnerships with private developers who would build and manage facilities, including, ultimately, the campus's south research park.

State bonds funded massive building programs, and the U of I was first in line to claim millions of dollars for buildings and programs billed as investments in intellectual and research infrastructure linked to economic development—jobs, in the political vernacular of Illinois.

The University of Illinois, for example, provided a blueprint to newly elected Illinois Governor George H. Ryan (1999-2003) that was intended to drive the "new economy" in a state where agriculture, manufacturing and financial services ruled. The U of I's blueprint was a document called "At the Crossroads: The State, the University and Tomorrow's Technology; A Plan for Economic Development through Advanced Technology Investment."

"At the Crossroads" laid the groundwork for a gubernatorial and legislative budget initiative called Illinois VentureTECH. In his combined 2000 State of the State and Budget address, Ryan proposed a five-year, $1.9 billion commitment of state funds to help develop more than $3.9 billion in technology-related infrastructure throughout Illinois. The setup to VentureTECH came a year before, shortly after Ryan took office, in his 1999 State of the State address.

"Illinois has always served as a crossroads," Governor Ryan said. "For two centuries, our location has helped make Illinois rich, as goods and ideas have moved faster and faster. First by water. Then by rail. Today by air. For each, in its time, Illinois was a dominant hub. But the new medium is neither water, nor steel nor air. It's information. . . . Illinois must invest in this technology-based innovation economy."

In 2000 the U of I was attracting about $340 million in federal research money, five times what the other public universities in Illinois brought in combined. In making its appeal for capital investment in research facilities, the university cited a combination of intellectual muscle, proven success, and strong reputations in engineering, computer science, chemistry, life sciences, including agriculture, and other fields to lay claim to nearly $300 million for construction and operations in eight new high-tech initiatives at the U of I (including pharmacy, medical imaging, and advanced chemical technologies at the Chicago campus).

As with the earlier packaging of facilities and programs for agriculture and veterinary medicine called "Food for Century III," Illinois VentureTECH did not deliver all it promised. But at its inception, the U of I was ready with a specific program and facility list, had begun to strengthen its existing relationships with such entities as the Illinois Medical District, the Illinois Coalition, and IBIO (the Illinois Biotechnology Organization), and had crystallized more than a decade of internal conversations into two big notions.

Fourth Mission: Economic Development

The big ideas: First, the University of Illinois should publicly and through formal action of its board of trustees claim a "fourth mission" of economic development in addition to the familiar triad of teaching, research, and public service long identified with the university's land-grant origins. And second, the Urbana campus should create two Science and Engineering Technology Commercialization Centers—one near the engineering (north) campus and one on the south (farm) campus.

In the end, the Urbana-Champaign campus partnered with private developers selected in 2000 in a contentious competition to create a single research park that was anchored by its first building, a Motorola software development facility, where sheep once grazed at the southwest corner of First Street and St. Mary's Road. Motorola has since vacated the seventy-four-thousand-square-foot charter building, now the Atkins Building, named for park co-developer Clint Atkins.

And economic development was added to the U of I's formal mission.

Convergence of Factors

As the campus embarked in 1985-86 on its first comprehensive North Campus Master Plan, three factors were evident.

The U of I was giving a higher priority to advancement and development, or private fundraising, in science and technology, the arts, and athletics. It recently had completed its first major fundraising campaign, which ran from 1979 to 1984, and had exceeded its $100 million goal by $32 million, and was preparing to launch a $1 billion campaign. The convergence of new pools of state money for capital expenditures tied, at least nominally, to economic development; private gifts; and private/public development partnerships would play out in campus plans and growth for the next two decades and beyond. Or two of the three would, as the State of Illinois slid deeply into debt.

Unlike the Sasaki "directional" plans (north, central, south, south farms), the last full campus plan—a kind of omnibus plan that revised and melded 1986-2003 plans—moved slowly. It was begun in January 2004 and took more than three full years to complete. It brought the entire Urbana-Champaign campus of seven thousand acres and hundreds of buildings, roads, sidewalks, farms, forests, and gardens into a single plan that from north to south reached some six miles.

Called "Campus Master Plan Update," it was endorsed by the board of trustees on March 13, 2007. It is credited to Sasaki et al. and covers the area south from University Avenue to Airport Road and east from Neil Street to Philo Road.

What is clear from the published schedule of activities leading to the report and from the report itself is a shift to the idea of "stakeholders" overtly participating and affecting the plan (and slowing it down); the involvement of the board of trustees earlier in the process (they review a draft one year into the process, which is two years before the plan goes to the board for approval); and the bureaucratization of the plan in its language. Sections of the report are identified as to author—for example, Sasaki Associates Inc. or Jones Lang LaSalle IP Inc.—and additional existing plans on athletics, retail, and transportation are rolled into the overall updated campus plan.

President White (2005-9) and Urbana-Champaign Chancellor Herman (2004-9), as their predecessors did for earlier plans, spoke of the goal of the 2007 plan in their shared foreword:

> Now, shortly after the turn of the twenty-first century, this campus plan update continues the focus on future campus growth needs. As it builds upon the historic framework of existing patterns of land use, circulation, infrastructure, and open spaces established in earlier planning efforts, it also provides recommendations for making wise use of limited resources relevant to the campus today and into the foreseeable future. Some issues involved in this update include traditional academic campus growth and redistribution needs but many seek to better integrate the campus with its surrounding communities. Connecting the University and its neighbors (whether through public/private development, economic development, transportation, or the landscape) not only supports institutional goals that build community partnerships but also serves to enhance the quality of life on and around campus.

North Campus

A bare twenty years had elapsed between the groundbreaking 1986 North Campus Master Plan and the 2007 omnibus plan, but the impact of the 1986 plan is still felt and can be used to demonstrate the grasp on the campus and the strategy planners employed to create what became a successful redevelopment of a homely and isolated portion of the campus.

Although the hurry-up North Campus Master Plan was begun in response to the Beckman gift, Sasaki Associates clearly established a pattern that the firm followed for successive planning slices of the campus. It included a snapshot of the existing study area, a set of objectives for the plan and—in simple language—the future: "Proposed Organization of the North Campus."

The plan also lays out design guidelines that, with minor modifications, are repeated in the 1986 and 1989 plans for the south and central sections of campus. The guidelines include straightforward standards (many of them reinforcing existing campus practices) such as architecture style sympathetic to existing buildings in height, orientation, and decoration.

The report cites the Quad—with its many divergent styles and hues of buildings—as a successful and unified space because the buildings are equally massive, directed or aligned toward each other and the grassy space they share as a front yard. Conservative and serene landscaping—styled in the late 1920s by Ferruccio Vitale and updated by Sasaki—further binds the Quad.

But even that most iconic space is not perfect: "The Foreign Languages Building . . . has a strongly divergent shape (narrow base, broad top) and texture (overall grain of detail, window, and solid area) and becomes a disharmonious element when viewed from certain points of view," according to the 1986 Sasaki report. It also blocks a full-on northside view of Smith Memorial Hall, the campus's first gift building (1921), formerly fronted by low-lying greenhouses. (A truth-resistant story says the basement of the Foreign Languages Building was built to withstand a nuclear blast, protecting PLATO computer labs. Not true, but one of many myths that persist for students and others.)

Among the most enduring and recognizable elements of the 1986 plan is the addition of about two thousand feet to the central or north-south axis of the campus, creating room for two new quadrangles and linking the north campus to the main one. As one travels due south from the front door of the Beckman Institute (which faces into the campus) to Springfield Avenue and on farther south in a straight line to Green Street (the Illini Union is ahead), the axis is strengthened. This powerful axial treatment significantly transformed the campus's look.

Ikenberry recalls his "meddling" in the transformation of Burrill Avenue, between Springfield and Green, into a vast open space with pedestrian walkways and landscaping around the former eyesore, Boneyard Creek.

Burrill, which had head-in parking on both sides of the roadway, was dug up for repair of steam tunnels that underlay most of the campus. Ikenberry believed that was the perfect opportunity to convert Burrill into greenspace. But campus officials said his proposal was outrageous and wrong for three reasons: the president was meddling in campus affairs, the campus didn't have the money to create a greenspace, and the campus didn't want to deal with the outcry from faculty and staff who would permanently lose their parking.

In the end, the Bardeen Quad was created—with private money.

North Plan as Example

Because subsequent plans reflected basic principles and approaches embedded in the North Campus Plan, it seems helpful to lay out the plan's objectives and organizing ideas in full.

Objectives of the North Campus Master Plan are listed below. The plan encompasses several specific proposals to accomplish these objectives.

- Create a clear image and high-quality ambience for the North Campus reflective of the quality of its academic programs. Issues of scale, density, arrival, orientation, architectural design, and landscaping will be addressed.
- Improve visual and physical ties to the central campus, and resolve the Green Street and Springfield Avenue "barriers."
- Develop spatial patterns that respond to the differing needs of teaching and research.
- Recognize and maintain strong relationship between the campus structure and the existing urban fabric of streets, uses, and infrastructure.
- Promote interaction of disciplines, recognizing the value of open spaces, bridges, and walkways.

- Develop a flexible plan that responds to the dynamic growth characteristics of scientific research facilities which can be phased.
- Develop a parking plan that does not detract from the pedestrian and visual experience of the campus.

The campus plan then laid out a "proposed organization" for the North Campus reflecting seven principal organizing ideas. These ideas, published here in full, are followed by bracketed summaries of what has happened in the intervening years as of fall 2016.

- Building on the historical organizational framework of the entire campus, the main axis that now extends from the Foellinger Auditorium south to the Stock Pavilion and north through the quadrangle to the Illini Union will be extended through the North Campus to the Beckman Institute site. A new series of open spaces will be created along the axis, with the Beckman Institute becoming the northern terminus.

  [*Update:* The axis is virtually and clearly visually complete; visitors to the fifth-floor tower room of the Beckman Institute can look north to south and see the spine—the straight-line axis that organizes the campus.]
- A new quadrangle north of Engineering Hall and east of Talbot Laboratory will be created when the Aeronautical Laboratory B and Electrical Engineering Research Laboratory, Electrical Engineering Annex and Burrill Avenue are removed. The new quadrangle will become the focal point of the academic and instructional core between Springfield Avenue and Green Street, and contain facilities such as the engineering library and classroom building.

  [*Update:* Once Burrill Avenue—a north-south street and parking lot that linked Springfield Avenue to Green Street—was torn up, the named buildings were razed, and Boneyard Creek was subdued, private money stepped in to build the Bardeen Quad, topped on the north by the Grainger Engineering Library and Information Center.]
- Land use will be based on patterns of instructional and research functions. The core area, including the undergraduate teaching complex, will be partially enclosed by areas of research activities. The teaching core will be centered within the area defined by Green Street, Springfield Avenue, Wright Street and Mathews Avenue, near the instructional area of the central campus. Computing and systems research will be clustered north of Springfield Avenue; materials and design research will be clustered east of Mathews Avenue; and advanced multidisciplinary research will be clustered north, along University Avenue.

  [*Update:* Engineering Hall, built for $162,000 in 1894 and fastidiously renovated for more than $15 million in 1998-2000, falls within those "teaching core" boundaries, as does the ingenious wraparound addition of the Digital Computer Lab on Springfield Avenue. But a major teaching building, the $80 million Siebel Center for Computer Science (2004), and the integrated teaching and research Electrical and Computer Engineering Building (2014) are well outside the teaching core neighborhood Sasaki promoted. It is clear the College of Engineering envisions a future where instruction and research are seamless. ECE, a net-zero energy building, fills the last remaining space of the Beckman Quad. And Everitt Lab, built in 1949 as the Electrical Engineering Building at the northeast corner of Green and Wright Streets, is under renovation until 2018. The project is budgeted for $55 million; the Department of Bioengineering Instruction and Research will occupy the space.
- The "Beckman Quadrangle" will be created south of the Beckman Institute, becoming the focal point of the research complex between Springfield and

University Avenues, and flanked eventually by associated research facilities.

[*Update:* Done and done; the Beckman Quad (Oval Allee of the North Engineering Campus) is complete.]

- The two new quadrangles will be joined along the central axis by a landscaped mall flanked by the new Microelectronics Center on the west and the Newmark Civil Engineering Laboratory and Digital Computer Laboratory on the east. New engineering laboratories eventually will be located on the Kenney Gymnasium site.

  [*Update:* The campus is not inclined to raze Kenney Gymnasium, built in 1902, or the Kenney Gymnasium Annex, designed by Nathan Ricker and built in 1890 as the Military Drill Hall. Both score well above 4.5 on a scale of 5.0 on the campus's historic preservation index. And the north campus, which is densely populated, is already short of recreational space for faculty, staff, and students. But instead of building a recreation center at the northeast corner of Springfield Avenue and Goodwin Street as the Sasaki plan recommended, the campus built a new public safety building there. A substantial student-focused 20,500-square-foot addition to Newmark in 2011 features classrooms, meeting rooms, and informal gathering spaces, and completes the building.]
- The planting and setback lines of "Presidents' Walk" on University Avenue will be repeated along the campus side of Wright Street, recognizing the future importance of that street as a visual and pedestrian route between the North Campus and the central campus and as a "gateway" into the North Campus.

  [*Update:* Wright Street is unchanged, with small businesses on the west side.]
- Most surface parking will be removed, and a system of landscaped open spaces, pedestrian routes and bicycle routes will be established. Parking structures are planned, and are critical from an aesthetic standpoint, as well as being a reflection of land value in a campus setting.

  [*Update:* A six-level parking structure fills the block bounded by University Avenue to the north, Clark Street to the south, Goodwin Avenue to the east, and Mathews Avenue to the west. The ground floor on the south of the parking structure (campus side) contains some 21,300 square feet of available retail space—storefronts and sidewalks; the north some twenty-one thousand square feet of office space. The campus has failed to attract and install any retail tenants in the $31.8 million structure; the Parking Division moved out of the nearby Public Safety Building and fills part of the vacant office space facing north.]

Dramatic Change

The North Campus Master Plan was ambitious: it was predicated on growth approaching 80 percent, or 1.7 million gross square feet of new/expanded building space over twenty years. In fifteen years beginning in 1985, more than $200 million in new construction and major remodeling was accomplished. After decades of neglect, the Engineering Campus burst with new and expanded buildings, and Boneyard Creek, which sliced through the north, was turned into an amenity.

South Campus Plans, a.k.a. Name Confusion

As the Urbana-Champaign campus intensively planned and re-planned itself from 1985 to 2007, the geographic nomenclature and area boundaries changed. What had been the "South Campus"—south from Armory Avenue to St. Mary's Road, and including the South Quad—became an extension of the Central Campus, and the "new" South Campus began at Florida-Kirby Avenue and ended at Airport Road in Savoy. This renamed South Campus is thirty-four hundred acres on five square miles of land, almost 80 percent occupied and used by the College of Agricultural, Consumer, and Environmental Sciences with additional intensive use by the Division of Intercollegiate Athletics, Campus Recreation and, east of Lincoln Avenue, existing married student housing. An ambitious plan to redevelop the married student housing complex failed.

1986 South Campus Plan

On September 11, 1986, mere months after the board of trustees received and adopted the seminal North Campus Master Plan, the board approved the South Campus Master Plan, an area of 550 acres bounded by Armory Avenue on the north, St. Mary's Road on the south, Lincoln Avenue on the east, and the Illinois Central Railroad tracks on the west.

This plan was the second in the Sasaki series and followed the same format as the north plan right down to the identical design guidelines and general call for "better visual organization of the campus." Unlike the north plan, the South Campus Master Plan did not call for major land acquisition (indeed the planning area is almost landlocked) but did suggest moving athletic and recreation fields farther to the edge of the campus, a trend well underway. The freed-up space would be transformed into an academic core, primarily on the north portion of the master plan area. Recreation, housing, and support uses would spread out to the periphery.

(Several years later, a freestanding intercollegiate athletics plan, "Heritage Master Plan: Division of Intercollegiate Athletics," would supersede and elaborate upon the Sasaki south plan. Fueled by private money, the Division of Intercollegiate Athletics would build an office building, outdoor track, separate soccer and softball stadiums, and tennis facilities in the area generally laid out in the 1986 plan.)

But in 1986, larger questions loomed: Could the South Campus, which would contain the university's best examples of Georgian revival architecture, a raggedy east-west military axis, and ample open space, be planned into submission?

As Ikenberry and Everhart put it in their foreword to the 1986 South Campus Master Plan:

> Shortly after the turn of the [nineteenth] century, leaders at the University of Illinois showed great foresight in laying plans for the development of the South Campus, then dotted with wood-frame farm buildings and a handful of agricultural research facilities.
>
> In 1911, state funding was granted for the Armory, which inspired Daniel Burnham—who made no small plans—to introduce the idea of a strong east-west alignment of buildings heading east from the Armory. Nonetheless, most campus construction continued to center on the Main Quadrangle.
>
> University growth surged after World War I. But before building Mumford Hall, David Kinley Hall, the Library and the Architecture Building, the University commissioned Charles Platt to revise a campus plan. His influence is evident today: he firmly established the extension of the north-south axis into the South Campus, established the east-west or "Military Axis" and chose the Georgian style for future buildings.
>
> The inexorable march south of academic, residential and recreational facilities, local streets and parking lots from the mid-1930s to the present sometimes ignored the Platt Plan. One goal of the present effort is to rediscover the genius of that earlier design.

Sasaki planners worked with the assumption that by 1995 the campus would build nearly one million square feet of new building area—about half for the College of ACES. That would grow to 1.8 million square feet of new space by 2000 and 2.5 million square feet into the next century, doubling the building area on the South Campus.

This 1986 South Campus Plan had to accommodate not only a half-dozen independent colleges, with little in common, but a smorgasbord of non-college units. The college/department occupants of the South Campus are ACES, Education, Commerce and Business Administration (renamed Business), Law, Environmental Studies, Applied Health Studies (now Applied Health Sciences), and Library and Information Science, now Information Sciences, or the Illinois iSchool. The non-college users on the South Campus are the University Library, McKinley Health Center, Illinois Natural History and Geological Surveys, Abbott Power Plant, south garage and car pool, athletics, student housing, and central stores and food stores. The Division of Intercollegiate Athletics also has most of its facilities on the south edge of campus, split by Kirby/Florida Avenue.

As Sasaki saw it in 1986, the South Campus was being asked to accommodate two million square feet in new additions with no opportunity to sprawl north, east, or west. The planners sought "consolidation and cohesiveness, rather than expansion or sprawl."

North-South and East-West Axes

The north-south axis envisioned for the South Campus in the 1986 Sasaki plan was intended to replicate the classical quality of the central Quad by planting formal rows of trees on each side of the space from Gregory Drive (south side of the main Library) to the Stock Pavilion.

By contrast, the plan would create a mall of open space aligning east-west with informal landscaping, bringing life to the old Military Axis, which is not well developed. The northern edge of the mall would follow the south façade of Huff Hall, the Architecture Building, the Commerce Building (now Wohlers Hall), David Kinley Hall, and Mumford Hall. The south edge of the new mall would follow the north façade of the Education Building and buildings to follow. (In fact, the new architecture building, Temple Hoyne Buell Hall (1995), is aligned slightly farther north from the imaginary southern edge of the proposed mall, which terminates at Flagg Hall. Flagg Hall in 2010 was part of a major redevelopment of

FIGURE 6.2. McFarland Carillon, a 185-foot bell tower, was built in 2008-09 on the South Quad. It was designed by Fred Guyton of Peckham, Guyton, Albers & Viets. The carillon has forty-nine bells and can be played by a keyboard or controlled by a computer with five hundred pre-programmed songs. (Photo by L. Brian Stauffer, University News Bureau.)

FIGURE 6.3. Colorful art outside the Carl R. Woese Institute for Genomic Biology depicts microbes that live by the trillions on human and animal skin, muscles, organs, and brains. The giant work, "Darwin's Playground," was created by Chicago artist Tony Tasset. A 1977 Illinois law established the Art-in-Architecture program, which reserves 0.5 percent of state building and renovation costs to purchase public art. (Photo by L. Brian Stauffer, University News Bureau.)

student housing in the area now occupied by the "Six Pack" and being replaced, one building at a time, by the Ikenberry Commons and Housing complex).

On the east, the Military Axis terminated (in 1986) at Turner Hall, which the planners called "a building which is not well designed to fit within the University context, and which has limited symbolic importance." And the western terminus was a row of trees, a windbreak that defined the western edge of campus in its early years, and the Peabody housing complex, "also an unfitting end if this axis is to become an identifiable campus open space." Since the plan was finished, the octagonal 2001 ACES Library, just west of Turner Hall, became the new eastern terminus on the Military Axis. Elaborate plans to remove parking and redevelop/landscape the entire axis were on hold as of summer 2016. But trustees in September 2015 approved a new signature building, the $48 million Design Center, to be sited on the east side of Fourth Street south of Huff Hall, creating a new western terminus.

Central Campus Master Plan

The third plan of the 1980s-1990s Sasaki series covers the smallest—but perhaps most significant—section of the U of I, the 207 acres comprising the Central Campus, which is bounded by Green Street on the north, Lincoln Avenue on the east, Gregory Drive on the south, and Fourth Street on the west. At its heart is the Quadrangle, unarguably the most iconic space of the Urbana-Champaign campus.

The board of trustees adopted the Central Campus Master Plan dated October 27, 1989, on November 9, 1989, with the same alacrity as the north and south campus plans.

This center of the Urbana-Champaign campus is heavily trafficked by pedestrians day and night—undergraduates in the so-called liberal arts core, library users, faculty and researchers in chemistry and life sciences, denizens of Campustown eating and drinking establishments, residents of nearby Greek houses, worshipers at the churches and religious foundations on the west side of the core, and off-campus visitors to the Krannert Center for the Performing Arts.

Parallel streets form a tidy grid that transportation managers alter year to year to little effect. Sasaki planners, in fact, make few suggestions or recommendations about parking and motor traffic and the few they made have been implemented in the quarter-century since the plan was approved.

The plan posits a 40 percent growth in building space—2.2 million gross square feet—from the then-existing 5.4 million gross square feet. It proposes new green spaces, pedestrian malls, extensive tree-planting program, and a vast "public-related uses zone" to the east.

South Farms: Moving Again

Well more than a century ago, livestock roamed what is now the Quad. The main agriculture building—the mammoth 1900 Davenport Hall—is centered on the east side of the Quad. The peach orchard was south of Davenport . . . but not for long. The campus began almost immediately to move south, buying up land and moving its own production agriculture, livestock, horticulture, and forestry operations south, south, south in waves.

By the time the South Farms Master Plan was approved September 13, 1990, the so-called South Farms comprised twenty-seven hundred acres devoted to agriculture, veterinary medicine, the state surveys (now pulled together in a unit called the Prairie Research Institute), campus recreation and athletics, and police and fire training institutes. The College of Agricultural, Consumer, and Environmental Sciences, like the College of Engineering before it, was on a mission to replace, renovate, or relocate many of its facilities. But agriculture has unique challenges: ongoing or long-term research in production agriculture—food crops, biomass, trees, turf—means living things in the ground cannot be moved willy-nilly, and soil types and drainage must be considered, as well as supporting roadways and buildings.

The 1990 plan also sites a proposed research park for the northwest corner of Windsor Road and South First Street; in fact, the park's first building opened instead in 2001 at the southwest corner of St. Mary's Road and South First Street, three-quarters of a mile closer to campus. And it sites a new and expanded arboretum (elaborated in a separate 2001 plan) east and south of the President's House on Florida Avenue, after several moves. Immediate land needs in ACES were 1,588 acres, including moving the apple orchards onto 105 new acres far southeast of the campus.

Beef and Sheep

Within five years of the South Farms Master Plan and internal "South Campus Modernization Project," sheep and cattle were rustled from handsome old barns just south of the Assembly Hall (now the State Farm Center) to up-to-date pole barns near Race Street and Old Church Road. The $10 million complex is four cattle barns, a sheep barn, and office building and machine/feed shops.

This move, as others, responds to the growth of the Research Park and a more generalized fussiness about animal management, including handling waste and housing live pigs, cattle, and poultry away from homes, workplaces, and entertainment venues, like the State Farm Center.

Research Park

The new millennium marked the long-awaited entry of the Urbana-Champaign campus into the research park business. With a research contract/grant portfolio of hundreds of millions of dollars, available land on the south campus, management and control structures in place, and a private-sector development partner, the park has grown to fifteen buildings on more than two hundred acres.

Read about the "Research Park" on the companion Web site (sidebar 6.1).

The Apple Orchards

The campus's first apple orchard—with one thousand varieties—was planted in 1869, about where the Armory is today. Like so many elements of the agricultural enterprise—livestock on the Quad, corn near the Observatory, sheep at the Research Park—the orchards have been on the move, bobbing ever farther south and east into Urbana. Read a short history of the Apple Orchards on the companion Web site (sidebar 6.2).

CHAPTER 7

The Neighborhood

Sleep, Eat, Pray

The life of a young man drawn to the new Illinois Industrial University, an all-men's school that opened in a single building in late winter 1868, was full of everything except fun. Not only did the university pioneers have to wear a cadet-gray uniform reminiscent of West Point—standing collar, single-breasted vest, dark-blue welt on the outside seams—but they had to do two hours of manual labor a day, drill three hours a week, and march to and from mandatory chapel. This on top of attending classes, studying, and preparing their own meals.

Warp speed to today: a record 44,800 students in fall 2016 (33,467 undergraduates, and 24 percent of all students from outside the United States) and almost eleven thousand faculty, professional, and support staff together, creating a learning and living community that fills a sprawling and vibrant campus.

What links the earliest and the most recent cohort of U of I students is youth—a potent stew of energy, recklessness, imagination, restlessness, idealism, silliness, eagerness, and rebelliousness. The Urbana-Champaign campus, as many of its Big Ten peers, remains a residential university, or as one recent U of I president put it, "a classic campus," dominated by eighteen- to twenty-four-year-olds.

In times past, ambitious young people would champion causes: a new name, legalizing social Greek organizations, forming an athletic association, and ending mandatory chapel. The twice-monthly *Illini* simply and boldly printed the name "University of Illinois" on the newspaper's masthead in 1881, four years before the state legislature acted on the name change. In 1887, students drafted a constitution for the Illinois Intercollegiate Athletic Association, wrangled faculty approval two years later, and two more years after that raised money to build a sports field—Illinois Field—on the north campus.

The story of the place of the University of Illinois, yesterday and today, is also a story of life in that place. For every hour spent in the classroom, lab, or library, more hours are spent simply living: In the twenty-first century, that means working low-pay jobs, hanging with friends, working out at the ARC, cruising the Green Street circuit, eating pizza, drinking beer, and, maybe, going to church or synagogue, all the while electronically and chronically hooked to smart phones and social networks.

What follows is a fragmentary and episodic look at life in the 'hood back in the day.

Sleep

The puffing steam engine shrieked to a stop, and the family of four descended from a railcar into the gloom of a Champaign midnight. They were met on the platform by the bearded, stern-faced regent of the brand new Illinois Industrial University, John Milton Gregory (1867-80). Taking the mother's bawling infant in his arms, Gregory led the family to their temporary new home on University Avenue.

"He marched ahead and we followed," Frances Potter recalled many years later in the U of I alumni magazine, "stumbling along over the ups and downs of the board walks. We had thought that we knew what mud was, but surely we had never seen real mud until we walked in Champaign."

It was the winter of 1868, and Potter's father had arrived in Champaign to teach. Instead, he ended up supervising the boarding hall at the new school's dormitory. The Champaign-Urbana area lacked rental housing, and Gregory wanted "the boys coming from home for the first time" to have "a good home at reasonable rates." So began the university's first experiment in student housing.

The University building—popularly known as "the Elephant"—served as the school's dormitory, its library, its classrooms, its offices. The early prospects were not encouraging. Frances Potter termed the Elephant "a large, plain, red brick five-story structure set down flat in the black Illinois mud, with not a tree or shrub, a spear of grass or a fence. It was as desolate a place as it is possible to imagine," she said.

In March 1868 dozens of students began arriving at the fledgling school, and many of them—including the future "Poet of the Prairie," James Newton Matthews—took lodging at the University dormitory.

Sixty-five rooms on the top two floors of the Elephant were set aside for student housing. The rooms, which held two occupants each, were small—fourteen feet long by ten feet wide—and unfurnished. The cost was modest: $4.00 per term. The university also opened a hall for women students, who were first admitted in 1870, featuring "a parlor, dining room, kitchen, laundry, and music room," but this was short lived.

The university's first student housing venture began to end on an April night in 1880 when a windstorm—some say a tornado—ripped off the west wing of the Elephant. Soon enough, the board of trustees declared "the old Dormitory" unsafe for occupancy. It was razed the following year after an arson attempt. And the university would not return to the business of student housing for a complex of reasons spanning nearly forty years.

Local residents already had opened boardinghouses that catered to the growing student population. Longtime dean of men Thomas Arkle Clark considered some boardinghouse operators honorable stand-in parents, earning "the greatest respect by all classes of citizens" because they treated student boarders well.

"They took the keenest personal interest in students and gave many of the comforts and kindnesses of home for the $2.25 or $2.50 a week which the undergraduate student handed over for his board," Clark wrote. "Some of these sensible and level-headed women did quite as much in the training and disciplining of the raw fellows . . . as did the men who were in the regular faculty."

Clark said that in the early days some students—the cool kids—lived in boardinghouses far from campus—in the "more attractive part of Champaign about the [downtown West Side] park" or in Urbana near the business district. This pattern changed around the turn of the century when most students began to cluster in houses near campus.

Clark told a story about a student who, before going off to college in 1903, received and took advice on where to live from his much-older brother. "Now, Alexander," the brother cautioned, "don't make the mistake of getting a room near the University. If you want to make a good social start, get a room on West Hill street near the Presbyterian church, where the better class of students live. Keep away from the East Side." So Alexander rented a room on West Hill Street,

FIGURE 7.1. Aerial view, looking north, of the Illini Village temporary housing complex at the University of Illinois. Note the Mount Hope Cemetery to the left of Illini Village and the greenhouses, Freer Hall, and Busey and Evans Halls in the distance. (Photo dated February 1946. Photo courtesy of University of Illinois Archives 0003960.)

only to discover that there wasn't "another student within a mile of him and that all the better class of students were living on the once despised East Side."

Greek Housing Boom

Beginning in the early 1900s, many socially ambitious students lived in fraternity houses on Green Street and sorority houses on John Street. Banned for years, Greek organizations finally were OK'd by the board of trustees in 1891 and soon spread rapidly into neighborhoods nearest the campus.

In 1908 the members of Phi Kappa Psi launched a new fraternity district south of John Street in what was called the "Chalmers Street wilderness" when they erected a brick Jacobean period revival house at 911 South Fourth Street. The sorority district underwent a similar migration, moving east from its original John Street center into Urbana, leapfrogging the nascent Quad.

FIGURE 7.2. Kappa Kappa Gamma sorority house. (Photo by Karyl Wackerlin.)

The 1920s witnessed a Greek house building boom. At its peak between 1926 and 1928, some twenty-six chapter houses were built at a cost of about $2 million. These mansion-like structures were a smorgasbord of architectural designs ranging from Tudor revival to Georgian and neoclassical, with a few exotic Chateauesque, French eclectic, Italian renaissance, and Mission specimens.

"With the recent progress in sorority and fraternity building, Illinois can now boast one of the most beautiful campuses in the country, as far as the chapter houses of the national organizations are concerned," the *Daily Illini* bragged in 1929, near the end of the construction boom. "Few chapters of any organization have any more lavish and pretentious residences in any school than they have at Illinois."

The *Daily Illini* claimed that this explosion in Greek housing had "eliminated, to a large extent, the necessity for University dormitories of the type that were recently constructed at the University of Wisconsin and other campuses."

Even so, the university by this point had already reentered, timidly, the business of student housing. In 1916, construction began on what would become Mary E. Busey Hall, the result of years of agitation to provide suitable living places for women. President Edmund J. James (1904-20) insisted that the new colonial-style structure be called a residence hall and not a dormitory, the latter term sounding to him too much like a "ten-cent-a-night hotel." (The same semantic tussling continues to this day.)

Women's Housing

Though completed in 1917 at a cost of $218,000, the Women's Residence Hall would not house even a single woman for two years. First it was used as a barracks for World War I aviators enrolled in a newly established School of Military Aeronautics, and then it served as a hospital for patients struck down by the great influenza pandemic of 1918.

On September 22, 1919, the residence hall, "dreamed of for nearly a half century by Illinois women," finally opened its doors to 120 women. The university later furnished additional housing for women in the form of Davenport House on Wright Street and the so-called West Hall (later renamed Laura B. Evans Hall) adjacent to the Women's Residence Hall and completed in 1925.

Houses run by religious denominations also provided rooms for women, including the Episcopalian-run Osborne Hall, Presbyterian House, Bethany Circle, and Congregational House. The university encouraged the formation of several cooperative houses for women: Alpha House, Campbell Cottage, and Beta House. In co-ops, students share in household duties such as cleaning, menu planning, and cooking to keep costs down.

But for a half-century the university let men fend for themselves. Besides living in fraternities and boardinghouses (and, increasingly, apartments), male students had the option of living in one of the four private dormitories—College Hall, Granada Club, Illini Hall, and Newman Hall—that together could hold about 645 men.

The lack of university housing for men troubled U of I President Harry Woodburn Chase (1930-33). "We have a most unusual problem on this campus and one about which we are doing very little," Chase wrote to James White in 1931. "I refer to the conditions under which sixty-three per cent of our men's students live who are not members of fraternities in terms of housing, eating and social contacts. I think we are doing less for these people than the great majority of American universities." Chase was correct: 1936 figures show that only two Big Ten schools, Illinois and Ohio State, did not have university-owned men's dormitories.

At Last, Men's Housing

It was left to the administration of Arthur Willard (1934-46), Chase's successor, to tackle the issue. Backed by an organization of independent men, university officials stood up to fraternities and boardinghouse operators and pushed for a men's residence hall. Despite opposition, the first university men's dormitory in sixty years rose on the Parade Ground just west of Huff Gym. The Triad, consisting of three four-story colonial-style buildings (later named Clark, Lundgren, and Barton Halls), opened its doors to 364 male students in September 1941. The *Daily Illini* welcomed the new residence hall, calling it "a practical advance toward solution of the vexatious independent housing problem."

The Willard administration also created a centralized Division of Student Housing and a list of "approved housing" but did little to address the issue of housing segregation. In the 1910s Jewish fraternities and sororities arose on campus, offering new housing options to Jewish students who were sometimes discriminated against by local landlords. Shortly after West Hall (later Evans) was completed in 1925, Jewish women started flocking to that dormitory. In 1936 Abram Sachar, director of the Hillel Foundation, asked

Dean of Women Maria Leonard to prevent the segregation of Jewish women students. Reporting to President Willard in October 1936, Charles Havens of the Physical Plant Department wrote that the "Jewish girls refuse to live anywhere except in West Hall when they learn that there are more Jewish girls there than in any of the other units." And, he continued: "The problem has been in evidence for the past few years and has in most cases been settled by giving the girls their choice sooner or later. With as large a percentage of Jewish girls in West Hall, the Gentile girls are anxious to move to the other hall."

Black Students, Pre–World War II

The housing situation before World War II was especially difficult for African American students. Barred from most boardinghouses, African Americans had two options: live in the private homes of local black families, often far from campus on the north side of Champaign-Urbana, or join a sorority or fraternity. In the 1930s two African American organizations—the Alpha Kappa Alpha sorority and Kappa Alpha Psi fraternity—owned houses that accommodated large numbers of black students. In school year 1938-39, fourteen of the thirty-six African American women at the university lived at the Alpha Kappa Alpha house at 1201 West Stoughton Street in Urbana, while twenty-four of the sixty-five black men at the school lived at the Kappa Alpha Psi house at 707 South Third Street in Champaign.

The university had taken "an unofficial interest" in helping these organizations acquire their homes. Assistant Dean of Men Charles R. Frederick, though, had expressed concern over Kappa Alpha Psi's move into the heart of the fraternity district, fearing that white "fraternities will eventually create an incident in their efforts to harass the negro group."

The university itself discriminated against African Americans, forbidding black students from living in the residence halls. In a 1937 letter to a Chicago politician, President Willard indicated a willingness to change this discriminatory practice, saying that a dormitory planned for the west hall of Memorial Stadium would be open to "white and colored boys alike." This dorm project, however, never got off the ground, and it wasn't until after World War II that the university residence halls were desegregated.

In September 1946 newly elected U of I president George Stoddard (1946-53) declared the university had a responsibility to house racial minorities. This is "more than a pious gesture," Stoddard told the board of trustees. "It is a statement and clarification of university policy."

Military Impact

World War II threw the university housing scene into chaos. Servicemen invaded the campus, and rooms had to be provided for them. Navy officers settled into the Busey-Evans Residence Hall, taking the place of the evicted women undergraduates. Navy men also roomed in the new Men's Residence Halls, now fenced off and guarded, and in the Old Gym and Annex on Springfield Avenue that had been converted into a combination barracks and classroom. In the summer of 1943 more than three thousand trainees in the Army Specialized Training Program also descended on the campus, further complicating the housing situation. Forty-four fraternity houses and the upper floors of Illini Hall and Newman Hall ultimately were mustered into service as living space for the army men.

The housing crisis only worsened after World War II. The G.I. Bill propelled thousands of veterans to the university en masse, and these men, often with families in tow, needed places to live. Early in 1946 the housing problem reached almost unmanageable proportions. Thousands of new admissions applications poured into the registrar's office, threatening to swell an enrollment that already approached ten thousand, but at the time "the visible supply of housing" reportedly could only accommodate 10,400 students.

(Fall enrollment in 1946-47 topped 18,000 and was an all-time high. Of the total 18,378 students, 12,524 were men. In 1948-49, men composed 15,137 of the total 19,277 enrolled in the fall. In 1946-47, the U of I undergraduate division at Chicago's Navy Pier enrolled 3,403 men, 443 women; in 1948-49, 3,549 men were enrolled, 625 women. The Galesburg undergrad division enrolled 400 men and 32 women in 1946-47, and 927 men and 152 women in 1948-49.)

Postwar, desperate university officials scrambled for housing space anywhere they could. The west great hall of Memorial Stadium, the Men's Gym Annex, and the Ice Arena, fresh off service as a training rink for the Chicago

FIGURE 7.3. Stadium Terrace, the university's temporary housing to handle the overflow of students and families after World War II, as viewed from the power plant with Memorial Stadium in the background. (Photo dated December 1946. Photo courtesy of University of Illinois Archives 0003719.)

FIGURE 7.4. High-rise retail and student residential buildings line Green Street looking west in 2015. Private investment in Campustown changed its face, following the private-public taming of the Boneyard Creek, which routinely swamped its banks and Green Street. (Photo by Darrell Hoemann.)

Blackhawks, were drafted into duty as dormitories that could house one thousand students. Most significant, the university obtained 275 prefabricated houses for veterans and their families, erecting them at two sites: the Stadium Terrace complex northwest of Memorial Stadium and the Illini Village complex south of the Sigma Nu and Alpha Tau Omega houses on Pennsylvania Avenue. And the barracks-like Parade Ground Units were built to accommodate about thirteen hundred single male students.

The university had bought time, but it was clear that the world had changed. In a time of burgeoning enrollment—and not just veterans—the school no longer could rely on private owners to be the primary providers of student housing.

Between 1946 and 1966, university officials oversaw a colossal housing program. Some twenty-five halls and apartments housing thousands of students were built: Lincoln Avenue Residence Hall (1949); Green-Goodwin Student-Staff Apartments (1950-51); Noble Hall (1953); Flagg Hall (1953);

FIGURE 7.5. Stores and cars along Green Street looking east toward Wright Street and Altgeld Hall. (Photo dated ca. 1922. Photo courtesy of University of Illinois Archives 0002186.)

Taft Hall (1957); Van Doren Hall (1957); Allen Hall (1957-58); Gregory Drive Residence Halls (1958): Garner, Forbes, and Hopkins, and Orchard Place Apartments (1959); Peabody Drive Residence Halls (1960-61): Scott, Snyder, and Weston; Daniels Hall (1960-61); Orchard Downs Apartments (1961); Pennsylvania Avenue Residence Halls (1963): Carr, Blaisdell, Babcock, and Saunders; Illinois Street Residence Halls (1964); Townsend and Wardall; Florida Avenue Residence Halls (1966): Trelease and Oglesby; and Sherman Hall (1966).

Several of these new residence halls were high-rises. Twelve-story Wardall, the first high-rise dormitory on the U of I campus, soon had some tall companions, including the sky-scraping Sherman (for graduate students), Trelease, and Oglesby Halls. Encouraged by the university—and the market—private developers also began to build soaring "luxury dormitories" in the mid-1960s: Europa House, Bromley Hall, Hendrick House, and Illini Tower. Clocking in at seventeen stories, Illini Tower was the tallest structure

FIGURE 7.6. A snowy Green Street looking west in the 1920s. (Image undated. Photo courtesy of Champaign County Historical Archives.)

in Champaign-Urbana until dethroned by the twenty-one-story, aptly named Century 21 apartment/office building in the early 1970s. Illini Tower since 2008 has been owned and managed by Campus Living Villages Pty Ltd., which owns, manages, or is developing university housing from Texas to Australia, Utah to Great Britain. With some thirty thousand beds under contract at about fifty institutions, Campus Living represents the globalization of what once was a mom-and-pop operation of boardinghouses.

Independence Days

The university's ambitious program of dorm building largely came to an end in fall 1965—one year into the arrival of the first class of baby boomers—when officials said the school had enough housing to match enrollment. By then, students increasingly were living in apartments that had begun to mushroom around campus. This trend accelerated dramatically in the 1970s and the 1980s with the diminishment of *in*

FIGURE 7.7. Old picture of 600-614 block of Green Street looking northwest. (Image undated. Photo courtesy of Champaign County Historical Archives.)

loco parentis, the long-held belief (leading to rules) that the U of I should act as its students' parents. At the onset of this period, students with ninety credit hours (of 120 or so needed to graduate) or more could live outside of certified housing, but by 1983 this exemption had been broadened to include students with only thirty credit hours—namely, most sophomores. Freed from the mandate to live in university-approved housing, many students, sophomore year and above, headed for apartments and all the freedom they promised.

Private developers both responded to this trend and helped create it. New high-rise apartments on Green Street and Springfield Avenue illustrate this continuing dynamic. They often are mixed-use buildings with retail at street level and commercial offices and apartments above. The high-rises

FIGURE 7.8. Green Street 600-614 block looking north 1997. (Photo courtesy of Champaign County Historical Archives.)

(and somewhat older private buildings in the campus living district) also boast urban luxuries and convenience: built-in cable and internet connections, washers and dryers, microwave ovens, security systems, and underground parking.

By the fall of 2015, tall residential-retail buildings under construction or planned on both sides of Green Street from Wright Street west to Neil Street and on First, Second, Fifth, and John Streets had significantly altered the skyline of Campustown. Those projects, estimated at nearly $187 million in new construction for 2015-16, according to the *News-Gazette*, would add more than eight hundred units of private living spaces to Campustown. And Champaign city planner T. J. Blakeman calculated that the population density in the university district already "rivals Chicago's most densely populated neighborhood, Streeterville, on the city's near north side." It's "a shocking statistic," he said.

The university meanwhile is midway through a multimillion dollar project to replace, building by building, the Peabody and Gregory Drive residence halls—the famous "Six Pack." Three residential units of the Stanley O. Ikenberry Commons and a contemporary dining area already are finished and, when complete, the complex will house more than three thousand students. With the ongoing work on the Ikenberry Commons, the new seven-story, super-green replacement Presby House, the huge addition to Newman Hall (Newman North), the eight-story Green Street Towers, the mammoth twenty-four-story 309 E. Green, the tallest building in Champaign-Urbana, a slew of new fraternity houses, and those big new complexes on and near Green Street, students now have more choices where to live than ever, all close to the campus itself.

Eat

Just before 8 A.M. on March 23, 2011, a fire tore through the building on Green Street that housed the Pitaya clothing boutique, Mia Za's Café, and Zorba's, sending a plume of pitch-black smoke billowing into the air. The blaze started on the second floor and quickly spread to the roof. By 8:30 that Wednesday morning, a portion of the roof had been eaten away by flames and caved in. It took firefighters nearly two hours to contain the fire, but by then the building was largely destroyed. Several days later, partial demolition of the remaining structure began. It was the end of an era: Pitaya and Mia Za's Café had moved into the building during the last decade, but Zorba's, a campus institution famous for its gyros, had occupied this space since 1973; in spring 2012 Zorba's fans lined the block when the business reopened in a good-looking reproduction/salvage. Before the fire, the building had been a fixture in the heart of Campustown—the 600 block of Green Street—since the 1920s.

FIGURE 7.9. Ikenberry Commons dining area. (Photo by L. Brian Stauffer, University News Bureau.)

The 2011 fire was a dramatic incident in the century-long history of Campustown. In the earliest days of the university, Campustown did not exist. The plain campus of the Illinois Industrial University occupied a no-man's land between Champaign and Urbana, separated from them by a vast expanse of prairie and cornfields. Most students roomed in one of these sleepy towns and did their shopping there.

Boardinghouses soon popped up in the open spaces between the university, which consisted of a handful of buildings, and the towns. But it wasn't until the early 1900s that what is known as Campustown developed. The organization of the first fraternities and sororities provided the impetus. The fraternities invaded Green Street, moving into modest frame homes adjacent to the campus. According to longtime dean of men/students Fred Turner, "practically all the houses on Green street from First to Wright street were at one time fraternities." The sororities similarly colonized John Street. "This movement has made a compact community of students within six blocks of the campus, with very few living farther away," the 1918 *Alumni Record* noted. Businesses eventually emerged to cater to the needs of this compact community, and Campustown was born.

Enter "Fast Food"

"Quick lunch counter" establishments—the early-twentieth-century version of fast-food restaurants—were among the first businesses to open in Campustown. Places like "Tite-Wads" on Mathews Avenue, "Kirks" on Goodwin, "The Cave" on Green, and "Zeke and Dykes" on Sixth catered to students who were hungry and in a hurry.

The dean of men—the "matriarchal, patriarchal Thomas Arkle Clark"—strongly disapproved of these cheap eateries where the talk was loud, the tableware was dirty, and the food was barely edible. "Eating at such places is almost certain to develop bad manners and bad digestion," Clark said. "A stranger who should drop into one of these eating places when a meal is in progress would scarcely believe that he had come upon a group of educated young men who are striving for higher education, higher standards of living, higher ideals."

Black students, already hard pressed to find convenient housing, were barred from most campus-area eateries for decades even though state law prohibited racial discrimination in restaurants. Some campus restaurants, while not expressly forbidding blacks, discouraged them through deliberately bad service.

"Even in the place where I work," Jacob Goldstein, a U of I undergraduate, told a friend in 1929, "the boss told us that if any colored person came in, to take our time about waiting on them and give them poor service because he doesn't want to encourage their trade. . . . Sometimes those fellows wait fifteen or twenty minutes before they get any service and I really feel sorry for them."

As late as 1938, a survey reported that African American students had to trek 1.5 miles from campus to find restaurants that would serve them. A notable exception was the university cafeteria in the Woman's Building (1905-46, now the English Building), which, however, offered only lunch. This longstanding discrimination finally ended in 1946 thanks to a picketing campaign waged by a multiracial group of students and community members. (The University YMCA, already building a progressive reputation, later led a three-year campaign against Campustown barbers who refused to service African Americans.)

Campustown Pioneers

In 1907 George N. Cunningham constructed the first commercial building in Campustown at the northwest corner of Green and Wright Streets. Six years before, Cunningham had opened a student supply store in a thirty-year-old frame house located on the site. The old house, though, was unsuitable as a shop. "In the faraway days of 1901 the house had its disadvantages as a market-place for books," wrote local historian H. F. Harrington in a pamphlet about the Cunningham Brothers' business. "For one thing the room that held the books was only 10 feet wide by 12 feet long, hardly large enough to enclose a professor's library."

So in 1907 Cunningham moved the old house back from the street and built in front of it a substantial two-story brick structure. In addition to the supply store, the new Cunningham Block featured a post office, a confectionery, a billiard parlor, a tailor, a barber shop, and other enterprises that gave "a business air and activity to this corner such as it has never enjoyed before." In January 1916 a fire nearly destroyed the building and the new one erected in its place ultimately would house Follett's bookstore. In 1997 this last structure was demolished and replaced by a modern brick-and-limestone Follett's, one of eight hundred college bookstores owned by the privately held textbook company. Follett's pulled out of the local market in 2013 and local developer JSM, a titan of Green Street, has other commercial tenants in the vacated space.

After the Cunningham Block was built, Campustown didn't exactly boom. O. K. Barton, who opened a real estate office near campus in 1907, claimed that there was little activity in "University district property" until 1915. Barton said he and several other Campustown business pioneers were initially "the laughing stock of downtown merchants who believed we would never succeed."

Barton and his peers would have the last laugh, all the way to the bank. "Lots along Green street sold for $2,500 when first laid out," the real estate man reported in 1928. "Today the same lots are worth from $15,000 to $20,000." Inflated to today: $196,000 to $261,000. But simple inflation cannot explain the reported $2 million paid for a busy corner in Campustown where a high-rise apartment building with ground-floor retail was built in 2013-14.

As early as 1918, a university publication claimed that Campustown could supply students with their everyday needs. But a full-scale building boom would not hit the university district until the 1920s. Organized by Barton and his friends, the University District Building and Loan Association fueled this boom by providing financing for construction, which centered on Green Street, between Wright and Sixth.

Campustown businessmen here applied both initiative and a flair for publicity, using their own money to finance the widening of the street, lobbying for the installation of electric lights, and sponsoring a baseball team. During homecomings, the Green Street merchants illuminated the thoroughfare with a thousand or so orange and blue bulbs—a gaudy show of Illini boosterism. The *Daily Illini* applauded this garish display: "Anything which shades or tints the ugliness of modern practicality—and everyone will agree that Green street buildings were built with an eye to nothing else beside[s] practicality—should be welcomed."

By the end of the 1920s, businesses were popping up all around campus: west of Sixth, on Daniel between Wright and Sixth, on the corner of Lincoln and Nevada, and on Goodwin. (The Goodwin Avenue mini-district on the west side of the street would fall to the U of I's Chemical and Life Sciences Lab in the 1990s.) Even Collegiate Cap & Gown (now Herff Jones), founded in 1926, was located in Campustown until moving in 1939 to North Market Street near downtown Champaign.

Food and Drink, Then and Now

Some of the university's most famous eating and drinking places originated in the 1920s and 1930s, including Prehn's, Bidwell's, and Kam's, long before corporate food and drink such as McDonald's, Wendy's, and Starbucks arrived on the scene.

Paul Prehn was a campus legend, and, as the *Daily Illini* said, his life read like "the sort of tale Horatio Alger would have enjoyed writing." Confronted with the need to earn money for his poor family, Prehn entered the professional wrestling ring at age sixteen. After winning the light-heavyweight championship of the Allied Forces during World War I, he returned stateside and landed in Champaign, reputedly with only three cents in his pocket. He quickly obtained a job as the U of I wrestling coach and went on to guide the team to seven Big Ten championships. In 1929 he was elected president of the national boxing commission.

Despite these accomplishments, Prehn was probably best known on the U of I campus for his string of confectioneries owned in partnership with L. Donnelly Babcock, his brother-in-law: the original Prehn's at Sixth and Green Streets (opened in 1921, closed in 1941, and turned into a drug store and restaurant); Prehn's on Oregon and Goodwin (opened in 1928); and Prehn's on Daniel (opened in 1930). Costing $85,000 to build, the Oregon Street store was the showplace of the Prehn shops. With an eye-catching Spanish-style exterior of yellow stucco and red tile trim, the interior continued the theme with a balconied Spanish court and a gushing fountain. It was leased to a Chicago businessman in 1944 and renamed "The Flamingo." By 1947 it had closed and then reopened as Prehn's-on-Oregon; the operator was the nephew of Paul Prehn's sister, Effie Babcock. In 1966, Prehn's on Oregon became Treno's restaurant, another longtime campus institution. It is now an Espresso Royale coffee shop; the southern section of the space is The Bread Co., an eclectic restaurant. Both feature many of the original architectural and decorative elements. Following the repeal of Prohibition in 1933, Prehn's, as other campus confectioneries, started selling beer.

"Don't burn down Bidwell's . . ."

Bidwell's, which opened on Wright Street in 1919, was a popular confectionery turned watering hole, probably because it was willing to serve beer to underclassmen. In the early 1940s an appreciative Allan Sherman, campus cutup and future bestselling song parodist, even honored Bidwell's in verse. "Burn down Memorial Stadium,/ And Huff Gym as well . . . /But PLEASE/ Don't burn down Bidwell's," the song begins.

Around this time Bidwell's attracted the notice of U of I officials, thanks to a series of incidents involving intoxicated students, including football star Alex Agase. Dean of Men Fred Turner went so far as to call for Bidwell's to close. "If there is anything at all that we could do to have the place declared a public nuisance and closed I believe we should do it," Turner wrote President Arthur Cutts Willard (1934-46) in May 1942. "The operators of the establishment are without conscience as to what goes on there as long as they are not hurt financially, and skate along the narrow edge of 'within the law' and 'it is all right if you can get away with it.' We have had numerous disgraceful affairs come from there and I fear it is inevitable that a real tragedy or minor scandal will arise from the place."

Bidwell's survived until the late 1960s. By then, Don Ruhter, the *Daily Illini*'s Campus Scout, estimated that the bar was "probably netting more from coffee sales than beer sales."

Kam's

Kam's is one classic campus watering hole still standing. It has ranged up and down the 600 block of East Daniel Street for more than eight decades and survived family-business breakups, Prohibition, and a shift in the food-and-drink culture. It survived comic (then-student) Arte Johnson riding a horse into the place one Spring Carnival and professional hedonist (then-student) Hugh Hefner hanging around. It reveled in its standing as one of *Playboy*'s "Top Five" campus bars.

In 1929 Martin, Gordon, and Dick Kamerer opened two pharmacies, one at Lincoln and Nevada and the other at 602 East Daniel (now an Espresso Royale). In the early 1930s Martin added 608 East Daniel—site of Kamerer's Annex—to their growing business empire. According to John "Jack" Kamerer, Martin put his two younger brothers though pharmacy school, and they ran the family drugstores. Martin and Helen Kamerer ran Kamerer's Annex, nicknamed Kam's by students. The brothers split up the businesses in the 1930s.

The original Kam's housed a basement dining room that specialized in fried chicken from birds raised in west Champaign and served to students looking for a good meal before the U of I built dorms and offered meal contracts. During Prohibition, Kam's served near-beer. Martin Kamerer also contracted with the Army Specialized Training Program during World War II to serve late-night snacks of hamburgers, milk

FIGURE 7.10. From left, Martin and Helen Kamerer and Helen's brother, Leo Gordon, host the visit of the Budweiser Clydesdales and wagons at Kamerer's Annex (later known as Kam's) in the early 1950s. (Image ca. 1952-1954. Photo provided by Kamerer family.)

shakes, and ice cream to soldiers on campus. And in the 1950s Kam's brought in a local Italian restaurateur, Dom Buttitta, who made pizza in the basement.

Long before Kam's gained its reputation as the "Home of the Drinking Illini," a slogan coined in the 1970s by bar manager Mel Coleman, Kam's poured a lot of coffee for bridge-playing students and sold homemade donuts.

From 1959 to the early 1970s, Kam's was owned by Gene Fiedler and Leo Gordon, Helen Kamerer's brother. Down the block from Kam's was restaurant Marty K's. In 1958 the Kamerers rented the restaurant to football legend Stan Wallace, who ran it as Stan's Gridiron until 1975.

Jack Kamerer took over the space at 618 East Daniel, demolished an apartment house that shared the lot, and renovated the bar to triple its size. He oversaw the bar and food operations until 1981, when an investor group leased the business, which finally was leased to Eric Meyer. The KAM'S name and Home of the Drinking Illini slogan are part of the deal. The Jack Kamerer family still owns 616-618 East Daniel and its adjoining lot. He said student life and the business changed dramatically in the late 1960s and early 1970s as the U of I loosened its social controls over student life and housing.

In March 1966 Kam's, the neighborhood's foremost student bar—especially for Greeks—was the target of an outrageous and botched raid. Twenty-nine agents with the Illinois secretary of state's office raided the bar one Friday night. In search of fraudulently altered drivers' licenses, they apprehended some seventy students and charged fifty-two. Neither U of I nor local police were alerted to the raid, which followed correspondence and visits the preceding month to campus by investigators from Secretary of State Paul Powell's office. (Powell later was discredited, postmortem, when a shoebox full of cash was found in his Springfield hotel room.) Resolutions, petitions, rallies, demonstrations, and the inevitable lawsuits followed. One rally featured the ultimate political odd couple: campus leaders of the John Birch Society and Students for a Democratic Society jointly lambasting Powell, who was at Lincoln Square in Urbana to address a luncheon connected to an auto show.

House of Chin

The ghost of the House of Chin, a little bar and Chinese restaurant, remains visible to the curious who will risk traffic to stand in the middle of Sixth Street close to Green, facing south, and crane their necks up and to the east to catch a sliver of the old roofline of a modest three-story white house embedded in food and drink establishments that have been remodeled and rebuilt over the past three decades at that location.

This was a neighborhood of white frame houses with front porches and steeply pitched roofs. When it opened in 1964, the House of Chin was a business-in-a-house; in the 1960s customers sat on the porch facing Sixth Street to drink beer or sloe gin.

George Chin, a Chinese immigrant, transformed the Louie Lee Laundry (later the House of Chin Laundry, 1946-64) at 706 South Sixth Street into the House of Chin bar/restaurant. At the time, it was the only Chinese restaurant in Campustown. The family lived on the third floor above the second-floor restaurant and the first-floor Asian-styled bar called the Bamboo Lounge.

The bar eventually expanded to take in the Chin front porch populated by the "porch people." One porch person recalled those days: "It was fun and a bit bizarre. We'd sit out there in warm weather, drinking beer and spotting friends we knew walking or driving down the street. Sometimes we'd jump out on the street and drag them in. More well-intentioned people got sidetracked that way. To this day, I've never seen anything like that arrangement."

The porch era ended in 1968, when George Chin expanded the restaurant onto the porch space. The House of Chin survived in one incarnation or another into the 1990s. George Chin died in 2006 at age eighty-four; by fall 2016 the Clybourne, the last in a series of businesses to occupy the House of Chin building, had vacated the space.

Gone or Not

By the early 1970s, bar-hopping had become a favorite pastime of undergraduates, and Campustown provided plenty of venues. On the night of March 3, 1972, alone, an estimated two thousand students, "their hands barely able to hold a glass of beer after a strenuous week of notetaking," crammed into nine campus bars offering something for everyone. The bars included the Wigwam, "a down-home bar" catering to "the longer haired people"; the Red Lion, a pub attracting "all types"; Murphy's, the favored lair of graduate students then and now; Dooley's, "the best place to meet girls"; and

FIGURE 7.11. The rooftop of long-gone House of Chin is still visible from 6th Street between Green and John Streets. New construction wrapped around the existing structure, leaving the core house intact. (Photo by Karyl Wackerlin.)

Whitt's End, "the best place to meet boys." In subsequent decades, the bar names may have changed but Campustown bar-crawling remains popular.

Nuts for Spudnuts

Of course there's much more to Campustown than the bars.

Take the important food group of doughnuts and coffee. A midcentury campus area favorite called Spudnuts, a franchise doughnut operation based in Salt Lake City, Utah, first appeared locally at 513 Goodwin Avenue, Urbana, in March 1955. Spudnuts—as the name implies—were doughnuts made with potato flour. The aroma wafted through the east campus from a small shop later demolished in the name of science. The Goodwin Avenue store was followed in 1959 by one at 612 East Daniel Street in Champaign, another in 1965 at 119 South Race Street, Urbana, and finally at the Country Fair Shopping Center on Mattis Avenue in Champaign. The stores featured fresh bakery products and coffee.

But Campustown was not all beer and doughnuts.

Since the earliest days the university district has furnished "all the ordinary needs of the students": men's clothing at Schumacher's; sporting goods at Bailey & Himes; books and school supplies at Follett's and the Illini Union Bookstore; flowers at Campus Florist, where Anne Johnston has presided since 1940; records at Record Service and Record Swap; DVDs at That's Rentertainment; coffee at Espresso Royale in a wonderful dark brick building reclaimed from a hot dog shop that was painted bright yellow and red (and earlier was a Kamerer property), pizza at Papa Del's and Garcia's; gyros at Zorba's; groceries at Schrumpf's; and movies at the Co-Ed Theatre. Or at least most of a student's needs. When Schrumpf's closed in the 1990s a grocery store wouldn't return to the campus area until 2008 and is not so centrally located. Video streaming knocked off That's Rentertainment in 2015. And there hasn't been a movie theater near campus since the shuttering of the Thunderbird Theater in 1998 and the Co-Ed in 1999.

Anne Johnston has owned and operated Campus Florist at 609 East Green Street almost nonstop since 1940; the business was at a different location for six months in 1940-41. In a 2009 interview with Marie Wilson, then a U of I journalism student, Johnston said major cultural shifts—informality in how students dress, few events that require corsages, and customers just buying flowers and plants for themselves for no special occasion—have changed the business.

Change also came to Bailey & Himes. It opened at 606 East Green Street in 1920, expanded its factory on campus, and had other stores in Urbana, downtown Champaign, and the west part of the city. The business operated until 1979 when Don Himes, son of Shelby Himes, one of the company's original owners, dissolved it.

Don Himes said the company was a pioneer in sporting goods, working with U of I coaches and faculty to develop new products, such as a basketball without a lace that was manufactured by Rawlings, removable football cleats, and other equipment for track, basketball and football. The factory, which closed in 1958, made gym uniforms and chenille letters for varsity letter jackets. Himes said the factory made the original Harlem Globetrotters uniforms. This was long before former Illini basketball point guard Mannie Jackson rescued the Trotters from bankruptcy in 1993. Don became president of the company in 1965 when Shelby Himes died, and he closed the business in 1979 in the face of competition and a changing retail landscape of sports superstores catering to growing recreation and athletic gear markets.

Today many students bring cars to school and can travel off-campus to shop. That was not always the case. Between 1926 and 1953, the U of I enforced a no-car rule. In those days, students with limited mobility absolutely depended on Campustown businesses to provide everyday needs and an occasional new sweater.

Now these businesses face stiff competition from the covered malls and strip malls that have blanketed the area since the opening of Lincoln Square Mall in 1964. One block of East Green Street—the north side only—tells the story of both variety and necessity. In 1960, according to Jack Kamerer, the businesses from 602 to 624 Green were: Green Street Pharmacy, Capitol Restaurant, Bailey & Himes, Erber's Camera, Heller's Studio, Daniels A1 Printer, Hoffmann Music, Co-Ed Theatre and Southern Apartments.

In recent years Campustown has undergone revitalization or become a commercial strip that lacks character, depending on one's point of view. University officials, the city of Champaign, and local businesses combined effort and money to create the Campustown 2000 project that gave Green Street between Wright and Fourth an $8 million facelift. The street was narrowed to three lanes, the sidewalks were widened, and benches, fancy trash cans, fencing, planters, trees, and banners were added to beautify the streetscape. Since then more upscale businesses have arrived to Green Street, including Urban Outfitters.

Fast-food restaurants have also gone upscale, with Taco John's being replaced by the likes of Chipotle, Panera, and Potbelly. McDonald's, which has been in and out of the market for decades, is back in a JSM location. And, most dramatic of all, those high-rise apartments soaring over Green Street have forever altered its face.

On the east campus, near the Krannert Center for the Performing Arts, private developers have brought in a few shops and restaurants to what was a retail desert.

Pray

Writing in 1930, Arthur Ray Warnock, a former U of I assistant dean of men, claimed that the University of Illinois led all American colleges in two ways: the size of its Greek system and its "plan of religious instruction" via the sectarian foundations. "It is rather interesting that a so-called pagan state university should be a leader in an effective form of religious guidance," Warnock said. Both the Greek system and the religious foundations would help shape the physical and social and moral environment of the U of I campus.

Much earlier the university could be criticized for being too religious rather than godless. Jonathan B. Turner, the great champion of the national and state land-grant movement, was alarmed when he learned that John Milton Gregory, a Baptist clergyman, had been appointed the first regent of the Illinois Industrial University, as the U of I was called at its launch.

But Gregory insisted the university should be nonsectarian. "I am not even a Baptist inside of University walls," he wrote in one letter. "I am simply the servant of science and sound learning—of industrial and Christian education." The new regent tried to hire faculty members from various religious denominations—"men of all communions," as he termed it—but all of these denominations were Protestant.

"The University was at the outset avowedly Christian but nonsectarian," Winton Solberg writes in *The University of Illinois 1867-1894*. "Theoretically it opened its doors to all beliefs and to none; actually it was a Protestant institution."

End of Chapel

Gregory and his successor Selim Hobart Peabody (1880-91) both believed religion was a positive force and required students to attend daily chapel services. Even in the 1860s, the very dawn of the new university, many undergraduates found chapel to be boring and a waste of time. As early as December 1869, a mere twenty months after the school opened, students asked to be excused from chapel, but the faculty would "grant relief only for conscientious scruples," Solberg wrote. Professors themselves rarely attended chapel.

Student opposition to compulsory chapel grew. In 1885 Foster North, a senior in the School of Natural History, mounted a full-scale challenge to the system. The agnostic son of an agnostic father, North had impatiently endured chapel as a student and finally reached his breaking point. "I used to mentally damn—yes, god damn—old Peabody and his damned old prayers," North would recall in 1942. Just a few weeks before graduating, the headstrong senior skipped chapel, and Peabody suspended North indefinitely. North appealed unsuccessfully to the board of trustees, the regent, and the Illinois Supreme Court to regain admittance to the university. Finally, in 1914, the university awarded North a bachelor of science; he promptly returned the degree because a Roman Catholic priest had officiated at the commencement ceremony.

The chapel controversy had been rendered moot long before the North case. In March 1894 acting regent Thomas Burrill (1891-94) called for the end of university chapel, saying that "the time now set for the chapel exercises" interfered "with better arrangements for classes." The trustees agreed with Burrill, who later conceded to president Andrew Draper (1894-1904) that most students would not miss the services, and Draper himself dismissed chapel as irrelevant—"really a bore to everybody."

Draper, in fact, had outlined his views of the "new education" at the University of Illinois—which married science, democratic purpose, and a spiritual dimension—in a speech delivered to a national association of university officials in early 1903 in Springfield.

The work of the university, he said, "nourishes the life of the spirit, but it neither submits nor objects to any creed: it is not for free thinking which has no havens or anchorages; it is for freedom in a faith based upon scientific facts and logical thinking, and encourages worship in any form. It stands for all men and equality of opportunity; its sympathies are as high as heaven, and as broad as the boundless universe of matter and of life."

YMCA/YWCA

During Draper's administration, religious work on the campus was largely the province of the Young Men's Christian Association and the Young Women's Christian Association. The campus YMCA was organized on February 3, 1873, and the YWCA followed nearly twelve years later, in 1884. Hoping "to form in the University a center of Christian life and activity," the Christian associations sought to achieve this goal through an ambitious program of religious meetings, Bible study, missionary work, and community service.

During the Draper years, the YMCA experienced phenomenal growth: between 1896 and 1904, while male enrollment at the university grew by some 280 percent, YMCA membership expanded by more than 400 percent. The YWCA's rates were even more impressive: between 1900 and 1904 the number of women belonging to the YWCA went from 165 to 370, up some 124 percent. During this period, 63.5 percent of women undergraduates, on average, were members of the YWCA.

Signaling they were here to stay, the Christian associations moved into a house on the southwest corner of Wright and John Streets in 1899.

(A little-known fact: from 1884 to 1955, the YMCA-YWCA published a handbook about the university and its host communities, Champaign and Urbana, including a list of churches, and advice about registration and life as a student. This calendar/handbook, eventually called the "I-Book," is now published by the Illini Union Board.)

At this time, 1899, there were only two churches located within a half-mile of campus: the Methodist-run Parks Chapel, on Mathews and Springfield (where University High School stands now), and the Disciples of Christ–affiliated University Place Christian Church at 606 East White Street. Both churches soon would have bigger and better quarters, the University Place Christian Church moving to a big new building on the southwest corner of Springfield and Wright in 1903, and Parks Chapel, renamed Trinity Church, being rebuilt as a handsome Gothic edifice in 1906.

Following these pioneers, many other religious organizations began to build near campus. By 1918 the U of I campus was ringed with churches: the Unitarian Church at Oregon and Mathews, built in 1908; the George McKinley Memorial Church (Presbyterian) at John and Fifth, opened in 1912; and the University Baptist Church at Fourth and Daniel, a distinctive, white-columned Greek revival structure erected in 1916. In addition, the Methodists were then busy buying up the block bordered by Green, Goodwin, and Mathews as a site for a social center (completed in 1921) and sanctuary for the nation's first Wesley Foundation at an American university.

James C. Baker, minister of the Methodist Trinity Church, was a strong proponent of the foundation idea. Shortly after he took charge of Trinity in 1907 at age twenty-eight, Baker grappled with the problem of "filling the gap [in religious instruction] left by state institutions." The minister came to believe religious foundations chartered by the state as educational institutions could be that bridge. The basic idea had been suggested by U of I president Edmund Janes James in his 1905 inaugural address when he predicted the establishment of "local colleges in close proximity to the State

FIGURE 7.12. The University YMCA at night as viewed from the east side of Wright Street. The YMCA, an organization that traces its history at the U of I to 1873, moved into the building in 1938. (Image dated 1937. Photo courtesy of University of Illinois Archives 0003574.)

University in which ample provision will be made for the instruction in religious subjects."

In 1913, the Wesley Foundation, "the first institution of its kind," was incorporated to provide just such "instruction in religious subjects," with Baker a member of the first board of trustees. Six years later, in what Winton Solberg calls "a relatively bold new departure," the university began accepting for full academic credit courses taught by the religious foundations.

All Faiths Welcome

During the 1920s religious foundations flourished on the U of I campus, their growth encouraged by the devout U of I

FIGURE 7.13. North side and addition to St. John's Catholic Newman Hall Chapel, designed in the Charles Platt red-brick-and-limestone style by James M. White and completed in 1927. Newman Hall was built as a residence for 325 men a year later and, after a 2008 expansion, houses six hundred male and female students. (Photo by Darrell Hoemann.)

president David Kinley (1919-30). "There is no complete education without religious training," Kinley, a Presbyterian, said. By the end of Kinley's decade-long tenure as U of I president, there were six foundations on the campus: Wesley (Methodist), Newman (Roman Catholic), Hillel (Jewish), McKinley (Presbyterian), Disciples of Christ, and Congregationalists.

The decade also experienced a wave of church construction: Community United Church of Christ (Congregationalist), Sixth and Daniel, in 1921; St. John's Chapel (Roman Catholic), Armory and Sixth, in 1927; and St. John the Divine (Episcopalian), Wright and Armory, in 1927. St. John the Divine was finally finished in 2008, with a partial knock-down and addition that increased congregational seating by 30 percent. Like many U of I and neighborhood buildings, St. John's had a "temporary" wing—that stood for decades until resolve met money and the building was completed. The Reverend Timothy Hallett, who oversaw the two-year, $2 million effort that involved adding twenty-inch-thick walls that enhance the church's historic reverberant natural acoustics, jokingly called the earlier church St. John the Unfinished.

The Illinois Disciples Foundation, long located at the corner of Wright Street and Springfield Avenue, moved to downtown Champaign in 2008 and sold its original building to local developer JSM that converted it into apartments.

FIGURE 7.14. Hillel at the Margie K. and Louis N. Cohen Center for Jewish Life, was built in 2007 on the southeast corner of John and Fifth Streets, replacing an earlier Hillel center, which was the first in the country. (Photo by Karyl Wackerlin)

The Newman Foundation

The Newman Foundation was the brainchild of the Reverend Father John O'Brien. A Peoria native, the newly ordained O'Brien arrived at the U of I campus in 1917 and quickly set about raising money for a foundation building. During a whirlwind publicity campaign, the energetic priest informed Illinois Catholics that the U of I enrolled "more Catholic students than all the state Catholic colleges combined." It is, he said, "the great pivotal, strategical center of the educational life of the state."

O'Brien's efforts drew the ire of the Jesuits, who believed the downstate Catholic foundation threatened their own colleges, including Loyola of Chicago. Baltimore Archbishop Michael J. Curley also opposed O'Brien's plan, saying it "enabled laymen to conclude that Catholic schools have no reason for being." But O'Brien persevered and oversaw the completion of St. John's Chapel in 1927 (U of I campus architect James White designed it in the style of Platt: all red brick and limestone) and the matching 325-bed Newman Hall a year later. Things did not end well for O'Brien: in 1938, as

FIGURE 7.15. Louis C. Tiffany stained-glass window at McKinley (Presbyterian) Church at Fifth and John Streets was a gift to the church from U.S. Representative/U.S. Senator William McKinley, whose father founded the church. The window is called "Good Samaritan." The church building is more than a century old. (Photo by Karyl Wackerlin.)

the Newman Foundation slid toward bankruptcy, he was forced to resign as chaplain of the Illinois campus. According to historian Solberg, Peoria Bishop Joseph H. Schlarman decreed on doctrinal as well as financial grounds "that the founder of the Illinois Newman Foundation was never again to celebrate Mass or remain overnight in the diocese."

Short-timer Rev. Roger Schoenbechler (1939-43) was replaced by the legendary Reverend Edward J. Duncan, who influenced campus, neighborhood, and Catholic development for more than four decades, 1943 to 1998. Monsignor Duncan died in 2012 at age ninety-six. Newman Hall expanded substantially in 2008 and now accommodates six hundred students. The St. John's Catholic Newman Center at the U of I is the largest in the country.

The story of the Hillel Foundation's birth also was a story of struggle. A group led by downtown Champaign clothier Isaac Kuhn spent long years trying to bring Judaism to the U of I, which had some 150 Jewish students in 1915. Kuhn and his associates had called for a rabbi "who can radiate Jewishness in all directions" to be sent to the U of I. Enter in 1923 the gentle giant Rabbi Benjamin Frankel. Charismatic and confident, Frankel was a man in a hurry, and he got things done fast.

In the fall of 1923, he organized the nation's first Hillel Foundation, named after the first-century Jewish scholar. The foundation's purpose was "to establish for the Jewish students of the University of Illinois a religious, moral, social and recreation center, to teach the principles of the Jewish faith, and to cooperate with other similar agencies in the cultivation of a moral and spiritual life." Frankel died at age thirty, a victim of heart disease, but his great legacy—the Hillel Foundation—lives on. As of 2015 there were some 605 collegiate Hillels around the globe. The Urbana-Champaign campus is rated a "Top 60" school by Jewish enrollment, an estimated 10 percent of undergraduates, according to hillel.org.

Religious Expansion

In the years since the earliest activity in the 1920s, the number of religious organizations on campus has multiplied, and so has the number of religious buildings. In 1930 the monumental McKinley Foundation building was dedicated; in 1938 the YMCA moved into its current familiar home on Wright Street (major remodeling in 2010-11); in 1950 the Hillel Foundation occupied a modernist structure at Fifth and John (in 2007, the building was replaced with the striking Margie K. and Louis N. Cohen Center for Jewish Life); and in 1959 the Methodists completed their soaring Wesley Sanctuary that looms over the corner of Green and Mathews. From the 1960s onward, many more churches have come to the campus area, including St. Andrews Lutheran Church, Twin City Bible Church, First Mennonite Church, and its neighbor, the Central Illinois Mosque and Islamic Center.

The decade of the 1960s was a challenging time for many campus religious organizations as some U of I professors tried to end the program of university-accredited courses taught by religious foundations. Until 2010 the Newman Foundation offered two for-credit courses through an arrangement with the university, with the foundation paying the salary of the instructor. Following a controversy over an instructor expressing in an e-mail a doctrinal viewpoint on homosexuality, the U of I ended this arrangement and assumed the instructor's salary.

Though many churches championed the civil rights cause early in the 1960s and won support from progressive-minded collegians, this allegiance began to wane in the late 1960s in part because, according to Rev. Richard Lundy, a former pastor of the McKinley Presbyterian Church, "most Christian denominations did not take a strong stand against the Vietnam war."

By the 1980s, religious participation on campus started to rebound, prompting the 1982 *Illio* (U of I yearbook) to proclaim "A religious revival in the 1980s." Today more than two dozen religious organizations and at least seven sectarian foundations serve the campus.

Thomas Arkle Clark, Über Dean

Thomas Arkle Clark was legendary—and controversial—as "dean of deans" in student affairs. He was dean of undergraduates, assistant to the president, and, ultimately, dean of men, where he exerted powerful influence with an outsized view of control and discipline, a staunch adherent of *in loco parentis*, which kept students under the thumb of the campus acting as parents. He was affiliated with the U of I from 1885 to 1931, a year before he died. Read a mini-bio of "Thomas Arkle Clark" on the companion Web site (sidebar 8.1).

Orchard Downs

Married students, many with children, were left to negotiate the local rental and real estate market as they flooded onto campus immediately at the end of World War II and long after. Predictably, local landlords objected, but the campus developed the Orchard Place/Orchard Downs complex by a since-abandoned "design-build" process that handed planning and design roles to contractors. Read about "Orchard Downs" on the companion Web site (sidebar 8.2).

The Christian Science Building

The Christian Science Building at Fourth Street and Gregory Drive was designed by Paul Rudolph, a leading modernist with an international reputation. It was not a campus building, but its location and architectural prominence put it squarely in the U of I's orbit. It lasted a mere twenty years before falling to the wrecking ball. The campus didn't buy the land then either; a local developer built an undistinguished apartment building on the corner. Read "The Christian Science Building" for more on the companion Web site (sidebar 8.3).

CHAPTER 8

Gifts and Givers

Donor Buildings

> I think there will be two hundred thousand dollars to put into the building, and that ought to be a sufficient sum of money to really erect a great music building, and when constructed, I want it to stand alone as a monument to the memory of Mrs. Smith.
>
> —Letter from Thomas J. Smith to a Champaign friend, August 4, 1913

Thomas J. Smith, Civil War hero, successful small-town lawyer, and wealthy landowner, leaned into the task at hand. He would write a memorial booklet about Tina, his beloved wife, whose dead body lay near him in the big Victorian house on University Avenue in Champaign, Illinois. It was 1903.

Fourteen years later, Smith laid the cornerstone on the Tina Weedon Smith Music Building—a monument to his late wife and the first donor, or gift, building erected on the campus.

"Capt. Smith was the largest single financial contributor to the University of Illinois in all its history," wrote the *Daily Illini* on April 17, 1918, in reporting his death the day before in Battle Creek, Michigan.

"He has not only paid his share of taxes toward the support of the University on a large property for many years, but he finally presented to the University a munificent gift of 770 acres of the best farm land in Champaign County, the proceeds of the sale of which should go to the erection of a Music Hall on the campus of the University."

In the nearly one hundred years since Smith Memorial Hall opened, some thirty gift buildings and athletic venues, ranging from a state-of-the-art computer science center to a tidy softball field, have been donated to the University of Illinois at Urbana-Champaign by individuals and family foundations. Fully three-fourths of the gift buildings and arenas have come since 1980, and most contributions covered from a third to a half or more of the cost of the project. Each of them represents not only a commitment of substantial financial resources but a sign of trust and affection toward the U of I, its leadership, and its aspirations.

The love story of Thomas and Pauline "Tina" (Weedon) Smith that yielded Smith Memorial Hall flows from the story of Capt. Smith, who served the Union during the Civil War and migrated to central Illinois, where the new Illinois Industrial University would be chartered in 1867. Smith would serve the University of Illinois as an elected trustee, 1897 to 1903, during the presidency of Andrew Sloan Draper.

But it was Edmund Janes James, Draper's successor at the university, who secured the gift of farmland and cash that would make possible the music hall. And it was James, whose sixteen-year presidency was marked by vigorous campus planning, ambitious building, and high academic aspirations

FIGURE 8.1. Captain Thomas J. Smith, U of I trustee and husband of Tina Weedon Smith, donated land and cash to build a music hall in his wife's memory. (Photo dated ca. 1895-1900. Photo courtesy of University of Illinois Archives 0003715.)

FIGURE 8.2. Smith Memorial Hall was named in honor of Tina Weedon Smith, a southern belle who married a northern Civil War officer. (Image undated. Photo courtesy of University of Illinois Archives 0003397.)

for the young university, who accepted the compromise that left Smith Memorial Hall a standalone building instead of one linked to the Auditorium, as planners had suggested.

Thomas J. Smith was born in 1839 in Virginia and moved as a boy with his parents to Ohio; he studied law in Louisville, Kentucky, just before moving to Clay County, Illinois, where he taught and in 1859 was elected superintendent of schools as a Republican. But he resigned his term to enlist as a private in Company F, 98th Illinois volunteers.

War service suited Smith. He rose from orderly to captain of his own company. On duty in middle Tennessee, a Confederate stronghold, Smith first met Pauline Weedon, some dozen years his junior and a month short of fifteen years old.

Smith described the afternoon of March 6, 1863, when he spied Tina—nicknamed for her diminutive stature, including a size 2½ shoe—perched on her mother's kitchen table with her legs hanging down.

"Whether she or I spoke first I cannot say, but our meeting in that informal way brought on some lively talk, which soon developed the fact that she liked the Rebels and hated the Yankees," Smith wrote in his memorial tribute.

By the following January, the couple—she fifteen and he twenty-six—were married and en route to Champaign, where Smith's brother lived. Tina was to live with Judge Smith's family while Capt. Smith returned to active duty in Tennessee, Kentucky, and Mississippi until war's end, his wife periodically visiting. At one point, learning that Tina was seriously ill, he went AWOL to fetch her in Champaign and take her to her family in Murfreesboro; the irony is that he was assigned as a judge advocate of the military commission to try cases of desertion and other military crimes. He was arrested and held for eight days and then sent back to his commission work right after. The Civil War had created shortages of all sorts—including lawyers in uniform.

At war's end the couple settled in Champaign, where Smith opened a law practice. He served as city attorney from 1866 to 1868 and from 1881 to 1887 was "master of chancery" for Champaign County. He acquired substantial farmland, the currency of a wealthy Illinoisan. The couple joined the First Methodist Episcopal Church, and she became an important hostess in Urbana-Champaign's social whirl. The University of Illinois—a single secondhand building east of downtown Champaign in the twin city of Urbana—opened in 1868.

"She possessed that rare and distinctive Southern trait [of hospitality] to a remarkable degree," Mrs. Smith's pastor said at her funeral. "She was the charm of any circle, genial, graceful, captivating, easily the presiding genius, the peerless queen among host of admirers."

The couple had built their house at 407 West University Avenue; it could seat two hundred for dinners and parties, which the couple hosted often. The house faced north and was directly across the street from the heart of West Side Park, Champaign County's first park, consisting of 12.5 acres donated to the city in 1854. In the early years, residents pastured their cows on the fenced-in rectangular green for thirty-five cents a month. Soon, prominent citizens would outline the park on three sides with their Victorian and Edwardian mansions.

The park was two blocks from the city center that throbbed with commerce fed by the rich Drummer soil laid down by glaciers millennia before and only recently uncovered from its blanket of tall prairie grasses. In the summer, brass bands and singers, orators and politicians, including Teddy Roosevelt, would climb up into the park bandstand. The Smith home was razed in the mid-1960s to make room for The Oaks at 407-409 West University Avenue, which overlooks the 2008 reconstruction of the bandstand.

In keeping with their status, the Smiths traveled widely in the United States and Europe. Mrs. Smith had bouts of neuralgia and throat trouble, but travel always perked her up. In 1871 Smith went to the nation's capital on business accompanied by his wife. President Ulysses S. Grant and his wife, Julia Dent, hosted the Smiths for dinner, the president escorting Tina Smith into the White House dining room.

"When dinner was over, Grant gave Tina a bouquet of flowers from the table," according to a 1982 history of Cannon County, Tennessee. "She kept them the rest of her life, and when she died they were placed among the rest of the flowers around her coffin."

The illness that led to her death began as the couple was returning by rail from their summer vacation at White Sulphur Springs, West Virginia; Culpeper, Virginia; and Washington, D.C.

In his memorial, Thomas Smith describes her last illness in gruesome detail, five days of abscesses and pain and morphine, with four doctors attending and women friends, such as Mrs. F. K. Robeson—the wife of a major downtown retail general store's owner—hovering. At her death, Tina Weedon Smith was dressed in "her black spangled net, over white silk under dress, white stockings, and white sating [*sic*] slippers with white bows in her hair." She was laid in a metallic casket in the front end of the parlor, flowers overflowing the University Avenue house.

Her death, in the year after his six-year term as University of Illinois trustee ended, marked the beginning of Capt. Smith's determination to build an appropriate monument to Tina Smith. "It shall be my purpose to live only to perpetuate the memory of my dear and loving departed wife," he said in 1903.

The president of the University of Illinois and the director of the School of Music, which opened in 1895 (although there had been piano and voice instruction dating to the 1870s), conspired to encourage the gift of music. Before she was married, young Tina Weedon played piano and sang for her Yankee suitor, according to the 1984 Cannon County history.

"Her favorite song was 'I Dreamt I Dwelt in Marble Halls.' She did not play or sing well. But Captain Smith thought she could. It may have been then and there that he resolved he would come as close as he could to giving her the equivalent of marble halls," wrote Robert L. Mason.

On November 9, 1917, Capt. Thomas J. Smith laid the cornerstone of Smith Memorial Hall, which was materially finished in 1920-21 and dedicated in 1922. He also endowed music scholarships, which still are awarded to women students from Illinois, before dying in early 1918 at age eighty-two.

❖ ❖ ❖ ❖

The University of Illinois Foundation, the fundraising arm for the three-campus institution, was charted in 1935, just as the nation began its slow recovery from the Great Depression. Its goal was simple: raise private gifts and invest funds on behalf of the university, as a separately chartered, not-for-profit organization.

Among its earliest gifts: barberry bushes, a collection of old commencement programs, and some *Illio* yearbooks.

But things were looking up, according to a brief history of the foundation produced for its fiftieth anniversary.

John N. Chester, whose endowment continues to support the visual arts at Illinois, made the first major gift: Sir Walter Raleigh's *History of the World*, a valuable old book. Merle and Emily Trees followed that with some paintings by old masters. In 1939, just four years after it was chartered, the foundation launched its first major fund drive to build, equip, and furnish the Illini Union.

A chart of private giving drawn from U of I comptroller's reports shows the value of gifts: \$3.2 million from 1895 to 1935; \$1.8 million, 1936 to 1940; \$2.4 million, 1941 to 1945; \$23 million, 1961 to 1965; \$50.4 million, 1971 to 1975; and \$256.3 million, 1981 to 1985, which encompassed the university's first major capital campaign, Campaign for Illinois, which ran from 1979 to 1985 and exceeded the campaign goal of \$100 million by \$32 million. The second campaign, Campaign Illinois, ran from 1991 to 2000 and raised \$1.53 billion; and the third, Brilliant Futures, ran from 2003 to 2011, and raised \$2.267 billion. A new campaign will launch soon to coincide with the 150th anniversary of the University of Illinois's charter.

New buildings or significant additions, playing fields, monuments, and gardens are among the gifts the U of I has received over the past century. But most private giving is not for bricks and mortar, being designated instead for professors, student scholarships and fellowships, library materials, and to keep WILL on the air. Still, the Urbana-Champaign campus has notable buildings and public spaces made possible by men and women who love the Illini Place.

Smith Memorial Hall

Designed by James M. White, the long-time campus supervising architect, and George E. Wright, the 1921 building is a fine example of Beaux-Arts classical style, a flamboyant and rich expression that originated from the Ecole des Beaux-Arts in France in the late nineteenth century.

Smith Memorial Hall, east of the Auditorium on the main Quad, has a classic and imposing white stone façade with columns. Its main performance hall seats 650 on the floor and 450 in the upper balcony; there is mahogany woodwork throughout.

The building contains studios, classrooms, and nearly one hundred practice rooms for students and professionals associated with the School of Music.

Smith Memorial Room, an Italian renaissance drawing room with fireplaces, a trio of crystal chandeliers, and heavily detailed ceilings and doorways, is used for chamber music and harpsichord recitals. It has two marble fireplaces each inscribed with SMH for Smith Music Hall. Oil portraits of the Smiths used to hang above the mantles; now they are in stairwells outside the room. Smith Memorial Room was the music library from 1940 to 1972; the library is now in the Music Building, south of the Krannert Center for the Performing Arts.

The building has more than seventy-six thousand square feet. An elevator was installed in 1940, and a west wing was added to the building in 1953. Smith is a registered historic landmark; a campus committee ranked Smith Memorial Hall 4.45 on a 5.0 scale for historic significance.

Smith Hall is one of the most elaborately decorated buildings on the campus, including lines from the English poet William Cowper ("There is in souls a sympathy with sounds. . . .") and composer names carved into the sides and front of the building: Bach, Beethoven, Haydn and Palestrina (Giovanni Pierluigi de Palestrina, a sixteenth-century composer of sacred music). Edmund J. James had surveyed four thousand educators and musicians to gather names to inscribe inside and outside the building; once again, lack of money prevented most of the planned decoration.

Frederic Stiven, director of the School of Music, understood the immediate and enduring impact of Capt. Thomas Smith's donated land and money to underwrite the building to honor his late wife. "To Illinois belongs the honor of being the first state to put its School of Music on the same basis as the other colleges of its great University," he wrote.

Smith provided about $215,000 for the building. Fully furnished—including a new Steinway piano—the building cost $462,625, according to "Rediscovering Smith Hall" in the winter 2014 edition of the School of Music magazine, *Sonorities*. The building's 2008 "book" or replacement value is about $18 million.

Memorial Stadium

On a mild and sunny Saturday in November 1920, more than twenty thousand fans, including some two thousand dads (this was the first Dad's Day), packed the wooden bleachers at tiny Illinois Field to watch the Illini and Buckeyes battle for the Big Ten football championship. Unable to obtain seats, tens of thousands more milled outside the fences while the game raged. The two evenly matched teams remained deadlocked in a scoreless contest until the last seconds of the game, when Ohio State quarterback Harry Workman heaved a "Hail Mary" from the fifty-yard line to tight end Truck Myers, who raced eighteen yards for the touchdown and the win. The Ohio State fans went wild, and more than thirty thousand of them stampeded through the fences and "swarmed over the field, carrying the Buckeye champions off the gridiron in a triumphant procession behind the Scarlet and Gray 100 piece band," in the words of the *Daily Illini*.

This game, more than any other, pointed out the inadequacy of the Illinois Field "lumberyard" and the desperate need for a large-scale football stadium to accommodate the growing number of fans. Harvard and Yale Universities already had big stadiums, and Ohio State itself was in the middle of a million-dollar stadium campaign. Why shouldn't Illinois climb on the bandwagon? Taking the ball and running with it, George Huff, the beloved athletic director, and Robert Zuppke, the fiery Illinois football coach, spearheaded a furious drive to build a stadium that would

FIGURE 8.3. Memorial Stadium was built with contributions from students and alumni as a memorial to the U of I students who died in World War I. Besides football (and earlier, track) Memorial Stadium has held commencements and an occasional concert. (Photo courtesy of Fighting Illini Athletics/Division of Intercollegiate Athletics.)

be both a football arena and a memorial for the Illini who perished in World War I.

Organized early in 1921, the Stadium Fund Drive—"the university's first public attempt to secure private financial support for a major project," according to the historian Maynard Brichford—targeted first the students' purses and wallets. Expertly managed by alumnus Samson Raphaelson, future author of "The Jazz Singer," fundraising committees with some twenty-five hundred members "lived and breathed Stadium" day and night, and employed picnics and parades, posters and publications to persuade students to help "build that Stadium for Fighting Illini."

The effort culminated in a "monster mass meeting"—complete with bands, airplanes, and artillery—held on April 21, 1921, in two places: the Gym Annex and the Auditorium. Some seven thousand students turned out to hear eleven speakers, including Huff and Zuppke, make final pitches for the stadium. Zuppke's sentences "zigzagged" across the wide expanse of the Gym Annex like "lightning," and, when he closed his remarks by asking for $1,000 donations, the buzzing crowd fell silent. Suddenly, a student from the international section—the students were seated by county, state, and nation—stood up and said, "I will give, sir!" His name was R. L. Cavalcanti, and he was from Latin America. The

FIGURE 8.4. Coach Bob Zuppke with players. The Memorial Stadium football field is named for Zuppke, head coach for twenty-nine seasons. (Photo courtesy of Fighting Illini Athletics/Division of Intercollegiate Athletics.)

logjam having been broken, a flood of donations ensued. When the student campaign ended on May 1, some $665,000 had been pledged.

"What you have started, our alumni will finish," Huff had told the students at the April 25 meeting. And finish they did. Huff and Zuppke barnstormed the country during the spring and summer of 1921, speaking to alumni clubs from Seattle to New York City and most points in between. Their "oratorical fireworks" paid off: in late December, Huff reported that a total of $1,642,000 in stadium pledges had been received. Some eight thousand alumni and a similar number of students had made pledges.

In the spring of 1922 a swampy south campus field was chosen as the site for Memorial Stadium, and construction began the following autumn. Champaign's very own English Brothers Company oversaw the gargantuan construction project, managing an army of as many as thirty-six hundred workers. Steel, concrete, brick, and limestone for the structure were brought to the site via a railroad spur line branching off the nearby Illinois Central tracks. In the end, thirty-two hundred tons of steel, forty-five thousand tons of sand and gravel, twelve million pounds of cement, and 1.2 million bricks (all from Danville's Western Brick Company) were used to build Memorial Stadium.

Holabird and Roche, a famous Chicago firm then acting as an architectural consultant for the university, designed the classical revival structure. The firm was a natural choice for the Memorial Stadium commission: John Holabird had just designed the Municipal Grant Park Stadium (later Soldier Field), which would open in the very same year as Memorial Stadium. According to Holabird's son, his father had gotten the idea for Memorial Stadium's tower ramps from the Bramante spiral staircase in the Vatican Museum. Architectural historian Allen Weller called the stadium's exterior "an imposing shell which cleverly introduces a majestic colonnade in harmony with the Georgian buildings designed and erected at the same time." With its two main stands extending for 548 feet, the stadium at first could comfortably seat some fifty-six thousand people—a capacity then exceeded in the Big Ten by only Ohio State's The Horseshoe. Doric columns lining the east and west sides of the stadium are engraved with the names of 184 Illini—one name per column—who gave their lives during World War I. Additional columns honor the unknown Illini dead, a graduate from the universities of Chicago and Michigan, and the World War I–era Students' Army Training Corps.

Though not yet completed, Memorial Stadium hosted its first football game on a drizzly, raw Homecoming Saturday in early November 1923. Senior Logan Peirce was an awestruck witness at the mammoth stadium's "baptism of rain," which featured a muddy match-up with bitter rival Chicago. "Dear, the spectacle here Saturday was beyond my powers of description," Peirce raved in a letter to his girlfriend. "It was wonderful! 62,000 people jammed into the stadium. Chicago, with their maroon colors, formed an enormous C in the east bleachers. The players looked like midgets—but you could see wonderfully well." The Illini defeated Chicago in the "Mud Bowl" by a score of 7-0, and that night "the campus was nothing but a wild howling mob of half crazy homecomers," with the booze "floating around everywhere."

Memorial Stadium was officially dedicated on October 18, 1924. The most ardent Illini fan couldn't have asked for a more "thumping" dedication. On that warm Homecoming afternoon, Harold "Red" Grange galloped into the history books, scoring five touchdowns on the ground (and throwing a pass for a sixth) against a heavily favored Michigan team. Grange's phenomenal performance that day helped put college football on the national map and turned the newborn Memorial Stadium into an instant historic landmark.

The stadium ushered in a golden age of Illinois football: between 1923 and 1929 Zuppke-led teams won three Big Ten championships. "A gift of the alumni and people of Illinois, the stadium was the key factor in the 'golden' era of Illinois football," Maynard Brichford wrote. "From 1923 to 1930, football began producing substantial profits on the field, in the grandstands and in the accounting office."

Over the years Memorial Stadium has undergone many renovations, beginning in 1928 and 1929 when the West Hall and the south "horseshoe" stands were built. In 2008 the $121 million "Illinois Renaissance" renovation installed skyboxes, extended and improved the concourse areas, and added a five-thousand-seat structure to the stadium's north end.

McKinley Hospital and Health Center

When U.S. Senator William B. McKinley, still considered among Champaign's most accomplished citizens, died on December 7, 1926, the next day's edition of the *Daily Illini* captured the essence of the tenacious businessman, politician, and philanthropist: "His genius for making money was exceeded only by his genius for giving it away."

A Petersburg, Illinois, native, McKinley attended the Illinois Industrial College, which later became the University of Illinois, for one year before he left due to lack of funds. In

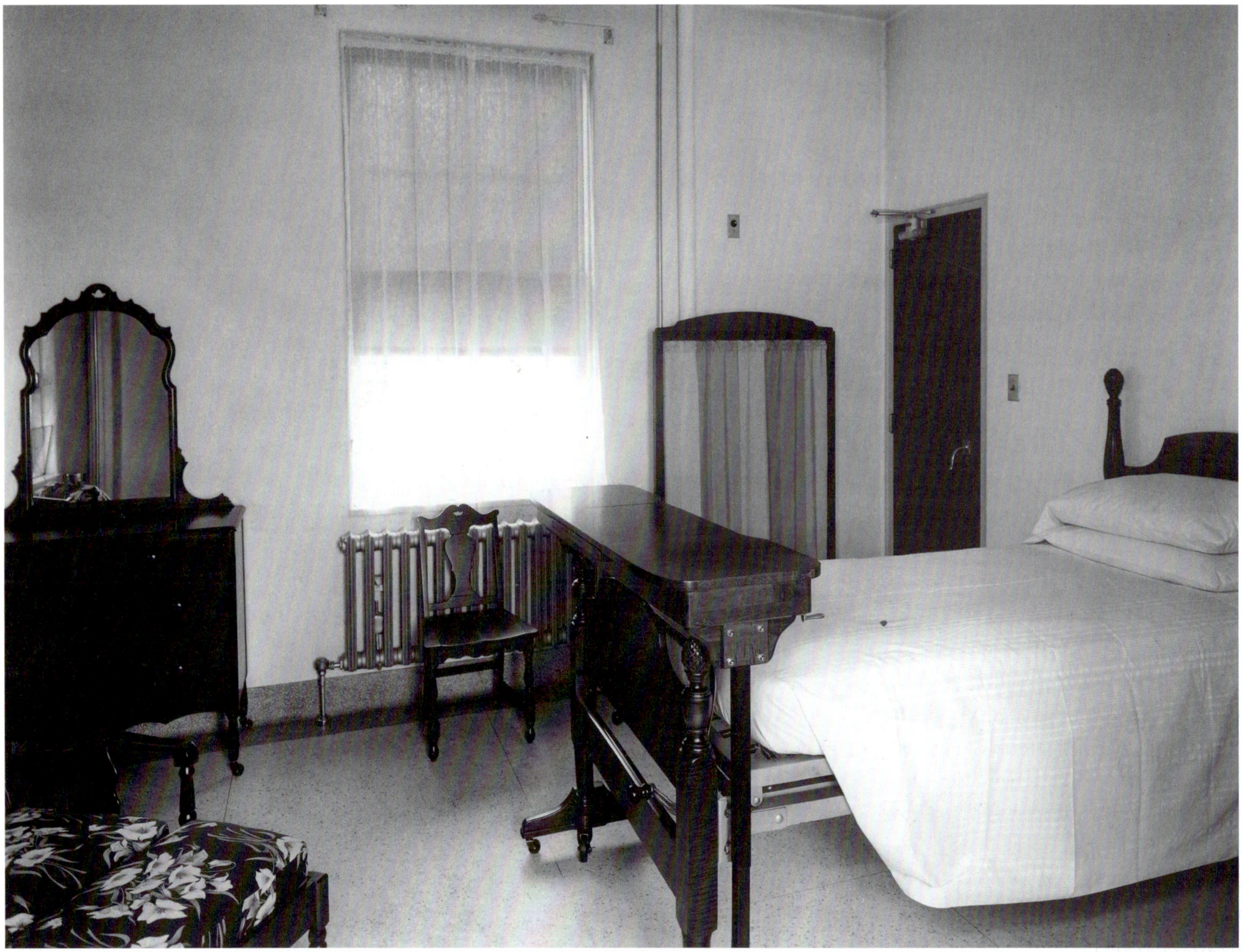

FIGURE 8.5. Typical room in McKinley Hospital, built in 1925. (Photo dated 1942. Photo courtesy of University of Illinois Archives 0001816.)

the 1880s he was involved in private banking during a land boom that went bust, leaving McKinley broke and down but not out.

Tapping into interest and experience in the public utilities industry, he built the Champaign Water Works, Illinois Power and Light Co., and the Illinois Traction System, an electric "interurban" and freight railroad line that covered more than five hundred miles across central Illinois. The line, which was reportedly the largest interurban railway in the world, operated from the 1890s to the 1980s.

With business running smoothly, the restless McKinley then "blundered into" politics. "Things went on without me. So when it was suggested to me that I run for Congress, I accepted just for something to do. I never regretted it," he told the *Washington Post*. He was elected to the House of Representatives in 1905, reelected six times, and served one term as a U.S. senator. He held key committee posts in the House and Senate, and managed the national campaign of William Howard Taft for president in 1912.

McKinley was considered one of the wealthiest members of Congress, and he was also one of its most generous. His personal secretary indicated he donated between $10 million and $12 million in public and private philanthropies, especially to educational and religious institutions. He helped establish the Young Men's Christian Association building in Champaign, and the Young Women's Christian Association building and the McKinley Memorial Presbyterian Church and Foundation, both on campus. Those organizations have served the local and university communities alike.

At Illinois, his alma mater, which he later served as a member of the Board of Trustees, he established a loan fund that helped more than five thousand students, endowed a chair in economics of public utilities, and, in 1917, gave $100,000 to construct a new hospital on the Urbana-Champaign campus. McKinley twice committed additional funding to the project, contributing more than $200,000 for the much-needed hospital.

FIGURE 8.6. U.S. Senator William B. McKinley, elected in to the Senate in 1920 after several terms as congressman, was a University of Illinois alumnus, a Champaign banker, an electric power and transportation magnate, and a university trustee. He provided all the money to build McKinley Hospital (now McKinley Health Center) on Lincoln Avenue. (Photo courtesy of U.S. Library of Congress, Harris & Ewing Collection.)

The McKinley Memorial Hospital was dedicated on February 13, 1926. The 42,700-square-foot facility supplanted the university's student hospital in the twice-remodeled Floriculture Service Building. At McKinley, students and faculty paid a modest membership fee annually to receive low-cost care at the hospital.

The new facility also put to rest memories of isolation facilities, or "pest houses," that were established to treat patients with contagious diseases, such as scarlet fever during a 1914 epidemic. By 1950 McKinley Hospital had wards and private rooms to handle up to eighty student patients, as well as a contagious ward with forty-seven beds. The facility has been expanded, renovated, and modernized since, and it continues to serve tens of thousands of University of Illinois students, faculty, and staff annually, but now only as an outpatient clinic, not a hospital.

Allerton Park and Retreat Center

For sheer scale, worth, and beauty, no single gift to the University of Illinois can match the Allerton properties: the country home, the farms, the woodlands, the gardens, and the outdoor artwork that surprises and delights.

FIGURE 8.7. Robert Allerton in the lower garden at his estate in rural Monticello. (Photo dated ca. 1915. Photo courtesy of University of Illinois Archives 0004225.)

One of the University of Illinois's crown jewels, Allerton Park and Retreat Center is located in rural Monticello, twenty-five miles west of Champaign. The U of I has owned it since October 1946, when Robert H. Allerton deeded his Georgian mansion and almost half of his twelve thousand acres to the university.

Allerton had lived in his "summer home" since 1900, when he was twenty-seven and looking for something to do with his life after having abandoned his artistic studies in Europe. His millionaire father, Chicago pork packer and banker Samuel Allerton, had suggested that Robert manage the Piatt County farmland the family used as a fattening-up station for livestock heading to the Chicago Union Stockyards. But the property needed a home suitable for the young man who in 1906 would be named by the *Chicago Sunday Tribune* as "Richest Bachelor in Chicago."

Construction on the mansion, situated along the Sangamon River, began in mid-1899. William Mavor, the same contractor responsible for buildings erected at Chicago's 1893 World's Columbian Exposition, supervised the 150 laborers. The mansion was constructed using bricks previously employed as ballast on a ship from Holland. Limestone came from Bedford, Indiana.

The "summer home"—modeled after a Surrey, England, mansion (Ham House)—cost Robert Allerton's father some $50,000. The exterior was finished in 1900. The original parapet was removed a few years later in favor of a more watertight roof. The mansion's first floor, about thirty-two thousand square feet, follows an "H" plan and includes a gallery twenty feet wide by ninety feet long. The majestic mahogany stairway, the Pine, Oak, Butternut Rooms (each named for its clad walls), a library/music room, and a conservatory radiate from the gallery.

Allerton used the landscape as his canvas, combining his love of art and nature to create walking trails and

FIGURE 8.8. The main house at Allerton Park was built in 1900 and is listed on the National Register of Historic Places. (Photo by Michael Holtz.)

formal gardens. Before finishing the Brick Wall Garden where *Girl with a Scarf* stands, he wrote to a friend, "The paths are gradually being made. They improve everything awfully." Other gardens stretch from the Fu Dog Garden at the north end of the Park, past the *Death of the Last Centaur* beyond the Sunken Garden, to the *Sun Singer* at the park's south end.

Allerton encouraged his friends and family to wander by installing a cable bridge that connected the main property with the timbered area south of the Sangamon River. Called the Lost Garden, the area included a double allée of Eastern Red Cedars, a teahouse pavilion, and more statues.

The sphinxes near the pool are from the architect's designs, but Allerton purchased many other statues from Asia and Europe. Some were commissioned, such as the two full-size limestone *Primitive Man* sculptures, as well as a stone reproduction of Auguste Rodin's original bronze casting of *Adam*. (Robert purchased the bronze casting from

FIGURE 8.9. Allerton Park's Fu Dogs, twenty-two in blue ceramic, two in green ceramic, and one in granite, depict mythological Asian art lion dogs. They are Buddhist guardians that ward off evil spirits from temples, homes, shops, and cemeteries. Robert Allerton purchased them in 1932 from European and American art dealers. (Photo by Michael Holtz.)

FIGURE 8.10. Allerton bought Lil Auer's *Girl with a Scarf* at the Chicago Art Institute's 1941-42 Exhibition of American Painting and Sculpture. The four-foot-tall modeled concrete sunbather was the last piece Allerton added to his collection of outdoor sculpture. (Photo by Michael Holtz.)

Rodin's studio, then donated the original to the Art Institute of Chicago, where a wing is named after his father.) The current statue is a second reproduction.

While living on his Hawaii estate during World War II, Robert Allerton, then in his seventies, decided to donate most of his Monticello property to the university after the war ended. He no longer wished to be burdened with maintaining it.

In October 1946 Allerton sold most of the house's furnishings and donated the proceeds to charity. He deeded the mansion and fifty-five hundred acres of his property to the university, specifying it should be used as a public park and research center. He didn't care if the mansion were demolished, as long as the gardens and sculpture flourished. He and his adopted son, John Gregg Allerton, lived permanently in Hawaii until Robert Allerton died in 1964.

The park offers eighty acres of formally maintained space and fourteen miles of hiking trails. More than two miles of formal hedges run through the gardens.

Allerton Park and Retreat Center has earned a number of awards: in 1970, the National Park Service granted National Natural Landmark to eleven hundred acres in honor of the stream valley ecosystem and forests; the park and center are on the National Register of Historic Places; the American Institute of Architects lists it in "150 Great Places in Illinois"; and in 2007 it was voted as one of the Illinois Bureau of Tourism's "Seven Wonders of Illinois."

As Bruce Branham, director of Allerton Park, says: "People like the mansion but they come for the park. It's a unique place."

By Maureen Holtz, co-author (with Martha Burgin) of *Robert Allerton, The Private Man & The Public Gifts.* Author of *Allerton's Paradises, Monticello: Images of America* and *The Last Resort.*

The Krannert Center for the Performing Arts

On a cool and overcast day in May 1967, seventy-nine-year-old industrialist Herman C. Krannert shuffled to a window on the top floor of the twelve-story Illinois Street Residence Hall to get a bird's-eye view of his and his wife, Ellnora's, latest gift to the university—the Krannert Center for the Performing Arts, then under construction.

It was a chaotic scene abuzz with activity. An army of helmeted men toiled in a muddy, rugged landscape of nine and a half acres filled with building materials and construction equipment. Rising out of the ground and dominating the

FIGURE 8.11. Allerton Park's *Adam* is based on an Auguste Rodin bronze inspired by Dante's *Inferno* Allerton purchased in 1924 and donated to the Chicago Art Institute. Allerton had a stone copy made for his gardens. It was damaged in transit but installed, and then it was toppled and damaged beyond repair by a park visitor in 1975. The current *Adam* is a copy made that lacks the power and artistry of the original. (Photo by Michael Holtz.)

FIGURE 8.12. Herman and Ellnora Krannert, front row at center left, at the Foellinger Great Hall opening of the Krannert Center for the Performing Arts on April 19, 1969. The Krannerts also helped underwrite the Krannert Art Museum at the U of I. Herman was a U of I class of 1912 mechanical engineering graduate who made his fortune in corrugated boxes at the Inland Container Corporation, which he founded. Eleven buildings in Illinois and Indiana, mostly at universities and hospitals, bear the Krannert name. (Photo courtesy of the Krannert Center for the Performing Arts at the University of Illinois Urbana-Champaign.)

view were four rectangular red-brick-and-white-limestone monoliths in various stages of completion—Krannert's four theaters. In a few years, they would showcase high culture at the campus built in the cornfields of central Illinois.

It was fitting that the theaters had such pronounced, boxlike forms. Krannert had made his estimated $100 million fortune in the cardboard-box business as the founder of the Inland Container Corporation. The 1912 U of I graduate already had given his alma mater an art museum, but the couple (she graduated in music from Brenau College in Florida) surpassed that by donating about $13 million for the performing arts center. It took

FIGURE 8.13. Krannert Center for the Performing Arts, made possible with a $16 million gift by the Krannerts, was designed by U of I architectural alumnus Max Abramovitz. The center has four performance venues with a total seating capacity of about four thousand. (Photo by Karyl Wackerlin.)

about six years for the problem-plagued $21 million project to go from concept to reality.

"The University has done much for us and we wanted to do something for it," Krannert said of his generosity.

Krannert had wanted the center's architecture to be not too contemporary. Fellow Crane High School and U of I graduate Max Abramovitz, the architect of the Assembly Hall and other modernist masterpieces, stuck to his guns and came up with something that looked like (in Abramovitz's own words) "an aircraft carrier." The center's design garnered a fair share of praise—and some criticism—over the years. The *New York Times* called it "one of the most ingeniously worked out art complexes anywhere, integrating four theaters around one common lobby and merging their backstage facilities in ways that should save time, money and nervous systems." *Women's Wear Daily*, on the other hand, thought the center "a bit weird-looking—rather like multiple slabs of red brick cheese."

But none could quibble that the Krannert Center dramatically transformed its east campus neighborhood. More than forty modest frame structures, mostly rooming houses and a business or two, had occupied the two-block area that would be the center's site. In 1964 and 1965 the university employed eminent domain to acquire all of these properties for the center and was on its way to gobbling up most of the land east of the Quad and west of Lincoln Avenue.

"KCPA had far-reaching implications on the direction and focus of campus growth," said Eugene S. Pitcher, a long-time U of I real estate administrator, in an interview in 2009. "These are with respect to its siting in the east campus neighborhood, how that influenced physical growth in campus as a whole, elevating the stature of the campus (and the region for that matter) and attracting/retaining especially faculty in all disciplines, but also students."

What Abramovitz immodestly called "a prairie Acropolis, rising with grandeur above the rolling plains of Illinois" finally opened on April 19, 1969. "I imagine that during the next 100 years this (KCPA) will be a place of great interest and excitement," Herman Krannert predicted.

Unfortunately, the building started to fall apart almost immediately. Many of its seventy thousand ceramic roofing tiles, many attached vertically, blew off in the wind, the lobby's hand-glued teakwood floor developed cracks, and the roof leaked. A late-1970s $2.5 million renovation revitalized the center; another to repair exterior brick started in 2014.

The center hosts some three hundred performances each year. Among them: the Ellnora Guitar Festival. As the publicist for KCPA wrote: "What better name could there be for a culmination of riffing, sizzling, picking, bedazzling artistry from around the planet? Ellnora would be grinning with glee."

Krannert Art Museum and Kinkead Pavilion

Herman C. Krannert made a fortune as an industrialist, but his—and his wife, Ellnora's—love of art made the University of Illinois a cultural paradise on the prairie.

The couple made a monumental splash when they announced a $10 million gift to Illinois on July 24, 1964, to create a breathtaking performing arts center, the Krannert Center for the Performing Arts, which opened in April 1969. Only a few years earlier, however, the Kranners donated $1 million to construct the Krannert Art Museum, which opened in 1961, on the expanding south campus. And Ellnora provided another $1 million in 1965 for the museum to acquire historic artwork.

The couple's contributions include *Parable of the Prodigal Son*, a stained-glass window of French origin, circa 1215-25; Bartolomé Esteban Murillo's *Christ after the Flagellation*, circa 1670; and Thomas Gainsborough's *Portrait of the Honorable Anne (Batson) Fane*, circa 1786. They also commissioned the statue *Initiation* by Mirko (1961) that stands at the main entrance to the museum.

Building on its educational mission, the Krannert Art Museum partners with and serves U of I faculty, staff, and students as well as the public from local communities and beyond. More than 132,000 visitors annually take in the museum's permanent collection of ten thousand works of art, from ancient Egyptian to contemporary, in ten galleries.

The forty-eight-thousand-square-foot Krannert Art Museum, the second-largest fine art museum in the state and a leader among university art museums, was designed by architect Ambrose Richardson in a style reminiscent of the late work of Ludwig Mies van der Rohe, the highly influential German-American architect who resided and worked in Chicago for more than three decades.

Richardson, of course, also designed the law school across Peabody Drive from the museum, further breaking

FIGURE 8.14. Krannert Art Museum, designed by architect and faculty member Ambrose Richardson in a minimalist, modernist architectural style, was completed in 1961. (Photo by Karyl Wackerlin.)

the back of the predominate Georgian revival architectural style of the south campus.

Kinkead Pavilion

Fittingly, the name of another U of I alumni and industrialist, William S. Kinkead, is tied to an addition to the Krannert Art Museum that opened in 1988. The William S. and Anita H. Kinkead Pavilion, airy, glassy, and adorned in copper and marble, beefed up the building's size to sixty-three thousand square feet.

The Kinkead Pavilion, which linked new exhibit space, offices, and study and storage area across two stories to the east and a tad south of KAM, earned Lawrence Booth of the Chicago firm Booth/Hansen & Associates an architectural award for the design. The pavilion incorporates neo-Egyptian decorative elements in an overall postmodernist design.

FIGURE 8.15. Krannert Art Museum Kinkead Pavilion, a 1988 addition to the Krannert Art Museum, is a postmodernist building that doubled the size of the museum, making it the second largest in Illinois. (Photo by L. Brian Stauffer. University News Bureau.)

William Kinkead, who attended Illinois in 1919-20, was founder, president, and chairman of the board of Kinkead Industries Inc. from 1928 to 1977. His company was sold to the United States Gypsum Corporation, better known as USG Corporation, the largest manufacturer of gypsum products in North America. A gift of $3.9 million from the William S. Kinkead Charitable Fund and Kinkead Unitrust supported construction of the Kinkead Pavilion.

He also gave his alma mater much of his personal art collection, including works from French poster artist Henri Toulouse-Lautrec and contemporary Chicago artist Leon Golub.

The Krannert Art Museum and Kinkead Pavilion are just south of the western terminus of a planned 1927 east-west corridor that linked the original Illini Grove near Lincoln and Pennsylvania Avenues along Lorado Taft Drive on

FIGURE 8.16. Levis Faculty Center opened in 1972 as a place where faculty and staff could meet, eat lunch, and have meetings. Other than a few offices, it is largely unused today. (Photo by Karyl Wackerlin.)

the north side of Memorial Stadium. Plans for lush gardens and fountains along the axis were long ago abandoned as buildings encroached on the corridor. University trustees approved in 2015 a $48 million Design Center on Fourth Street just south of Huff Hall.

Levis Faculty Center

Nothing could stand in the way of campus development—not even the faculty. The Faculty Club lost its first clubhouse in the 1950s when the university secured the property for the site of Burrill Hall on Goodwin Avenue, across from what later became the Krannert Center for the Performing Arts, as the campus began its march east.

The all-male Faculty Club then merged with the University Women's Club and occupied the latter's digs at 1201 West Oregon Street. This cramped arrangement was less than satisfactory: the frame home didn't have near enough space for the current 732 members. Clearly, a new clubhouse was needed that could accommodate the nearly seven thousand eligible members of the faculty and staff.

Margaret H. Levis came to the rescue of the beleaguered faculty that lacked an adequate place for socializing and recreation. A 1914 LAS graduate, the former Margaret Harris married William E. Levis, a 1913 College of Law graduate, in the summer of 1915. Mr. Levis made a fortune as a glass manufacturer, and he gave back to the U of I by establishing loan and scholarship funds. In 1957 he was one of the first three Illini to receive an Illini Achievement Award. Levis died in 1962, but Margaret carried on her husband's philanthropic efforts.

Approached by U of I officials in 1968 to fund a faculty center, Mrs. Levis agreed to contribute $1 million to the project if the university would raise an additional $600,000. Announcement of the gift, however, stirred controversy. The Young Faculty, a group of assistant and associate professors, protested the gift and its planned use, arguing the money could be better spent elsewhere. An assistant professor in architecture called the proposed faculty center "yet another inflexible bastion against the increasingly evident and long over-due crumbling of the 'hallowed halls.'" Members of the group personally lobbied Mrs. Levis, attempting to persuade her to donate to some other purpose. She was not deterred.

Supporters of the faculty center weathered the storm, the additional money was raised with some difficulty, and the building was finally completed in 1972.

Designed by Harry Weese, a Chicago architect known especially for his brutalist-style Washington Metro stations, the four-story, brick-and-glass Levis Faculty Center exudes a very groovy 1970s vibe: its modernness fits the setting, with the futuristic Max Abramovitz–designed Krannert Center for the Performing Arts just west, and the spare, sleek Ambrose Richardson–designed Illinois Street Residence Halls just north. Like Richardson, Weese was a refugee from Skidmore, Owings, and Merrill—the iconic architecture firm renowned for its modernist masterpieces.

By the turn of the present century a "faculty club" seemed an artifact of an earlier time; the Levis Faculty Center was used for occasional meetings, small conferences, and special events. For a few years prior it housed the campus Visitors Center and ombudsman. By early 2016 the building was partially occupied by some administrative offices and a small academic program.

Beckwith Residence Hall

Who was the mystery man Guy Miner Beckwith, and why did he leave the university the bulk of his roughly $1 million estate in 1966 for the building of a residence hall? University officials at first were as amazed as anyone by this bequest out of the blue.

George Bargh, President David Dodds Henry's administrative assistant, and John Templin, the university's assistant legal counsel, eventually remembered a man who visited the campus sometime between 1960 and 1963. The sixty-something Beckwith—a farmer—had expressed a desire to bequeath his estate to the university. He was deeply interested in his family history and apparently wanted "to perpetuate his name," according to Templin. Bargh took the visitor from Will County on a grand tour of the campus and set him up at the Library, where he could undertake his genealogical research.

He was a reader and a traveler, curious and eventually successful.

Ruth Harstedt, Beckwith's sister, was shocked by her brother's gift to the university. "He didn't consult the family when he made out his will," she related. "He did it on his own." The sixty-eight-year-old Beckwith seems to have left his wife Wilhelmine—a native of France sixteen years his junior—out of the loop as well. In his will he left her only $30,000 and the farmhouse. The university, on the other hand, was given five parcels of prime Will County farmland and securities worth hundreds of thousands of dollars.

Beckwith's widow ultimately secured half of the estate for herself, but university officials didn't complain much: half of something is better than nothing. The university sold a ninety-eight-acre parcel of Beckwith land in 1969 for $105,000, and then in 1978 an additional 254 acres realized

FIGURE 8.17. Beckwith Living Center opened in 1982 to meet the residential needs of students with disabilities who required personal assistants to perform basic activities of daily living. The U of I was a pioneer in providing educational, athletic, and personal growth for those with disabilities. The center is now used by a fraternity, but its function lives on at Nugent Hall. (Image dated 1981. Photo courtesy of the University of Illinois Archives 0003707.)

a surprising $710,584 at auction. By then, the board of trustees had earmarked the Beckwith money to go to a residence hall for students with complex physical disabilities. Such a facility was desperately needed. At the time students with severe disabilities were housed in a decrepit frame home that had room for only about ten students on the first floor and their aides on the second and third. It was called "Tanbrier" for the color of its exterior paint when it opened in 1961, a sly reference to Greenbrier, a southwest Champaign nursing home that for about two years took on a handful of disabled students who needed help in their daily lives, such as dressing, hygiene, and eating.

The two-story, $1.5 million Beckwith Residence Hall, located at the corner of John and Second Streets, was dedicated in May 1982. Among those attending were President Stanley Ikenberry, Timothy Nugent (the director of UIUC

FIGURE 8.18. Nugent Hall opened in 2010 as part of Ikenberry Commons that is replacing the "Six-Pack." The first floor houses Beckwith Residential Support Services Program for students with severe physical disabilities. The new building is named for Timothy J. Nugent, who founded in 1948 at the U of I the first comprehensive living and learning center in higher education for students with disabilities. (Photo by L. Brian Stauffer, University News Bureau.)

rehabilitation-education services who had long lobbied for this facility), and Wilhelmine Hursh, Beckwith's widow. In a touching gesture, Hursh presented the university with the Beckwith family Bible.

Beckwith Hall would provide housing for more than 150 students during the course of its twenty-eight-year existence as a dormitory. It was a two-story building with twenty sleeping-study rooms, kitchen, dining room, library, and lounge all on the ground floor. The second floor contained apartments, laundry, medical facility, and offices for live-in staff and married students.

In 2010 Beckwith's role as an accessible and supportive residence ended and was taken over by the Timothy Nugent Residence Hall, named for a national force in disability rights who charted the campus's course as a leader starting in the late 1940s. But Guy Beckwith's contribution to the goal of fully integrating disabled students into the campus lives on. First-floor students at Nugent Hall who require considerable assistance with daily living receive help through the Beckwith Residential Support Services programs.

Lester H. Swanlund Administration Building

Four decades had passed when Maybelle Leland Swanlund reconnected with the University of Illinois from which she had earned a bachelor of arts in library science in 1932. The Great Depression was deep—U of I enrollment and state support had fallen dramatically since 1929—but the young woman from Galchutt, North Dakota, with a bachelor's degree in education from Mayville State College, aimed high. She chose the U of I, she later said, for one reason: "It was number one. It still is."

She had brought her life savings to Urbana-Champaign, where the bank she trusted her money to failed just months after she arrived. She told the library school she had to leave for financial reasons; school officials patched together work and loans to get her through her master's degree. And she never forgot.

En route to a career as a high school principal and head librarian in Milford, near the Illinois-Indiana border, and Chicago suburban Lombard, she met Lester Swanlund at the university. He earned a bachelor's degree in accountancy, also in 1932, and the couple married four years later. A CPA, he joined the Brunswick Corporation, where he spent his entire career, ultimately on the board of directors and president of the Brunswick Credit Corporation. Lester Swanlund died in 1971; the couple lived in Atherton, California. They had invested in California real estate and stocks and she was interested—no, she was determined—to help the university build a new administration building for its president.

FIGURE 8.19. Swanlund Administration Building, completed in 1983, houses offices of the campus chancellor and other senior officials. It was built with a donation from 1932 U of I alumna Maybelle Swanlund in honor of her husband, Lester. (Photo by Karyl Wackerlin.)

In an interview in 2008, Stanley Ikenberry recalled vividly a stern letter from Mrs. Swanlund just months into his term as president, asking where were the plans for the building she wanted to underwrite. He was clueless until he read correspondence between her and the previous president, John E. Corbally.

So, Ikenberry and a vice president, Ronald Brady, created a dozen different proposals and flew out to California, where Maybelle Swanlund served persimmon pudding. She rejected all the ideas; she was interested in capital construction, not programs. Finally, she and Ikenberry decided there would be a new administration building, but for the campus chancellor, not the president. "The last thing I wanted to do . . . in my early years of the presidency was to turn around and build a palace for the new president," he said.

It was just two years after Lester died that Maybelle had rediscovered her alma mater. A brief biography in a newsletter of the University of Illinois Foundation explains: "After anonymously investigating giving opportunities at the U of I through her attorney, she decided on a memorial fund for her late husband. Her first major gift funded construction of the Lester H. Swanlund Administration Building. The first phase of that building was dedicated in 1983, and a rededication was held in 1987, after the completion of the fourth and fifth floors."

The administration building was designed by Kenneth Nelson, a 1960 U of I architecture graduate in the Champaign firm Unteed, Scaggs, Fritch, Nelson Ltd. The first three floors cost $2.3 million; the structure was built to accommodate the vertical addition of two floors, which would cost an additional $1.85 million. Located at the southeast corner of Sixth and John Streets in the heart of campus, the building houses senior campus officials and staff. Each floor contains two large suites joined by a short hallway with elevators; it is clad in Illini red brick and is highly utilitarian. The Taft House, where famed *Alma Mater* sculptor Lorado Taft had lived with his parents, was mounted on wheels and driven to southeast campus to make room for the Swanlund Administration Building in 1981.

Mrs. Swanlund followed this two-part gift with others, including in 1990 $3.5 million toward the renovation of Harker Hall, the campus's oldest classroom building that now is the headquarters of the University of Illinois Foundation. Then in 1994, one year after her death, the university announced a stunning $20 million bequest from her estate to establish the Swanlund Endowment Fund to support ten endowed chairs and academic program initiatives at the discretion of the chancellor.

"Few graduates of Illinois will leave their mark more clearly on the Urbana-Champaign campus than Maybelle Swanlund," Ikenberry said.

Foellinger Auditorium

By the time Helene Ruth Foellinger decided in 1982 to underwrite a major renovation of the Auditorium, the fate of the 1907 landmark had been in doubt time and again over its seventy-five-year life. Modeled after the Paris Opera, the domed structure, which anchored the south end of the main Quad, needed rescue from the ravages of time, inattention, and original-construction shortcuts.

Five years earlier, Miss Foellinger had provided the lead gift of $500,000 to establish the Illinois Endowment for the Performing Arts; the university dedicated the Great Hall of the Krannert Center for the Performing Arts in her honor and in memory of her late sister, Loretta Foellinger Teeple, Illinois class of 1936.

Helene Foellinger earned a degree in mathematics in 1932; the announcement of her $3 million commitment (plus interest earned) to save the Auditorium came at the fiftieth reunion of her class. A mere four years after graduation, she prematurely inherited the News Publishing Company of Fort Wayne, Indiana. She enlarged both the company and her own reputation for corporate savvy: *Parade* magazine in 1974 called her one of America's top ten businesswomen.

Decades earlier she had been a busy and successful U of I student: woman's editor at the *Daily Illini* newspaper; member of the student council; member of the tennis team; Phi Beta Kappa, Pi Beta Phi, Phi Mu Epsilon, Alpha Lambda Delta, and Mortar Board and Torch activity honoraries.

FIGURE 8.20. Foellinger Auditorium was designed by U of I alumnus and Boston architect Clarence Blackall, who also planned the Quad. The Auditorium, located at the south end of the main Quad, was dedicated in 1907. Thanks to the generosity of newspaper publisher Helene Foellinger, a 1932 U of I alumna, and the architectural skill of Walker Johnson, the signature building was finally completed and renovated in the 1980s. (Photo by Karyl Wackerlin.)

Working as reporter and editor of the woman's section of the *Fort Wayne News-Sentinel*, Miss Foellinger was barely twenty-five years old when her father, Oscar, suffered a fatal heart attack; overnight, she became publisher and general manager of the publishing firm. In a 1986 story in the U of I *Alumni News*, she said the transition from cub to boss was difficult. "I was very, very fortunate to have an extremely loyal group of people," she said. "I told them, 'I'm scared to death. I'm willing to try it if you're willing to try it.' Every one of them did."

Circulation grew. Within a decade she had bought a radio station, and in 1950 she created Fort Wayne Newspapers Inc., which printed both her paper and the rival *Journal-Gazette*. In 1980 she sold the business to Knight-Ridder, a newspaper chain.

She and her mother, Esther, had established a family foundation in 1958, and by the mid-1980s it had distributed at least $10 million in addition to her personal philanthropy. Fort Wayne benefitted: Junior Achievement, an outdoor theater, botanical conservatory, public library, and zoo. The journalism programs at Indiana University and Ball State University received significant gifts, too.

But it was the Auditorium in Urbana—the signature building designed by famed Boston architect Clarence Blackall, an 1877 Illinois graduate—that stands as Miss Foellinger's greatest legacy on the U of I campus. "I owe a lot of my alma mater," she said at the 1985 dedication of Foellinger Auditorium. "And restoring this monument expresses more than I can put into words."

Blackall was hired in 1905 to design an Auditorium, estimated to cost some $200,000. He told the board of trustees that the university needed not just a building design but a comprehensive plan for its buildings and grounds. The result, in 1906, was suggesting that the Auditorium should sit on a slight rise to the south and face University Hall, the northern terminus of what would become the Quadrangle.

The Illinois legislature, stunned by the estimated $200,000-plus cost of the proposed building, appropriated only $100,000. "This was so manifestly inadequate that here was considerable question as to whether it would be wiser to abandon the scheme," Blackall was quoted in a 1985 story in the *Illinois Alumni News*. Lost were a grand entrance on the north, a backstage or stage house on the south, a copper dome, and decorations in the vaulted entrance hall.

And the acoustics were flawed from the start; in 1923 Blackall himself criticized the building. "I just came too soon on the auditorium," he told University Architect James M. White. "My best wish for that building would be to have it go up in smoke some night and somebody would have a chance to rebuild it right." In 1938, as elements of the original structure deteriorated, Blackall—then eighty-one years old—agreed with some U of I officials who wanted to raze the building. "I think the University is doing quite right in taking it (the Auditorium) down, especially if it would lead to a worthy building at that end of the campus." And three decades later, Charles Havens, the longtime and imperialistic director of the physical plant, suggested tearing it down and building a high-rise classroom and office building on the highest point of the main campus. (See chapter 2.)

Loved, ignored, reviled, the Auditorium hosted countless lecture classes, movies, concerts, and guest speakers as plaster failed, the back wall bowed, and lighting and sound were measured as marginal. It took a generous alumna, a dedicated architect, and creative builders and craftsmen to restore the icon to a glory only imagined in the original plan.

Lead architect Walker Johnson, class of 1966, and four U of I graduates then working at Holabird & Root took on the challenge of rescuing the Auditorium. The work, which took almost two years, won Holabird & Root the 1985 Distinguished Building Design Award from the Chicago Chapter of the American Institute of Architects, which cited the project's successful marriage of "sensitive restoration with careful modifications."

The project seamlessly added some six thousand square feet to the rear of the building—the thirty-six-foot backstage reflective of Blackall's original design—that also corrected with new trussing a serious bowing of the wall from the largely unsupported weight of the south rim of the dome in the 1905 building. The original structure was tuck-pointed, the dome was covered in copper, a four-and-a-half-foot-high welcome-symbol pineapple added as a finial, mechanical systems replaced, interior redecorated, contemporary control booth added, acoustics adjusted. A front porch—a semicircular forecourt with limestone balustrades—was added.

A local contractor, Hank Hart, in 1989 wrote an article for *Art Bulletin, The Journal of Preservation Technology* that outlined the challenge of redoing the roof without soldered joints (for low maintenance) and restoring or molding new pieces. He also proposed the pineapple finial after observing pineapples on campus columns. "The pineapple, when finally designed, was made up of 75 sheets (of copper)—all pressed on the mold," he said. It weighed seventy-five pounds and took a block and tackle to move it into place.

Beckman Institute for Advanced Science and Technology

Terms such as multidisciplinary, interdisciplinary, and STEM (Science, Technology, Engineering, and Math) are common in contemporary academic vernacular.

Back in the 1980s, however, when University of Illinois alumnus Dr. Arnold O. Beckman and his wife Mabel made an eye-popping $40 million gift to create a sprawling institute on the far north side of the Urbana-Champaign campus that combined research in the physical and biological sciences to better understand human and artificial intelligence, multidisciplinary and interdisciplinary were nascent, and STEM was part of a plant.

The nearly three-hundred-thousand-square-foot Beckman Institute for Advanced Science and Technology, a four-story laboratory and a five-story office complex connected by a glass-covered atrium, changed all that after it opened in 1989.

"We are now in a stage of a new revolution—a new era in technology," Arnold Beckman said at the announcement of the couple's gift in 1985. "This is a unique and critical period and I would like to use what resources I have to help that along."

At the time, the Beckman gift was the largest in U of I history and the largest to any public institution in America by an alumnus.

The Beckmans' gift to the U of I, said James J. Stukel, president of the university when Arnold Beckman died in 2004 at age 104, "sparked the rebirth of the engineering campus at Urbana-Champaign . . . launching the campus into the highest level of multidisciplinary research, which dovetailed with Arnold Beckman's vision."

That vision began in earnest at the U of I, where he studied chemical engineering and chemistry in the early 1920s. It continued at the California Institute of Technology, where he earned a PhD in photochemistry in 1928 and remained as an instructor and then as a professor. He advanced his vision through invention of the acidmeter (designed to measure acidity levels in lemon juice), which was later called the pH meter and became one of the most useful tools in analytic chemistry. The pH meter was designated by the American Chemical Society as a National Historic Landmark and led to Beckman's induction in the National Inventors Hall of Fame in 1987.

Arnold Beckman's company, Beckman Instruments Inc., became an international leader in scientific instruments, with about ten thousand employees in more than fifty facilities worldwide. The company developed products ranging from an oxygen analyzer designed to prevent "blue baby" condition in premature infants to a Mars robot mission "rock smasher" to an electronic component called the Helipot that was used in early radar systems during World War II and later in computers, control systems, and home appliances. Beckman Instruments, and later Beckman Coulter Inc., continued to create instruments for the betterment of humankind. Beckman's companies did not venture far from his original focus on "the chemistry of life."

For his monumental contributions to science, industry, and philanthropy, Arnold Beckman received several honors, including the National Medal of Technology, the Presidential Citizens Medal, the Medal of Science, the Public Welfare Medal from the National Academy of Sciences, and the Lifetime Achievement Award from the National Inventors Hall of Fame.

Arnold and Mabel Beckman, largely through the Arnold and Mabel Beckman Foundation, contributed more than $400 million for scientific research and education; they have

FIGURE 8.21. Beckman Institute for Advanced Science and Technology, backed onto University Avenue at the north end of the engineering quad, houses interdisciplinary research in the physical sciences, computation, engineering, biology, behavior, cognition, and neuroscience. Its building was the impetus for the redevelopment, renovation, and extensive rebuilding on the two engineering quads, Beckman and Bardeen, north of Green Street. (Photo by Karyl Wackerlin.)

donated more than $60 million to the University of Illinois. Mabel Beckman died in 1989, four days shy of her eighty-ninth birthday.

Former Illinois president Stukel added, "Arnold Beckman was inventive and creative, and an ideal University of Illinois alumnus. He was a practical man, modest and unassuming, generous with his time, his energy and his personal fortune."

For his part, Beckman said, "I accumulated my wealth by selling instruments to scientists. So I thought it would be appropriate to make contributions to scientists, and that's been my number one guideline for charity."

Atkins Tennis Center and Khan Outdoor Tennis Complex

Once upon a time, Illinois tennis, like tennis at every level and around the world, was a polite game. The sport is physical and demanding, but manners—"quiet, please"—ruled the game.

Among Illinois tennis fans, however, there has been a lot to shout about. The Net Nuts, an energetic organization that makes their voices heard at Illinois tennis matches, are an outgrowth of the teams' rousing success. Highlighted by the Fighting Illini men's NCAA championship in 2003, Illinois's power on the court is matched by the excellence of its indoor and outdoor tennis facilities—the Atkins Tennis Center and the Khan Outdoor Tennis Complex.

Champaign residents and longtime U of I benefactors Clinton C. and Susan A. Atkins contributed $2.5 million in 1987 toward construction of the tennis facility, located just east of the baseball and track facilities on the south side of

FIGURE 8.22. U of I alumnus Shahid Khan and his wife Ann Carlson Khan funded the Khan Tennis Outdoor Complex. Khan is an industrialist who also owns the Jacksonville Jaguars National Football League team. (Photo courtesy of Fighting Illini Athletics/Division of Intercollegiate Athletics.)

FIGURE 8.23. At the Atkins Tennis Center groundbreaking, from left, Susie and Clint Atkins, women's tennis coach Jennifer Roberts, Athletic Director John Mackovic, and men's tennis coach Neil Adams. (Photo courtesy of Fighting Illini Athletics/Division of Intercollegiate Athletics.)

campus. The Atkins Tennis Center was dedicated in 1991 and was voted the "Most Outstanding Facility in the U.S." in 1992.

The fifty-eight-thousand-square-foot building houses six indoor courts, a viewing deck, pro shop, men's and women's team locker rooms, public locker rooms, offices for the Fighting Illini coaches, and eight outdoor courts to the west of the facility.

In 2013 the U of I and the Atkins Tennis Center hosted the 2013 NCAA Division 1 Women's and Men's Tennis Championships. That marked the first time a Midwest school had hosted the NCAA Tournament since the men's and women's championships were combined in 2005.

Besides serving as the indoor facility of the U of I men's and women's teams, the Atkins Center is open to the public and visitors in Urbana-Champaign. The center also hosts private and group lessons, clinics, elite junior and professional tournaments, and Fighting Illini Tennis Camps and Nike Tennis Camps.

Clinton Atkins was a local real estate investor and developer, co-founder of the Plastic Container Corporation of Champaign, and longtime philanthropist. He and Susan Atkins have been especially supportive of projects that serve the university and the community alike.

Matching that criterion is the Shahid and Ann Khan Outdoor Tennis Complex. The twelve courts were added to the east side of the Atkins Tennis Center in 2009, thanks to U of I alumni and donors Shahid and Ann Khan.

Shahid, president of Urbana-based Flex-N-Gate, a massive manufacturer of vehicle parts (more than twelve thousand employees in more than fifty facilities in the United States, Canada, Mexico, and other countries), is also the owner of the National Football League's Jacksonville Jaguars. He and wife Ann also funded the Khan Annex to Huff Hall and have endowed five professorships in the College of Applied Health Sciences Center on Health, Aging, and Disability.

Harker Hall

If misery loves company, the University of Illinois Foundation for decades commiserated with the U of I Alumni Association.

Both organizations, allied agencies designed to serve the university, bounced from building to building before finding a permanent place to call home. The Alumni Association built anew: the Alice Campbell Alumni Center on the east side of campus, fronting Lincoln Avenue.

The foundation, the fund-raising arm of the University of Illinois and its campuses at Urbana-Champaign, Chicago,

FIGURE 8.24. Opened in 1878, Harker Hall originally cost $40,000 and was the Chemistry Laboratory. After a 1993 gutting, restoration, and remodeling, it is the handsome home to the U of I Foundation. (Photo by Karyl Wackerlin.)

and Springfield, settled on Harker Hall, the oldest major building on the Urbana-Champaign campus. Before anyone moved in, however, the structure needed a little work.

The original building was the product of Nathan Clifford Ricker, the university's and the nation's first architecture graduate. He designed it while a professor of architecture at Illinois.

Constructed in 1878 as the Chemical Laboratory, the structure—three stories plus an English basement in the Second Empire style—housed one of the best and largest laboratories in the nation at that time. In addition to chemistry, the building was home to the Mechanical Engineering Laboratory from 1893 to 1895. Lightning sparked a fire in 1896, destroying the mansard roof and damaging other parts of the facility. (In some ways the lightning strike was fortuitous: Noyes Lab was built in short order.)

After the fire, which took down all but the four walls and part of the basement, a new pitched roof was installed, reducing the fourth floor to an attic; the original stairs were removed, and the north and west entrances to the building were reconfigured. From 1902 to 1927, the College of Law occupied the building, which was renamed Harker Hall in honor of Judge Oliver A. Harker, longtime dean of the college.

The College of Law left Harker for Altgeld Hall, but the Department of Entomology and the Department of Botany became new tenants. (Other tenants across the years included the offices of the *Daily Illini*, the Departments of Journalism and Military Science, a mechanical engineering lab, a cement lab and clay modeling lab in the basement with rows of modeled facial features, a third-floor room—moot court during the day—used for Episcopal church services in the late 1910s and early 1920s, and a Red Cross auxiliary bandage-rolling basement room in World War I.)

Located on the central campus quadrangle between the Illini Union and the Natural History Building, Harker Hall appeared on life support and was targeted by campus planners for demolition and replacement. That changed when Harker Hall was listed on the National Register of Historic Places in 1986.

The U of I Foundation, which has been raising money on behalf of the university since 1935, received generous support from alumni and friends to reconstruct Harker Hall as the first official home of the foundation. A $5.5 million reconstruction to restore the exterior to its original design—including a handsome mansard roof—and provide a modern interior for foundation staff began in September 1991. The 32,474-square-foot interior was completely refurbished in a style sympathetic to buildings of the 1870s. The foundation moved into its new home in November 1992, and Harker Hall was dedicated in the fall of 1993. It remains a prime example of adaptive reuse of a historic building.

Leading the financial support for the reconstruction and restoration of Harker Hall were generous benefactors Maybelle Leland Swanlund and William Karnes. In addition to her generous gifts that resulted in the Swanlund Administration Building and various endowed chairs and initiatives, Mrs. Swanlund's $3.5 million donation in 1990 toward the renovation resulted in a new plaza that provides a formal entry from the Quad and features a fountain, public seating, and exterior lighting.

William Karnes earned a bachelor's degree in accountancy at Illinois in 1933. He rose through the ranks at Beatrice Foods Company of Chicago to president and CEO in 1952 and retired as chairman of the board in 1976. Beatrice created an endowed fund at Illinois to honor Mr. Karnes, with income used to support the William G. Karnes Professorship in Mergers and Acquisitions in the College of Business. In addition to his close ties to Business at Illinois—he served as first president of the Business Advisory Council—Mr. Karnes was a longtime member and president of the U of I Foundation and vice president of the board of directors.

Grainger Engineering Library Information Center

Nearly a half-century after William Wallace Grainger, a pioneer in the worldwide distribution of electrical supplies and components, graduated from the University of Illinois, he made a first gift to his alma mater. It was 1966, and an extended drive of philanthropy began.

Between 1979 and 1998, the Grainger Foundation contributed nearly $26 million to the campus for physical improvements and academic awards. Notable was $18.7 million to build a technologically sophisticated engineering library hailed as both the biggest and the best in the country when it opened in 1994. The entire project cost $34 million.

"This is a great day in our history," said University President Stanley O. Ikenberry in 1991 when the library gift was announced. "The generosity of the Grainger Foundation comes as a welcome vote of confidence in our academic past and our future."

FIGURE 8.25. The Grainger Engineering Library Information Center, on the northeast edge of the Bardeen Quad, is the largest library in the U.S. devoted to engineering. It was dedicated in 1994. (Photo by Karyl Wackerlin.)

W. W. Grainger, a 1919 electrical engineering graduate, was a charter member of the U of I Foundation and its President's Council, which acknowledges its highest donors. He died in 1982. His family foundation, successor to the Grainger Charitable Trust and based in Chicago suburban Skokie, has given the university professorships and fellowships, a lecture series, several laboratories, help with an engineering quadrangle, and, in 1998, $8 million toward the historic reconstruction of Engineering Hall, the 1893 signature building on Green Street, which also housed the previous Engineering Library. Grainger gifts to the U of I total more than $37 million.

W. W. Grainger's son, David W. Grainger, succeeded his father as chairman of the board and CEO of the family company and as chairman of the family foundation. He made the library gift in his father's honor.

The Grainger Library is at the southeast corner of Springfield and Burrill Avenues with entrances on its north and south. Some had preferred the site be farther west to line up with the pronounced north-south axis of the campus. The building, more than 130,000 square feet on four floors, room for more than 330,000 volumes and seating for 1,200, was designed by Indianapolis architect Evans Woollen, as principal, and Kevin Huse of Woollen, Molzan and Partners, Architects. It opened March 15, 1994, with an electronic ribbon-cutting to highlight the building's embedded technological focus.

The building is sympathetic with Georgian revival: red brick, limestone trim around punched windows, chimneys on a high-pitched roof. "The style is pseudo-Georgian, but was homage to the earlier campus architecture of Charles Platt," Huse wrote in an email in 2008. "This style seems to us to be unique to the Champaign Urbana campus."

A central pavilion separates east and west wings; each wing houses a two-story reading gallery with natural light from the north and south. Most of the book collection is on the mezzanine of each wing. Circulation and information services are on the first floor. Anchoring the library is an electronic information retrieval system and online catalog linked to hundreds of national and global databases giving users access to 100 million engineering and physical science references.

Its south side faces onto the Bardeen Quad, which the Grainger Foundation helped underwrite with yet another $2.9 million gift. Seated near the south entrance is a charming, life-size, cast-bronze sculpture of a male student reading a book and dressed in khaki pants and blue sweater, shirt collar and cuffs showing, and penny loafers. J. Seward Johnson Jr. is the artist of the piece called *Computing a Future*, commonly called Engineering Bob.

"It's brought a lot of whimsy to the place," Tony Graziano, former associate dean of the College of Engineering, told the *Illinois Quarterly* magazine in 1997.

Temple Hoyne Buell Hall

Temple Hoyne Buell and Lawrence J. Plym, proud sons of accomplished families deeply connected to the University of Illinois, built on that relationship by financing the lion's share of an architecture complex on the south side of the Urbana-Champaign campus.

A 1916 graduate of the School of Architecture, Buell left an indelible mark as an architect, developer, and philanthropist. The grandson of Thomas Hoyne, a reformer who served as de facto mayor of Chicago for twenty-eight tumultuous days in the spring of 1876, and the great-great-grandson of Dr. John Temple, one of thirteen pioneers who incorporated the village of Chicago in 1833, Temple Hoyne Buell completed his graduate study at Columbia University before heading to France during World War I.

In the battlefield trenches, he was exposed to phosgene gas and later diagnosed with terminal tuberculosis. Buell moved to Denver, where, after a year, he regained his health and founded T. H. Buell and Company. By 1940 it was the largest architectural firm in the Rocky Mountain region, employing 150 people.

Buell designed more than three hundred buildings, many in "the Western Style" that changed the face of Denver. His work included the Paramount Theater complex; middle school, high school and college buildings; private residences, banks, and government facilities; and the *Denver Post* Building, along with many others.

In the mid-1940s, Buell had a vision. At an Urban Land Institute conference in Chicago in 1946 he presented his concept for a shopping center with parking lots encircling the stores. His plan was well received, but nothing happened until he created the Buell Development Corporation, which transformed a fifty-five-acre Denver dumpsite into Cherry Creek Shopping Center, spurring the shopping center boom of the 1950s and serving as a prototype for years to come. He became known as the "father of the American shopping center."

FIGURE 8.26. Temple Hoyne Buell Hall, dedicated in 1995, cost $13.8 million. It houses the graduate division of the School of Architecture, as well as the Landscape Architecture and the Urban and Regional Planning Departments. (Photo by Karyl Wackerlin.)

In 1988 Temple Hoyne Buell made an initial gift of $1 million to begin planning for the first and only building in the Midwest to combine study and research in architecture, landscape architecture, and urban and regional planning. Buell himself worked with architects and planners. A year later, he committed another $5 million through his foundation to make Temple Hoyne Buell Hall on the U of I campus a reality.

The $13.6 million, 85,400-square-foot building, which opened in 1994, contains hints of the traditional style of the campus's Georgian revival buildings in the same way as other nearby structures, such as the Agricultural Engineering

Building, the Education Building, and the Krannert Art Museum. Located at the intersection of two major axes of the campus—the main north-south axis extending from the Illini Union though the Foellinger Auditorium and the east-west axis, also known as the Military Axis—construction of Buell Hall substantially completed a century-old plan for the South Quadrangle.

Lawrence J. Plym Auditorium

Functionally linked to Buell Hall is the Lawrence J. Plym Auditorium, a unique gathering space with seating for more than two hundred. Sheathed in glass wall that looks onto a courtyard that faces Buell Hall, the Plym Auditorium is ideal for large groups, presentations, and meetings.

The Plym Auditorium, courtesy of a $1 million gift from Lawrence J. Plym, is another expression of the Plym family's ties to the U of I. Lawrence Plym's grandfather, H. O. Barber, was a member of the first class of the University of Illinois, 1868-69.

Lawrence's father, Francis J. Plym, graduated from the U of I School of Architecture in 1897. In 1910 a grateful Francis Plym endowed the Francis J. Plym Traveling Fellowships in Architecture. The fellowship, the single most prestigious professional award of its kind among schools of architecture in North America, supports professional development for U of I School of Architecture graduates. More than one hundred alumni have been honored with the Plym Fellowship since 1911-12.

Lawrence Plym, who attended Illinois before completing his bachelor's degree at Babson College in 1929, expanded the Plym Fellowship Award and endowed the Plym Distinguished Professorship in Architecture in 1981.

A manufacturing executive, newspaper publisher, and philanthropist, Lawrence Plym was president of Kawneer Company of Niles from 1940 to 1962, the Plym Company, Niles Broadcasting Company, and Star Publishing Company, and was vice president of Amax Inc. until his retirement in 1979.

Bielfeldt Athletics Administration Building

University of Illinois graduates Gary and Carlotta Bielfeldt have long believed in the total education of students—the body and the mind.

The Peoria, Illinois, couple and their family backed up that belief in a big way with support totaling $6 million to build the Bielfeldt Athletics Administration Building in the heart of the Urbana-Champaign campus's sports complex. Construction on the $7.2 milllion, forty-three-thousand-square-foot structure began in 1994 and it was dedicated on October 4, 1996.

Located on a rise between the Atkins Tennis Center and the State Farm Center on the south side of campus, the Bielfeldt Building unites the university's Division of Intercollegiate Athletics administration, several coaching staffs, and other functions, including the I-FUND, corporate relations, marketing, and sports information. In addition to offices, a lounge, library, and professional development and seminar room, the facility has locker rooms and training and exercise rooms.

The structure pays homage to other Fighting Illini facilities across campus. The arched roof is reminiscent of the Armory. Columns in the Hall of Fame Room (which is not outfitted for that purpose) remind visitors of Memorial Stadium. Window sills are similar to those at Huff Hall. The Bielfeldt's red brick ties it to most of the other buildings on campus, and the light blue exterior glass subtly connects to the school colors.

Gary and Carlotta Bielfeldt have maintained a close association with their alma mater for more than sixty years. Born in Anchor, Illinois, Gary K. Bielfeldt played freshman basketball and baseball and was a member of varsity football team for two years. He studied agricultural economics, earning bachelor's and master's degrees in 1958 and 1959.

He served on the U of I Athletic Board of Control from 1983 to 1985, is a former member of the Alumni Association's board of directors, and is life director on the U of I

FIGURE 8.27. The Bielfeldt Athletic Administration Building, located east of the State Farm Center (formerly Assembly Hall), opened in 1996. (Photo by Karyl Wackerlin.)

Foundation board of directors. He is managing partner of Bielfeldt and Company, a commodity brokerage firm in East Peoria. He has served on the boards of several financial institutions and was an elected director of the Chicago Board of Trade.

Carlotta Hagen Bielfeldt, from Sycamore, near DeKalb, was the U of I's homecoming queen in 1957 and earned a bachelor's degree in physical education in 1959. The couple's children—David, Linda and Karen—graduated from Illinois with degrees in agriculture-related fields.

In addition to the Bielfeldt family's support of athletics at their alma mater, they contributed $1 million in 1992 to endow the Office for Futures and Options Research and the associated Thomas A. Hieronymus Distinguished Professorship in Futures Markets. Hieronymus was Gary Bielfeldt' s former agricultural economics professor and mentor at Illinois.

Irwin Academic Services Center

The University of Illinois and alumnus Richard D. Irwin had a decades-long symbiotic relationship that continues to bear fruit for students on the Urbana-Champaign campus.

Irwin, a Missouri native who grew up in Chicago, studied commerce and law at Illinois, graduating in 1926. After publishing and sales work with A. W. Shaw Company and McGraw-Hill, focusing on college business and economics textbooks, Irwin set up his own operation, Business Publications Company, in 1933.

A few years later, Irwin landed a couple of big fish: Harold Lusk, a young University of Indiana professor who wrote a business law text that Irwin published for the next forty-seven

FIGURE 8.28. The Irwin Academic Services Center, formerly Kappa Alpha Psi and Sigma Pi fraternity houses, is a study-tutoring center for U of I athletes. The Tudor revival building opened as a study center in 1997, and the Irwin family financed a $4.6 million expansion in 2007. (Photo courtesy of Fighting Illini Athletics/Division of Intercollegiate Athletics.)

FIGURE 8.29. Jacqueline Marie (Irwin) Pipher with Athletic Director Ron Guenther (1992-2011). (Photo courtesy of Fighting Illini Athletics/ Division of Intercollegiate Athletics.)

years, and Philip Locklin, a renowned U of I professor whose *Economics of Transportation* was a standard in the field.

Business Publications was renamed Richard D. Irwin Inc. in 1940, and the Flossmoor (later Homewood) company's sales climbed from $168,000 to $3.6 million in 1960 to almost $20 million after owners Richard Irwin and his wife, Anne Marie, took the company public. In 1975, a decade after being approached by Dow Jones Company to merge, Richard Irwin agreed, and his publishing firm became a wholly owned subsidiary of Dow Jones. He remained chairman of the new subsidiary for two years before retiring.

Richard and Anne Marie Irwin generously supported the University of Illinois personally and especially through their Irwin Family Foundation. In 1996 the Division of Intercollegiate Athletics announced that the Irwin Family Foundation had made a $1.5 million gift to renovate a 1920s fraternity house, Kappa Alpha Psi, as an academic services center for student athletes. The remodeled fraternity house included individual carrels, study lounges, counseling rooms, a career-planning center, and offices.

Less than ten years later, the Irwin Foundation provided an additional $4.5 million to the DIA to double the size of the Irwin Academic Services Center.

Years earlier, the Irwin Foundation established the Richard D. and Anne Marie Irwin Fellowships for PhD students in the College of Commerce and Business Administration, now the College of Business. Many years later, the College of Business was again the beneficiary of Irwin Foundation largess. In 2014 the foundation made a $4 million gift to renovate the Surveying Building.

The 10,172-square-foot building nestled behind Wohlers Hall along East Gregory Drive will be known as the Irwin Center for Doctoral Study in Business. It will be tailored for business doctoral and postdoctoral scholars pursuing their research and teaching activities.

Richard T. Ubben Basketball Complex

The old chestnut "practice makes perfect" may be a stretch, but practice—especially a lot of it—probably makes better.

For the University of Illinois men's and women's varsity basketball teams, practice found a much better venue in the Richard T. Ubben Basketball Complex on the Urbana-Champaign campus. The two-story brick and stone structure, which includes two full-size practice courts, lockers rooms for players and coaches, lounge, and video, training, and weight rooms, opened in 1998, thanks in large part to the generosity of Tim and Sharon Ubben of Glencoe, Illinois.

The couple's gift honor's Tim Ubben's father, Richard T. Ubben, a 1929 U of I chemistry graduate and PPG Industries

FIGURE 8.30. The Richard T. Ubben Basketball Practice Facility is named for the father of Timothy Ubben. Richard was a 1929 U of I chemistry graduate. The Ubbens also made a major gift in support of the renovation of the State Farm Center, formerly Assembly Hall. (Photo courtesy Fighting Illini Athletics/Division of Intercollegiate Athletics.)

executive. Richard and his wife, Lucille, shared their deep allegiance to Illinois with Tim, a DePauw University graduate who earned an MBA at Northwestern. Tim Ubben founded Lincoln Capital Management, a Chicago-based investment firm, in 1967, retiring in 1999 as chairman. Sharon, too, is a DePauw graduate. She was a teacher and later owned a tour company, Hearts Desire.

The Richard T. Ubben Basketball Complex, considered one of the finest buildings of its kind in the nation when it was built, is located on South Fourth Street along the east-west axis that is the hub of all new athletic facilities on campus. The Ubben blends aesthetically with the Bielfeldt Athletic Administration Building, the Atkins/Khan Tennis Center, and other nearby facilities. It faces a pedestrian walkway that links the Bielfeldt with the baseball, soccer, and track facilities and the tennis center.

In addition to their support of the Richard T. Ubben Basketball Complex, Tim and Sharon Ubben made a $2 million gift in 2013 to name the Donor Recognition Wall in the State Farm Center (formerly Assembly Hall). They also contributed to the Illinois Renaissance of Memorial Stadium, completed in 2008, and have established several endowed scholarships for Fighting Illini men's and women's basketball.

Campbell Hall for Public Telecommunication and Richmond Journalism Teaching Studio

For almost eighty years, the University of Illinois Division of Broadcasting's WILL was a nomad operation.

That all changed in 1999 when the Campbell Hall for Public Telecommunication and the Richmond Journalism Teaching Studio were dedicated. Laid to rest were memories

FIGURE 8.31. Campbell Hall for Public Telecommunication is the operations base of three U of I public broadcasting stations—WILL-TV and National Public Radio stations WILL-AM and WILL-FM. (Photo by Karyl Wackerlin.)

of the woeful broadcast facilities of WILL (now Illinois Public Media): an old bakery, an aged rooming house, a former grain inspection station, a mobile home, several storefronts, and a handful of other ill-suited locations.

"When we learned that WILL was operating out of nearly a dozen different locations, we knew we had found a need that was begging to be filled," said Robert Campbell, a 1954 U of I commerce grad. So, he and his wife, Alice, who earned a juris doctorate at the U of I in 1943, made a $5 million lead gift that paved the way for construction of a nearly forty-one-thousand-square-foot building that houses Illinois Public Media's AM and FM radio and television studios, offices, and technical facilities, as well as community-accessible spaces. A striking glass-enclosed lobby is complemented by an adjacent outdoor plaza ideal for receptions and other events. The building is located on the northeast side of campus, on Goodwin Avenue between Clark and Main Streets.

Kim Rotzoll, who was dean of the College of the College of Communications (now College of Media) at the time of the Campbells' gift, said the couple has "done more for the public service arm of our college—that's WILL—than anyone in the history of the stations."

Robert Campbell, a native of Athens, Illinois, was the president of Robert Campbell Company in Los Angeles. Alice Campbell, who was born in Wyoming, Illinois, served as chief financial officer of the company. They had long and successful careers in real estate financing and mortgage origination.

In addition to Campbell Hall, the couple's lead gift helped establish the first permanent home for the U of I Alumni Association in its then-139-year history. Alice Campbell Alumni Center provides an attractive, welcoming space devoted to alumni and students of the Urbana-Champaign campus. The Campbells' other significant gifts to Illinois include the Alice Curtis Campbell Professor of Law, the Michael Aiken Endowed Chair in honor of the former chancellor, scholarships for the James Newton Matthews Scholars Program, and matching funds for purchase of bells in the Altgeld Hall Carillon.

Richmond Journalism Teaching Studio

Jack Commodore Richmond's roots ran deep in Champaign County, where his ancestors helped settle the land. He lived his entire life, ninety-three years, in the Richmond family's two-story wood-frame house on Church Street in Champaign that once was on the edge of town and surrounded by farmland.

His ties to the University of Illinois, his alma mater, ran equally deep.

As a student at Illinois, Jack Richmond's crazy-quilt job résumé included meat truck driver, wrecking crew and highway construction worker, model for U of I art classes, night clerk, corn detasseler, and hotel bar bouncer. He also boxed, competed for the U of I gymnastics team before an injury sidelined him, and established a formal weight-training program at the U of I.

After earning a bachelor's degree in agriculture in 1943, Jack Richmond served in the army, worked for the U.S. Soil Conservation Service, owned and operated a sprawling pine and spruce tree farm, and was a salesman for Marchant Calculators (later acquired by Smith Corona) before retiring in 1972. He became a successful private investor and, subsequently, a philanthropist.

A donor to the university since 1965, Jack and his wife, Marjorie Laird Richmond, contributed increasingly generous gifts to an array of programs and activities that benefited students at the U of I and the community at large while honoring Jack, Marge, and Jack's parents, Mildred and Arthur Dean Richmond. This list includes scholarships for the men's gymnastics team, endowing the Fighting Illini men's head basketball coach position, establishing the Richmond Family Gallery, a first-floor reception area in the Alice Campbell Alumni Center, and creating and endowing the Richmond Journalism Teaching Studio, which is linked physically and electronically to Campbell Hall for Public Telecommunications.

The Richmond Studio houses a computer graphics laboratory, a television teaching studio (classes include broadcast news production, advanced television news and digital technology in broadcast journalism), a control room, and a video playback room. Student newscasts from the studio can be seen on local television and worldwide on the internet.

"We could see the students and faculty in broadcast journalism had been using meager technical facilities for years," said Jack Richmond. "We decided to do something about it."

Jack Richmond continued to support the university until his death in 2011.

Spurlock Museum

For almost one hundred years, the university's museum languished on the creaky fourth floor of Lincoln Hall, its wealth of treasures, dating from the prehistoric to the present, hidden away in a building usually abuzz with activity just a few floors down. William Spurlock let in the light, allowing these valuable collections to be viewed in a setting well-suited to such wonders.

Retired Eli Lilly vice president William R. Spurlock, a 1924 U of I graduate, and his wife, Clarice, were world

FIGURE 8.32. William R. and Clarice V. Spurlock Museum is an ethnographic museum with documents, objects, and exhibits from ancient Mediterranean Africa, ancient Egypt and Mesopotamia, East Asia, islands in the tropical Pacific Ocean, Europe, and the Americas. (Photo by Karyl Wackerlin.)

travelers with a keen interest in the customs and cultures of the nations they visited. To a campus determined to properly display artifacts of history in a better setting, the Spurlocks seemed to be the right people to finance a museum, which was a long-held dream.

As charming and alluring as the fourth-floor World Heritage Museum was to grade schoolers on field trips to visit the past, especially the child-sized ancient Egyptian mummy, the space was unsuited for contemporary care standards and display. As early as 1913, curator Arthur Pease expressed "hope for an adequate and dignified building, exclusively for museum purposes." After being wooed by U of I officials, Spurlock ultimately agreed to underwrite the William R. and Clarice V. Spurlock World Heritage Museum.

"As Mr. Spurlock approaches his ninetieth birthday," his lawyer explained, "he has many fond memories of his long association with the University of Illinois beginning with his college days. He also thinks of the many times when he and Clarice journeyed to Champaign-Urbana to participate in University affairs."

The University received a $7 million donation after Mr. Spurlock's 1993 death. Designed by Nagle, Hartray, Danker, Kagan, McKay in a modern Georgian vernacular, the dignified fifty-three-thousand-square-foot brick-and-stone building was dedicated on September 26, 2002.

The Spurlock Museum houses some forty-three thousand artifacts, although, as with most museums and galleries, only a few thousand items are exhibited at one time. Five galleries spotlight the cultures of Ancient Mesopotamia, Ancient Egypt, and Africa; Ancient Greece and Rome; East Asia, Southeast Asia and Oceania; Europe; and the American Indian Cultures of North and South America. It also hosts special exhibits—for example, a recent one commemorating the centennial of the famous Crocker Land Polar Expedition of 1913-17, which was co-sponsored by the U of I.

The Spurlock also contains contents from what was the campus's Museum of Natural History, the 1874 Art Gallery that was founded by the first U of I regent/president, John Milton Gregory, and some casts owned by sculptor Lorado Taft.

The Reginald and Gladys Laubin Collection is more than nineteen hundred items that reflect American Indian cultures; the couple, who were dance performers, also donated their personal photos from the early 1900s through 2000.

Irwin Indoor Football Practice Facility

Just as University of Illinois commerce and law alumnus Richard D. Irwin amassed authors in his highly successful college textbook publishing business, his family foundation has assembled a list of Urbana-Champaign campus buildings that bear his name and reflect his deep appreciation of his alma mater.

In addition to the previously noted Irwin Academic Services Center for student athletes and the Irwin Center for Doctoral Study in Business, the legacy of Richard Irwin and his wife, Anne Marie, was burnished via a $7 million gift from the Irwin Family Foundation in 1999 to construct the Irwin Indoor Football Practice Facility.

The one-hundred-thousand-square-foot structure houses an eighty-yard football field used as a practice facility for the Fighting Illini, and it also serves as a venue for other varsity and intramural athletics and summer sports camps. The Irwin Indoor also accommodates banquets and other social functions.

The facility is located on the southeast corner of Fourth Street and Peabody Drive, just east of the Activities and Recreation Center (ARC) and conveniently near Memorial Stadium.

In 1986, the Irwin Family Foundation provided a $1.5 million gift to the U of I Division of Intercollegiate Athletics toward construction of a football coaching and training headquarters near Memorial Stadium.

FIGURE 8.33. Irwin Indoor Football Practice Facility, which contains an eighty-yard field, opened in 2000. It is located on the southwest corner of East Peabody Drive and Fourth Street, Champaign, close to Memorial Stadium. (Fighting Illini Athletics/Division of Intercollegiate Athletics.)

Eichelberger Field and Martin Softball Complex

To friends, she's known as "Shorty," but among University of Illinois athletics fans, she stands tall.

Lila Jeanne Eichelberger, in memory of her husband, Paul, has provided significant support (ongoing and deferred) to construct Eichelberger Field, a testament to the couple's fondness for and dedication to the advancement of women's athletics and softball in particular. Eichelberger Field, built into the side of a hill overlooking Florida Avenue in Urbana, seats fifteen hundred and features an inning-by-inning scoreboard over the center-field fence, sand-based infield, irrigation, lighting, batting cages and bullpens, and in-ground dugouts.

FIGURE 8.34. Alice and Rex Martin of Lakeside, Michigan, made possible the final phase of the U of I softball complex through their family foundation. The $1 million gift paid for a clubhouse, a permanent press box and concessions, and restrooms. (Photo courtesy of Fighting Illini Athletics/Division of Intercollegiate Athletics.)

The $2 million Eichelberger Field was dedicated March 27, 2001, and "Shorty" threw out the first pitch.

Eichelberger Field has attracted scores of fans, especially during the U of I Division of Intercollegiate Athletics' annual World's Largest Tailgate. An attendance record of 1,445 was set at one of these events.

Among the staunchest Illinois softball fans are Alice and Rex Martin. Alice, who earned an MBA at Illinois, threw out the first pitch in the season home opener in 2006. The couple contributed $1 million through the Rex and Alice Martin Foundation to complete the softball complex. Their gift funded construction of a permanent press box, restrooms, ticket booth, concessions, and a clubhouse that includes locker rooms for teams and coaches, players' lounge, equipment room, sports medicine training room, and weight-training and conditioning room.

Wohlers Hall

It was, Albert Harry Wohlers confessed, "the best job of selling" he had ever done. In the spring of 1941, a determined Wohlers returned to the university he had graduated from one and a half years earlier with the firm intention of making his college sweetheart, Jane Lindemann, his bride.

Not long before, Al—then on active duty in the armed services—had sent the patriotic Jane a stars-and-stripes sweater with his Delta Alpha Epsilon pin attached. Jane, a member of Tri-Delt sorority, promptly mailed the pin back to him. Even worse, the *Daily Illini*'s "Campus Scout"—a gossipy column that would eventually fall out of fashion—reported that Jane, who also wrote for the newspaper, was dating Joe Smith, Chi Phi and senior class president.

But Al Wohlers was a persuasive man—after all, the Chicago native and first person in his family to attend college had been a member of the U of I Debating Club and later would be a successful insurance man—and his mission succeeded. Jane said yes to his proposal, and the couple got married four days before her June 1941 graduation.

"The U of I was the source of everything for us," a grateful Wohlers later said. "I wouldn't have met Jane without the U of I. Without Jane, I don't know what would have happened. We were a good team."

Al Wohlers, who finished his World War II service as a lieutenant colonel in the U.S. Army Air Force, worked for insurance companies Continental Casualty Company and Youngberg Carlson before founding Albert H. Wohlers and Company, a successful insurance brokerage company that had clients in fifty states, Canada, Central America, Europe, and Asia. His teammate, Jane, was corporate secretary for the company.

FIGURE 8.35. Wohlers Hall, formerly Commerce West, was renovated and renamed in 2000. Albert Wohlers was a College of Business alumnus. (Photo by Darrell Hoemann.)

He also maintained a close relationship with his alma mater, serving on and chairing the College of Business Advisory Council. Additionally, he chaired the College's Entrepreneurship Committee for several years, playing a key role in establishing the Office for Business Innovation and Entrepreneurship. Former OBIE director and accountancy/finance professor Ivan Bull called Al Wohlers "the rock" and an "entrepreneur par excellence."

Almost sixty years after their college days—his degree was in economics, hers in journalism—the retired insurance executive and his wife showed their gratitude to the university with a $6 million gift for the renovation of Commerce West, then the College of Commerce and Business Administration's headquarters. The university responded by renaming the building Wohlers Hall in a September 2000 ceremony.

It was a total facelift and extensive renovation and updating for the thirty-six-year-old Commerce West. An entire new west entrance was created, classrooms and offices were upgraded and modernized for the internet age, and the mechanical systems were revamped. In addition, the structure's modern Georgian exterior was resurfaced to bring it into better conformity with the Charles Platt–designed Architecture Building and the College of Business's David Kinley Hall to its east.

Al Wohlers received a great deal of praise for his and his wife's generous gift, but the words that meant the most may have come from a former caddy of his, who at the time was a U of I commerce student. Apparently too shy to address Wohlers face to face, the student wrote a thank-you letter and surreptitiously placed it in Al's country-club locker. As it turns out, the two not only had a College of Commerce connection; they also were fraternity brothers. "It goes to show you that it really is a small world," Wohlers said.

The Wohlers family was also a major donor to the twenty-four-acre Lauritsen/Wohlers Outdoor Golf Practice Facility.

Albert Wohlers died in 2014, three years after his wife.

ACES Library, Information and Alumni Center

Two of the historic strengths of the University of Illinois are its superior libraries and breadth in agricultural academic disciplines.

When the College of Agricultural, Consumer, and Environmental Sciences (ACES) Library, Information, and Alumni Center was dedicated in 2001, it was another quality indicator of both the college and the University Library, and a major benefit for students, faculty, staff, and visitors.

The first agriculture library at Illinois was established in 1914 in Agriculture Hall (now Davenport Hall). The library held forty-six hundred volumes and had a book fund of $2,000.

The new College of ACES Library, which replaced the agriculture library housed in three floors of Mumford Hall, occupies the top four floors of an octagonal, five-level facility reminiscent of the historic round barns of the university's South Farms. Though presented and described as a "lantern" at architectural design reviews, the barn image persists. It is located south of the Animal Sciences Laboratory and west of Turner Hall in the heart of the historic ag district of the campus. The $21 million, fifty-two-thousand-square-foot, technologically advanced facility includes online resources, compressed stacks, study carrels, and group study rooms.

Private sources underwrote half the cost of the ACES Library and Information Center. The Isaac Funk Family Library occupies the top three floors. The Funk family of McLean County, Illinois, has been involved in the development of agriculture, notably through seed production, for more than a century and has deep connections to the University of Illinois.

The ground level contains the McFarland Student and Alumni Center. The center, thanks to a significant gift from alumnus H. Richard McFarland and his wife, Sally, honors Mr. McFarland's parents, Arthur Bryan and Jennie Wilkey McFarland. Arthur McFarland farmed near Hoopeston, Illinois, about fifty miles northeast of Urbana.

The lower level contains the Odell Information Center, four computer-centered instruction and multimedia labs. The center was made possible by a generous gift from Russell T. and Florence O. Odell. Russell Odell earned his bachelor's, master's, and doctoral degrees at Illinois and spent fifty-six years of his life on or near the U of I agriculture campus, including twenty-two years as head of the Illinois Soil Survey.

Dozens of other individuals and organizations contributed to the ACES Library, Information, and Alumni Center, including the College of Agriculture class of 1941, which

FIGURE 8.36. The octagonal Agricultural, Consumer, and Environmental Sciences (ACES) Library Building was completed in 2001 on the South Campus. (Photo by Karyl Wackerlin.)

funded a group study room in honor of ten of their classmates who died in World War II.

The success of the far-reaching campaign for the library—several lead and significant donors, followed by many smaller gifts from a host of alumni and friends—is the same model employed by the Alice Campbell Alumni Center and the futuristic Electrical and Computer Engineering Building.

Thomas M. Siebel Center for Computer Science

The list of highly accomplished computer science graduates of the University of Illinois reads like a *Who's Who* list on an international scale.

The cream of the crop includes Thomas M. Siebel, who earned a bachelor's degree in history in 1975 and an MBA

FIGURE 8.37. Thomas M. Siebel Center for Computer Science was completed in 2004 at a cost of $80 million, of which the Siebel family contributed $32 million. Siebel, then-chairman and chief executive officer of the software application company Siebel Systems, earned three U of I degrees—a bachelor's degree in history, a master's degree in business administration, and another master's in computer science. (Photo by Karyl Wackerlin.)

in 1975 before he received a master's degree in computer science in 1985. He later founded and served as chairman of Siebel Systems Inc., one of the world's leading business software companies with more than eight thousand employees in thirty-two counties, forty-five hundred corporate customers, and more than $2 billion in annual revenue when it was merged with Oracle Corporation in 2006. (Oracle was co-founded by Larry Ellison, who attended but did not graduate from the U of I.)

Befitting the international renown of computer science at Illinois, Siebel donated $32 million toward construction of the $80 million Thomas M. Siebel Center for Computer Science, a 225,000-square-foot structure of brick, copper, slate, and glass that allowed the Department of Computer Science to nearly double the size of its faculty and student body. The Siebel Center united computer science places faculty, researchers, and graduate and undergraduate students under one roof for the first time on the Urbana-Champaign campus.

The Siebel Center is a "computing habitat," a living laboratory of testing facilities, classrooms (all are fully automated and equipped with audio/video capture, intelligent whiteboards, wireless networking, HDTV displays and other advancements) and other spaces where the physical and digital infrastructures are tightly coupled with the human element.

"The University of Illinois at Urbana-Champaign is recognized as a global leader in information technology," Siebel said in connection with opening of the Siebel Center April 30, 2004. "I am one of the many people who have benefitted greatly from this leadership. It gives me great pleasure to play a role in the enhancement of this great resource."

While the Seibel Center facilitates breathtaking advancement of computer science and information technology inside, exterior elements of the building and its adjacent landscaping evoke traditional forms, ones that are consistent with the campus. Perched along tree-lined streets, the Siebel Center's brick masonry, overhanging eaves, and other structural touches provide a familiar connection to campus.

Yet, reflective of its high-tech mission, the Siebel Center also embraces edgy architecture. The inner courtyard features transparent glass curtain walls and an L-shaped design that "recalls the geode: an opaque, earth-textured exterior with a crystalline, refractive interior," notes Siebel Center co-architect Bohlin Cywinski Jackson. Expansive views and natural lighting in public spaces near the courtyard further enhance the visual experience of the Siebel Center.

The Siebel Center is a key component in the information technology sector on the northeast side of campus that also is home to the National Center for Supercomputing Applications. Those buildings are part of the engineering campus that includes the Bardeen Quadrangle and the Beckman Quadrangle. It is an area of approximately thirty square blocks, bounded by Green Street on the south, Wright Street on the west, University Avenue on the north, and Gregory Street on the east.

In addition to the Siebel Center gift, in 2007 Thomas Siebel and his wife, Stacey, pledged $100 million in deferred and ongoing support of science and engineering on the Urbana-Champaign campus. The Thomas M. Siebel Fund for Excellence emphasizes collaborative work that addresses major problems and opportunities facing humankind in this century, including the convergence of the computational and life sciences and breakthrough developments in energy and human health.

Starting in 2000, hundreds of graduate students in bioengineering, business, and computers at top schools in the United States, including the U of I, have received substantial awards through the Siebel Scholars program. In 2006 the Thomas and Stacey Siebel Foundation provided $2 million to the U of I to establish the Thomas M. Siebel Chair in Computer Science as well as $2 million for the Thomas M. Siebel Chair in the History of Science in the College of Liberal Arts and Sciences' Department of History.

Then, in October 2016, the couple committed $25 million as the lead gift to establish the Siebel Center for Design, at the historic western terminus of the Military Axis, on Fourth Street. The two-story, sixty-thousand-square-foot building is planned to be built by late 2018.

Siebel, a member of the U of I College of Engineering's Hall of Fame, has served on the college's board of advisors and is a director of the U of I Foundation. A 2008 Lincoln Academy (of Illinois) laureate, he has received many honors for humanitarian and philanthropic contributions, including the 2010 Woodrow Wilson Award for Corporate Citizenship in 2010.

The Chicago native is currently the chairman and CEO of IoT, an enterprise software company. He also founded and chairs the Thomas and Stacey Siebel Foundation, which funds projects in energy solutions, educational and research programs, public health, and the homeless and underprivileged.

Alice Campbell Alumni Center

When University of Illinois graduates Robert and Alice Campbell see a need, they fill it. The couple, told of the subpar conditions of the U of I's public broadcasting facilities, contributed $5 million to construct the Campbell Hall for Public Telecommunication, the first permanent home for WILL-AM-FM-TV (now Illinois Public Media). Campbell Hall was dedicated in 1999.

A few years later, the Campbells provided a $5 million lead gift to construct the first facility devoted to the U of I Alumni Association. The three-story, fifty-thousand-square-foot building at Lincoln Avenue at California Street and immediately south of the Hallene Gateway Plaza, includes a reception gallery, library, lounge, great room and banquet room, offices for Alumni Association staff, and conference rooms and an executive boardroom.

FIGURE 8.38. The Alice Campbell Alumni Center, located on Lincoln Avenue in Urbana on the east edge of campus, was dedicated in 2006. Private contributions completely paid for the project, with a lead gift from Alice Campbell. As of 2016-17 the Alumni Association is remodeling part of the building for a campus Welcome Center. (Photo by Karyl Wackerlin.)

The Alice Campbell Center, which opened in 2006, compliments the Urbana-Champaign campus's brick-and-limestone Georgian architecture, features two balconies, expanses of glass and central skylights, and a patio for outdoor activities. The center serves as the official welcome site to campus. It is frequently used for special events, such as Homecoming, reunions, and other activities. The banquet room and flexible meeting spaces are a draw for college and departmental alumni gatherings.

The $15.7 million Alice Campbell Alumni Center was funded entirely by private donations. The majority of the benefactors were U of I alumni; rooms and galleries throughout the building are named for them.

While the Alice Campbell Alumni Center is a recent addition to the U of I landscape, its mission as a welcome center for visitors to campus is ongoing—and evolving. In time for the university's sesquicentennial and after a $4 million repurposing of sections of the Alice Campbell Alumni Center, a new Welcome Center is scheduled to open in 2017.

The multimedia, interactive Welcome Center intends to explain the university by expressing the experience of the entire Illini community, from the sixty or so farmers' sons who were the first students, to the more than forty-four thousand students now on campus. The focus of the center is to convey the culture, history, and traditions that alumni, students, and faculty share.

The first phase, ground-floor reconfiguration of the Alice Campbell Alumni Center will include spaces for the Welcome Gallery and Café, Student Life Gallery, Memory Space, and Story Booth. Together, the two galleries will house fourteen "discovery boxes" that combine artifacts, photographs, and an interactive video display.

After the opening of the Welcome Center, the second and third phases of the development, covering the conversion of the building's second and third floors, will be completed.

Doris Kelley Christopher Hall

Doris Kelley's friends warned her that the U of I campus was big. And it was. The baby boom was en route to college, and already there were 25,611 students enrolled at Urbana-Champaign in fall 1963; by fall 1966 the figure was 29,120. "You'll just be a number there," one said. Even her uncle Dave, the family expert on all things educational, advised her to choose a smaller school. "Doris will be lost there," he predicted. But supported by her mother, Doris attended the University of Illinois and never regretted her decision.

Kelley at first found the sprawling and crowded campus a bit overwhelming, but the picture brightened when she found that all of her home economics courses were located at Bevier Hall and its environs. "It was as if I were attending a small school within a big school," she wrote in her autobiography. She graduated with a home economics degree in 1967, the same year she married Jay Christopher, and she later credited the U of I for having broadened her "culinary horizons."

Almost forty years after she graduated, Christopher was back on the once-intimidating campus for the dedication of Doris Kelley Christopher Hall. In the intervening years she had become a teacher, a mother of two, and a multimillionaire entrepreneur. In 1980, at home with two small children, she had wanted more. She and Jay borrowed $3,000 against his life insurance policy and in the basement of their suburban Chicago house founded a company that would sell professional-grade kitchen equipment, tools, and gadgets to consumers via in-home demonstrations called "kitchen shows." It was, she said in a 2005 NPR Motley Fool interview, an elaborated version (with food cooked onsite) of home shows pioneered by Tupperware. Her goal then, as it remained, was to make cooking easier and more efficient so families could get to the main course: family time gathered around the dinner table.

Christopher called her company The Pampered Chef, and by the 1990s it had grown into a $500 million business with

FIGURE 8.39. Doris Kelley Christopher Hall is a research and educational facility that is home to the Family Resiliency Center and the Department of Human and Community Development. It helps anchor the east campus. (Photo by Karyl Wackerlin.)

a sales force of tens of thousands. In 2002 she approached Berkshire Hathaway, whose owner Warren Buffett she believed would be attracted to the business, which had no debt, was well-managed, and whose product (kitchen tools and gadgets) was easy to understand, all qualities Buffett famously seeks in investments. Christopher's first meeting with Buffett lasted four hours, and he made an offer on the spot for what she has called "the things in the drawers and the cabinets" of the kitchen.

Christopher never forgot her school, and in 2002 she donated $10 million to the U of I for a center on family resiliency. That gift to the College of Agricultural, Consumer, and Environmental Sciences, which houses the Department of Human and Community Development, made possible a three-story, 23,700-square-foot building that opened in 2006. An interesting feature is a one-thousand-square-foot Family Observation Suite that permits researchers to study families in a simulated home environment.

"No question facing our society is as important as 'Why do some families succeed while others fail?'" she said at the Christopher Hall dedication in fall 2006. "After all, the family is the first and most basic unit of society."

Booth Hansen Architects of Chicago designed the building, which employs a glass corridor to link a mini-house to the main teaching and research space.

In April 2003 the Christophers also established The Pampered Chef Ltd. Endowed Chair in Family Resiliency at the U of I; in 2006 the couple expanded its support for the Family Resiliency Program with funds for dissertation research awards and additional faculty research grants and public engagement activities. She is a lifetime member of the Horatio Alger Association of Distinguished Americans.

J. D. Demirjian Indoor Golf Facility and Lauritsen/Wohlers Outdoor Practice Facility

Golf offseason in Illinois was not ideal. During the winter, when local fairways and greens were blanketed in snow and ice, Illini golfers had to practice in the dreary basement of Huff Gym where they drove balls into old racquetball nets and putted on a makeshift green a few feet away from a boiler room radiating one-hundred-degree heat.

"It was crammed. It was hot," Mike Small, Illinois men's golf head coach, told *Golfweek* in September 2008. "Back then, 20 minutes of practice was good."

And in the warm months, practice meant a trip to a local public or private course—all are welcoming, to be sure, and add variety—cutting into time to drive, chip, and putt.

Over ten years, the same decade during which Small's golfers routinely defied weather logic and climbed high in

FIGURE 8.40. The Demirjian Golf Practice Facility opened for use of the U of I men's and women's golf teams in 2007. (Fighting Illini Athletics/ Division of Intercollegiate Athletics.)

FIGURE 8.41. The Lauritsen/Wohlers Outdoor Golf Facility, opened in April 2015, was inspired by the practice area at the Augusta National Golf Club, home of the Masters Golf Tournament. (Photo by Darrell Hoemann.)

national rankings and won Big Ten titles, alumni and other donors made sure Illini golfers, both men and women, would have premiere indoor and outdoor practice facilities.

In 2004 the Demirjian family of Decatur and the family business, The DemirCo Group, committed $1.5 million to help build a cutting-edge indoor golf-training facility to compensate for cold and wet early spring and late falls, and midwestern winter. The gift honors J. Gerald "Jerry" Demirjian. Designed by RATIO Architects Inc. and completed in 2007, the $5.1 million, three-and-a-half-story-high, fourteen-thousand-square-foot building, located on St. Mary's Road across from the Atkins Tennis Center, won rave reviews from the outset. *Golfweek* joined the chorus, publishing an article highlighting Illinois's "dazzling practice digs."

Dazzling is not overstatement. Golfers at the Demirjian can tee off from one of six heated hitting bays that overlook an outdoor driving range; two of the bays contain state-of-the-art swing analysis machines to help correct that pesky slice or hook. Small said his squad hit twenty-five thousand balls at the Demirjian one winter. Players hoping to improve their short game are provided for as well: the facility contains a sixty-three-hundred-square-foot surface complete with greens and four types of simulated rough. When not practicing, golfers can relax in a fifteen-hundred-square-foot team lounge or adjust their golf clubs in a fully equipped golf club repair room. There's also an exterior terrace that connects to the lounge for meetings and events.

When announcing his family's gift, Richard Demirjian, class of 1988, had expressed the hope that the facility would help launch the Illini men's and women's golf teams to number-one rankings. Both teams have certainly been on the move. The women's team made it to the NCAA regionals two years in a row—in 2010-11 and 2011-12. As for the men's team, between 2009 and 2015 it qualified for eight straight NCAA championships (runner up in 2013) and also won the Big Ten championship every year except 2014.

Lauritsen/Wohlers

Two alumni families, three ex-Illini golfers, a course builder, and a national fund manager—ten donors in all—linked arms not only to underwrite a $2 million, twenty-four-acre outdoor practice area of fairways and greens connected to the Demirjian but also to create a $3.5 million endowment to keep it in top shape into the future.

Inspired by the Augusta National Golf Club, Coach Small and PGA Tour veteran Steve Stricker designed the practice area; the Wadsworth Golf Construction Company, led by Brent Wadsworth (class of 1952), built the practice facility, which contains different grass types and lies, target greens of varying distances, as well as putting greens (thirteen hundred square feet) and chipping greens, along with several wedge areas. Don Edwards, who played with Stricker on the 1988 Big Ten championship team, and his wife, Anne Sebastian Edwards, contributed key funds; Arthur R. Wyatt, a 1946-49 golf letter winner and longtime accountancy faculty member, was a donor; and Steven S. Wymer (class of 1985), managed the Fidelity Growth Fund since 1998 and is the lead contributor to the facility endowment through the Steven S. Wymer Facility Endowment Fund for Men's Golf.

FIGURE 8.42. Kay and James Lauritsen, co-lead donors to the outdoor golf facility. Golf professional and U of I alumnus Steve Stricker also contributed funds and consulted on the design of the facility. (Photo by Mark Jones, courtesy of Fighting Illini Athletics/Division of Intercollegiate Athletics.)

The name donors are James and Kay Lauritsen and the Albert Wohlers families, both familiar names in the Illini Place. Jim Lauritsen, class of 1958, was a founding partner of Bielfeldt, Lauritsen and Hagemeyer; the late Albert Wohlers, class of 1939, helped renovate the old Commerce West into Wohlers Hall.

The Chez Family Foundation: Center for Wounded Veterans in Higher Education

A dean's big idea met the right guy at the right time, resulting in a one-of-a-kind campus center to help 175 military veterans navigate their way through college, participate in research, receive academic and career counseling, and, for a dozen severely injured vets, live in private suites and receive daily living assistance on the University of Illinois campus.

FIGURE 8.43. The October 2, 2015, ribbon cutting for the Chez Family Foundation Center for Wounded Veterans in Higher Education. Alumnus Ron Chez provided one-half the cost to build the $14 million facility. The center is a single location focused on helping wounded veterans attending the U of I. (Photo by Joyce Seay-Knoblauch, University News Bureau.)

The Chez Family Foundation Center for Wounded Veterans in Higher Education opened on West Nevada Street in 2015, thanks to the Chez Foundation's $6 million lead gift.

When Ronald L. Chez, a 1962 Bronze Tablet scholar, toured the new Beckwith Residential Support Services Program in Timothy J. Nugent Hall with Tanya Gallagher, dean of the College of Applied Health Sciences, she mentioned a big idea: a center for disabled vets attending the U of I that needed a first pledge to launch. He pledged a bit at the time, he told the *News-Gazette* in 2012, but soon his family foundation decided to underwrite half the cost.

Chez is an army veteran who earned an MBA from the University of Chicago. His business is Ronald L. Chez Inc., a financial managing consulting firm in Chicago; he's also chairman of the board of EpiWorks, a compound semiconductor materials company in Champaign (acquired in early

2016 by II-VI Inc. for nearly $50 million) and an occasional executive movie producer for projects such as *Magic in the Moonlight*, a Woody Allen film.

Much like the Campbell Alumni Center, the ACES Library, and the Electrical and Computer Engineering Building, the $14 million Chez Center for Wounded Veterans relied on many donors—nearly forty individuals, family and corporate foundations, and companies to sponsors rooms and programs. They range from a motorcycle club (Make a Difference Dinosores) to a U of I trustee (Dr. and Mrs. Timothy N. Koritz), from former U of I trustee Thomas R. Lamont and his wife, Bridget, to the familiar Grainger Foundation and McCormick Foundation—and even a basketball coach (Mr. and Mrs. John G. Groce).

The state's Illinois Jobs Now! capital construction and economic development program added $4 million toward construction costs; former Illinois Governor Patrick Quinn signed the law creating the program.

Chez said vets deserve the benefits of the new center. "It's our honor to respect the great courage of people who have put themselves in harm's way and go off and defend our country," he said in 2012. "It's an obligation; I feel like it's an obligation," he said two years later. "I always said, 'If I was blessed with the opportunity, if I could, I would do things to benefit others.' I didn't come from a wealthy family at all, at all."

Chez came to the U of I on baseball scholarship as a physical education major; his playing was just so-so, but after switching to political science he graduated Phi Beta Kappa. His family foundation in 2009 made a "seven figure" gift through the U of I Foundation for college scholarships for inner-city youths.

The Chez Center comprises forty thousand square feet on three floors. It is a red-brick modern with Georgian revival elements, including limestone trim. It does not front onto Nevada but rather has a circle drive at its front entrance that faces to the east to accommodate wheelchairs and other devices.

The center reaffirms the university's standing as a forward-acting campus for people with disabilities established at the end of World War II by Tim Nugent, famed for his advocacy and persistence. Nugent attended the October 2, 2015, dedication of the Chez Center and died on Veterans Day, November 11, 2015.

CHAPTER 9

Icons

Introduction

A campus is a community of scholars, a collection of buildings, and an organized landscape. It is a place with purpose.

Professors impart knowledge—which changes, inexorably, by new discovery or interpretation—to successive waves of students. Researchers explore and shape the natural and manmade universe from molecule to moon and gene to petascale. Scholars explore the hidden meanings of obscure texts, archaeologists fan out across the globe, and artists paint and perform. Semesters and seasons pass, class cohorts arrive and leave, new alumni are minted in grand ceremonies with processions, trumpets, banners, regalia.

If a generation is twenty years—rapidly moving toward twenty-five years as childbearing is delayed—then eight back-to-back generations of students have passed through the place of the University of Illinois. By mid-2015, the Urbana-Champaign campus claimed some 453,085 living alumni, a population equal to that of a midsized U.S. city.

The earliest students of the Urbana-Champaign campus—fifty pioneers (all men) who matriculated in March 1868—studied, ate, and slept by gaslight in a single building on University Avenue. They and the generations that followed lived impressionable years as campus features grew up around them: vast lawns, chimes, gardens, benches, statues, playing fields, and stadiums that, in time, became iconic. These icons were powerful symbols of a time lived on the University of Illinois campus. Revisited years or decades later, they harbor emotional content and jog memories of an influential place and time. For those fortunate enough to work long careers at the Illini Place, echoes and shadows of the past are a daily presence.

What follow are small stories about a sampling of the most obvious campus icons. Many date to the twentieth century, a few have been significantly altered or lost entirely, and one—the Hallene Gateway—is a special tale of the past rediscovered, resurrected, and reborn in a new generation.

Key Spaces and Places

The Quad

The Quadrangle is arguably the campus's single most evocative and important space, a well-manicured front yard

FIGURE 9.1. University of Illinois Quad and Illini Union. The Quad is the center of the campus. It remains the center of activities and the U of I's iconic center. Thirteen buildings, housing mostly liberal arts and sciences disciplines, surround the Quad, which established the north-south orientation of the growth and expansion of the U of I. (Photo by L. Brian Stauffer, University News Bureau.)

flanked by beautifully scaled yet architecturally diverse stone and brick buildings, crisscrossed by heavily trafficked sidewalks, and lighted and landscaped up, down, and across its twelve-hundred-by-two-hundred-foot expanse. At its north end, the gleaming white and red-brick, colonial-style Illini Union; at its south, the domed and lighted Foellinger Auditorium.

The quadrangle is a staple of European and American college campuses. At the University of Illinois, the Quad sheltered turn-of-the-century coeds costumed as ears of corn or twirling in flowing spring gowns on May Day. The Quad has witnessed political protest, religious argument, fundraising, flag burnings, bake sales, pep rallies, movies, teach-ins, concerts, streaking (including students

FIGURE 9.2. Nathan C. Ricker, class of 1873, professor of architecture and dean of the College of Engineering, served the university from 1872 to 1917. He established the first curriculum in architectural engineering in 1890. He designed the Natural History Building and co-designed Altgeld Hall, and Harker Hall. (Photo dated March 19, 1924. Photo courtesy of University of Illinois Archives 0003333.)

parachuting naked onto the lawn), ticket selling, Hash Wednesday, dogs running free, friendly squirrels, bicycles off path, lovers snuggled under trees, and people of all ages dozing, eating, drinking, and, until recently, smoking.

But the Quad, as it came to be called, owes its existence to a singular event: siting the auditorium in 1905-6.

The question of where to build an auditorium arose in 1905, and new president Edmund Janes James (1904-20) turned the issue over to a commission that included an astonishing cast of characters, all alumni: famed Boston architect/planner Clarence H. Blackall, class of 1877; Chicago sculptor Lorado Taft, class of 1879 (who later would design the *Alma Mater* grouping); prolific and pioneering architect Nathan C. Ricker, class of 1873, and, University Architect James McLaren White, class of 1890, who served the campus and community for more than four decades.

Blackall not only designed the anticipated building, which would cost $96,000 and seat twenty-five hundred (later reduced), but in short order (by today's standards) unilaterally laid out a plan for further campus development—including a quadrangle whose southern terminus—on a slight natural rise—was the proposed auditorium. At the north were the 1896 library (now Altgeld Hall); Harker Hall, built in 1878 as the chemistry lab; and University Hall (sometimes called Old Main), which was built in 1873-74 and razed in 1938 to make room for the Illini Union. Blackall brought his campus plan to the board of trustees in early 1906. The board appropriated $250 for additional planning help in the person of John C. Olmsted of Brookline, Massachusetts, the nephew and later adopted son of Frederick Law Olmsted, who laid out New York's Central Park. Their plan is outlined in chapter 2 of this book, but the key placement of the auditorium defined a vital space that continues to be what the American Society of Landscape Architects calls "places of the heart."

The Quad contained at various times all of the essential disciplines of a contemporary university: library, law school, chemistry, agriculture, liberal arts, natural history, music, and commerce. The major exception is engineering, then as now sequestered north of Green Street.

Today's students, alumni, and visitors would not recognize a 1903 map of what became the Quad, nor the uses of its thirteen buildings still standing, all but one built between 1878 and 1931 and ten of them built by 1921. The Foreign

Languages Building, a modern design by Holabird & Root built in 1971, was the last new construction on the Quad. It fills the space between Smith Music Hall (blocking its grand entrance) and Davenport Hall that was formerly occupied by the Natural History Survey Lab and the agronomy annex and greenhouse, all of which were demolished.

Early pathways on the Quad were curvilinear, gently winding, and bending toward building entryways rather than the straight and diagonal sidewalks of today. Burrill Avenue, an actual roadway for carriages and cars, ran north-south onto the Quad from Green Street to near present-day Gregory Hall; it later was converted into a boardwalk or sidewalk on the Quad's west side. The Quad is slightly trapezoidal—it narrows to the south—rather than the rectangle it appears to be from ground level. An underground watering system keeps the grass green, and substantial elements of the 1928-33 Vitale landscaping plan—dwarf flowering crab apple trees, short yew hedges, and taller trees all anchoring massive classroom and lab buildings—give the Quad its serene and controlled look.

In 1898 the campus superintendent of buildings and grounds proposed an artificial lake of one and a half to two acres in the center of what is now the Quad—about 450 feet south of University Hall (now occupied by the Illini Union). "A lake at this point would act as a catch basin for a considerable territory laying south and west of this point," Nelson S. Spencer wrote to the members of the board of trustees. The lake would be layered with clay to retain the water at this naturally occurring low point, be crossed by a bridge ("which would also add to the effect"), and provide recreation: boats in the summer and ice skating in the winter.

Dutch elms that once arched over the north-south roadways and sidewalks of the Quad fell to disease, but the old-fashioned lamps and curved bench still harbors lovers, the Altgeld chimes peal the hours and familiar tunes, and the *Alma Mater* grouping near Green and Wright Streets forms a welcome party.

The Beckman and Bardeen Quads

The engineering campus, so integral to the sturdy academic reputation of the U of I, was ignored for decades, a confusing industrial zone not fit for campus tours. But the 1985 $40 million Beckman gift, coupled with intensive planning and widespread new construction and renovation on the north campus, yielded opportunities for creation of two new quadrangles that would be built in less than twenty years, public art included.

The jumbled north campus, which housed all engineering buildings, in the end would be turned into twin pedestrian-friendly spaces that linked old and new buildings and reinforced the strong north-south axis established in the first decade of the last century. The new quadrangles are the Beckman Quad or Oval Allee, just south of its namesake building, and the Bardeen Quad, honoring the campus's two-time Nobel laureate.

Beckman Quad

The sheer size of the Beckman Institute for Advanced Science and Technology—more than three hundred thousand square feet—called out for open space at its imposing front door and distinctive five-story glass-and-brick tower, which faced to the south and centered on a reinvigorated north-south axis or spine that is a central organizing principle of the campus.

And while Kenney Gym, built in 1902, and the Kenney Gym Annex (the 1890 military drill hall), were shown for demolition at various times, including in the 1986 Sasaki plan, they remain along Springfield Avenue in the literal center of the engineering campus. The other buildings that flank the Beckman Quad are, to the west (Wright Street), the Micro and Nanotechnology Lab and, to the east (Mathews Avenue), the Coordinated Science Lab, a chiller plant, the Hydrosystems Lab, Newmark Civil Engineering Building and, wrapped in 1988 with a clever $17.5 million addition,

FIGURE 9.3. The College of Engineering's north Beckman Quad and buildings, from left, the Electrical and Computer Engineering Building, the Beckman Institute for Advanced Science and Technology, and the Coordinated Science Laboratory. The Beckman Quad was dedicated on October 14, 2004. (Photo by L. Brian Stauffer, University News Bureau.)

the 1958 Digital Computer Lab. The last open space, at the northwest edge of Wright Street near University Avenue, is filled by a new $95 million Electrical and Computer Engineering Building that was approved by the board of trustees in early 2010 and had successfully raised about half of its own cost as of mid-2015.

The Beckman Quad/Oval has globe lights, rows of trees, and curved and straight sidewalks. Its most notable feature, however, took advantage of a then-new state law, which encourages "art in architecture" by mandating 0.5 percent of the state-funded portion of new or reconstructed public buildings be spent on art tied to the building.

The U of I also has an art endowment, the John Chester Needles bequest, that can be used for art, rare books, and the like. Needles was an 1891 graduate and active in the University of Illinois Foundation and Alumni Association.

The U of I commissioned DePaul University professor and environmental artist/sculptor Stephen Luecking, who created *Upwells* and its oval plaza south of the Beckman Institute. *Upwells* (shown on Luecking's own Web site as a $250,000 project) features a forty-foot granite-and-bronze sculpture, a globe on a pedestal, and three close-to-the-ground "calendar" fountains that rise like shallow domes on the plaza. The shadow of the Gnomon Spire strikes the center of the nearest fountain on the summer solstice; other shadows strike the other domes on the winter solstice and the spring and fall equinoxes. Locals call the five-part sculpture—aligned north-south—"Beckhenge" in wry homage to Beckman Institute and England's Stonehenge.

Bardeen Quad

One-third the size of the main Quad, the John Bardeen Quadrangle is an expanse of greenery bordered by the Grainger Engineering Library Information Center on the north, Engineering Hall on the south, the Mechanical Engineering Laboratory on the east, and Talbot Laboratory on the west.

A quadrangle on the engineering campus was outlined in the North Campus Master Plan prepared by Sasaki Associates Inc. and adopted by the board of trustees in 1986. That plan assumed eliminating buildings, closing and vacating Burrill Avenue—which had deteriorated into a homely parking lot and roadway—and landscaping the entire area, including the banks of Boneyard Creek. In spring 1994, space for the generic Engineering Quad was cleared with the razing of the Electrical Engineering Research Laboratory, which straddled the Boneyard and was routinely flooded by it, and the Electrical Engineering Annex.

Then, at the October 14, 1994, dedication ceremony of the Grainger Library, an announcement was made that the Grainger Foundation had donated $2.9 million to finish the Engineering Quad. President Stanley O. Ikenberry (1979-95, 2009-10) authorized the appointment of the Chicago architectural/engineering firm Joe Karr and Associates as consultant on the project. In the first phase of construction, walkways were laid out, new lights installed, and the grounds re-graded and landscaped in the area between Boneyard Creek and the Grainger Library. The second phase involved work along the Boneyard from Wright Street to the site of the old Fire Station, just north of Green Street.

In 1999 the trustees designated the Engineering Quad as a "memorial to the life and accomplishments of John Bardeen," a two-time Nobel Prize winner and a longtime U of I professor of electrical engineering and physics who died in 1991. On October 14, 2004, more than a hundred people gathered on the newly built concrete terrace north of Engineering Hall to witness the dedication of the John Bardeen Quadrangle.

Illini Union

Roger Ebert, the late movie critic, called the Library "the soul" of the campus and the Illini Union "the heart." It took a long time to get the heart beating—more than three decades—but it clearly was worth the wait.

The idea of the Illini Union began—as did so many things—during the administration of the legendary Edmund Janes James (1904-20). Shortly after coming to the U of I, James broached the idea of a union building to students. Four years later, he encouraged the formation of the Illinois Union, a student group dedicated to promoting "Illinois spirit by all possible means, more especially by the erection and maintenance of a club house." This "club house" or Union building would be a central but elusive goal of the Illinois Union for years.

"When the [Union] building comes, and it is certain to come," the *Daily Illini* confidently predicted in 1909, "it will be the one place at the University where Greek and Barb, lit and law, engineer and ag, Cosmopolitan and American may meet on neutral ground. Its privileges will be denied to none, and its benefits will be conferred upon all."

FIGURE 9.4. The Illini Union, dedicated by Eleanor Roosevelt on November 1, 1941, was built with a $525,820 grant from the federal Public Works Administration and a $656,000 loan, later repaid with student fees. The building was designed in the shape of an "I" to honor the university, but additions have changed its footprint. The building is a hub for students, faculty, and staff who use it for social, educational, and organizational activities. (Photo by L. Brian Stauffer. University News Bureau.)

Years passed, then decades, and university after university across the Big Ten and elsewhere erected elaborate Union buildings—Ohio State in 1910, Michigan in 1919, Wisconsin in 1928, Indiana in 1932, Texas in 1933. What about Illinois? For much of this period, the U of I's Union was housed in the old YMCA building (now Illini Hall)—a structure falling apart at the seams. In 1934 things got so bad the building's south wall had to be reinforced to prevent it from toppling over. "What this campus really needs," the *Daily Illini* declared that year, " . . . is a new Union building."

Newly elected President Arthur Cutts Willard agreed. He wanted a Union building, and quick. But the desire for an Illini Union wouldn't begin to take concrete form until the pivotal year of 1938. Early that summer the university came up with a financing scheme that combined a federal grant ($525,820 from the Public Works Administration) with a $656,000 loan from the Connecticut Mutual Life Insurance Company, backed by the newly chartered University of Illinois Foundation, which would lease the building to the university itself. The loan-lease deal represented the first major fundraising effort on behalf of the campus. Student fees later repaid the loan.

Not long after, a location was selected on the front door to the campus—a site made possible by the razing of University Hall earlier that year. The exact final location, some 120 feet north of the old University Hall footprint, was chosen to preserve the two towering bald cypresses near Harker Hall. And Howard Lovewell Cheney, a 1912 U of I graduate and the designer of more than twenty federal buildings, joined the project as consulting architect. Alumni architects, who felt the university had ignored them in the past, had urged an Illinois grad be appointed. And he was. "Six feet of ability, good looks and friendliness," Cheney helped push the project along.

After meeting with Cheney and Physical Plant Director Charles Havens in late July, Willard unilaterally decided that the Illini Union should have a colonial design. "I think it will look well and gives us a chance to create a building which will look old and traditional, even more so than Uni [Gothic University High School] Hall ever did," Willard said. He believed the colonial architecture was the most appropriate for "social and domestic purposes, such as are required of a union building." He got the design he wanted.

Headed by the expert draftsman John C. Leavell, a crew of more than a dozen worked hard on the Union's exterior design and plans in offices on the south floor of Engineering Hall, across Green Street from where the new Illini Union would rise. Already, by late September 1938, the Illini Union on the draftsmen's drawing boards looked remarkably like the Illini Union that students and alumni know and love today, complete with the thirty-foot-high cupola that contains two artifacts from University Hall—the old chapel bell and the clock that had been the gift of the class of 1878. University architect Ernie Stouffer, who also worked on the project, credited Leavell as being "largely responsible for the unusual detail both on the interior and exterior of the building."

The general design was settled fairly quickly, but the details consumed time and creative juices. "This building involves more detailed planning and study than any building we have on the campus inasmuch as each room presents a separate design problem within itself," Willard explained to an impatient federal official in November 1938. During the Christmas holidays, Cheney journeyed to the recently restored Colonial Williamsburg in search of ideas for the Union's rooms. The result: the Illini Union's ornate Ball Room, the ivory and blue Wedgwood Lounge, and the Pine Room, with its knotty pine walls, were modeled after rooms in the Williamsburg Governor's Palace.

Colonial Williamsburg also influenced the Union's exterior. The building's architects decided early on that the Union's red bricks should have the same rich coloring as those used at Williamsburg. Unfortunately, the Virginia red-clay brick was too expensive to ship, and the shale brick of local makers was a far cry from the Virginia product. Two venturesome firms experimented and came up with a close-enough color, Stouffer later reported. The Illini Union's bricks were manufactured one-half inch thicker than normal bricks because of the enormous scale of the building.

The final drawings and specifications for the Illini Union weren't finished until spring 1939, and construction would take nearly two years, plagued by a shortage of men and material. The $1.5 million Illini Union opened to the public on February 5, 1941. The reviews were uniformly positive. Architectural historian Rexford Newcomb called the Union the finest on the campus. Betsy Ross, president Willard's niece, remembered people being amazed by the magnificent structure and its lavish interior. "They tiptoed through," she said.

At the building's dedication on Homecoming Day, November 1, 1941, Governor Dwight H. Green called the Illini Union "the crowning achievement in the life of one of the greatest educational institutions in the world." James M. Cleary, president of the board of trustees, named the Union "the most important building on campus" and added that "although the building is dedicated, it is not completed," taking the opportunity to ask a captive audience to raise another $100,000 "to equip and furnish the Union." He emphasized that "students have the right to expect a stimulating, pleasant experience while they learn," and he left listeners to ponder the question, "What are laboratories without laughter?"

In 1962, a $6.9 million south addition doubled the Illini Union's size. And in 1993 the underused interior courtyard—a patio open to the wet and cold of Illinois—was enclosed, creating the Courtyard Café. It cost $2.46 million.

Victor Shelford Vivarium

The Vivarium was completed in 1916 at a cost of roughly $76,000; it is tucked away at the northwest corner of Wright and Healey Streets in Champaign. It was built especially for

FIGURE 9.5. The Vivarium, built in 1916, was known from 1933 until 1948 as the Experimental Zoology Laboratory. (Photo by Karyl Wackerlin.)

the work of zoologists Charles Zeleny and Victor Shelford, a pioneering ecologist, and in its early years housed both the Departments of Zoology and Entomology.

A vivarium, a "place of life," is a mini-ecosystem for studying plants and animals in a controlled environment.

Flanked by two greenhouses on each end, the main two-story brick structure, fronting Healey Street, contained eight laboratories, one office, and storerooms, and was connected via a passage to a building just north of it. A pair of greenhouses and screened houses were attached to this latter building.

The Vivarium's unassuming exterior concealed then-cutting-edge scientific equipment: seawater aquariums, refrigerator systems, and an apparatus for "temperature and humidity control in the study of insect life histories." Using this equipment to simulate various ecosystems, Zeleny, Shelford, and colleagues studied insects and animals under conditions that mimicked their natural habitats.

But for nonscientists and passersby, the Vivarium remained notable for the Teco pottery tablets attached to the building's exterior; the six-foot-high iron fence that enclosed its east side; and the ponds to its south.

Melvyn Skvarla, campus historic preservation architect, said a Chicago Teco expert believes the so-called "Fish Panels" on the east and west sides of the Vivarium were designed in an art nouveau style by William Day Gates himself.

Gates, a lawyer, was founder, president, and general manager of what started as a simple tile company in 1879 in Terra Cotta, Illinois, between Crystal Lake and McHenry. It later was renamed The American Terra Cotta and Ceramic Company and pioneered architectural terra cotta, such as drain tile, chimney tops, urns, finials, and the like. Soon the company veered into art pottery with natural and organic themes and a distinctive signature green glaze. Gates designed most of the Teco output, but several Prairie School architects, including Frank Lloyd Wright, also designed pieces suitable for the simple ornamentation they favored for their buildings.

Skvarla said U of I records show the panels are roughly 3' 6" wide by 7' 6" high. They were designed, made, and fired in 1915 and shipped to the U of I the following January. The valuable panels show stylized fish swimming under stylized waves; they have the familiar "Teco Green" glaze that appeals to collectors. Teco is shorthand for "terra cotta."

The outside ponds on the south side of the Vivarium originally were supposed to have been built at the same time as the building but were not completed until 1946, probably for lack for funds, a recurring theme at the campus. But there were ponds inside the Vivarium from the outset, and a forty-year-old male turtle called Illibuck was a temporary inhabitant of one of these ponds.

In 1924 the Fighting Illini defeated the Ohio State Buckeyes, and the hapless trophy turtle was hauled off to the Vivarium. But not for long. In January 1925 an enterprising *Daily Illini* reporter discovered that Illibuck had been moved to a home on West Hill Street, where he lived in a washtub. Illibuck died April 14, 1926.

Today, the Victor Shelford Vivarium houses faculty in the Animal Biology Department. Its ponds are filled in.

Fraternity Park

The plain, grassy plot long known as "Fraternity Park" has mutated from fairgrounds to private property to publicly owned Champaign Park District land over the last century. From the late 1880s until at least 1903, the land constituted fairgrounds that also hosted traveling one-ring circuses.

A 1939 *Daily Illini* story recalled a fight at the fairgrounds in 1901. The circus announced that an encore show would cost ten cents, but students in the audience refused to pay. "It was a struggle in which the forces of law and order (represented by police, circus hands, and townspeople) evicted an unwilling group of students from a circus tent and, with superior numbers, drove them out of the neighborhood," the story said.

FIGURE 9.6. Fraternity (or Frat) Park, the informal name of Washington Park, is surrounded by Greek houses. Fraternities were banned early until U of I trustees relented in 1891. During World War II, fraternity houses served as living space for U.S. Army soldiers. (Photo by Karyl Wackerlin.)

The land was later owned by George Washington Davidson, son of a Mahomet farmer. Fraternity Park was part of the landowner's Davidson Place Annex inside the Fairland Place subdivision in turn-of-the-century Champaign. When Davidson died November 26, 1914, his son and estate executor Thomas Meredith Davidson sold ten plots of land in Davidson Place Annex to settle his father's debts.

Park District planner and landscape architect Andrew Weiss said that in 1905 when Fairland Place was platted, title to 2.5 acres was given to the city for open space; there was no park district at the time. In 1984 the city sold some open space and "de facto" parks—including Washington Park—to the Park District, which had formed in 1914.

Fraternity and sorority houses have surrounded the property in recent decades, accounting for its vernacular name. Formally it is Washington Park and measures in at 3.53 acres, about 2.5 owned by the Park District, according to district aerial maps. Two rights-of-way still owned by the city, some twenty-eight feet inward from both the east and west sides of the park as we know it today, originally were envisioned to be "Clarkson Avenue" and "Gardener Avenue"—two unbuilt north-south streets. The park would have been a boulevard between the two avenues, running the entire block between Daniel and Armory.

The space now has two volleyball courts and a basketball court, and students use its grassy area for informal football and Frisbee games. In an otherwise dense neighborhood, the park is welcome open space.

Gregory Grove/Grave

John Milton Gregory, the first regent (now called president) of the university, had expressed the desire to be buried on the property of the school that he had helped launch in 1867 and led until 1880.

So, when Gregory died October 19, 1898, in Washington, D.C., at age seventy-six, the U of I Board of Trustees—four members had been students of the "distinguished deceased"—made certain his wish was honored. Gregory's body was brought to the university, lay in repose in the rotunda of the Library (now Altgeld Hall), and then was placed for a short time in a vault in Mount Hope Cemetery before being buried south and east of the then-Library.

In October 1912 President Edmund Janes James (1904-20) recommended that "the grave should be marked in some appropriate and simple manner by the Trustees of the University at the expense of the University." A little more than a year later, the trustees accepted the suggestion of Supervising Architect James M. White that a glacial boulder excavated during the construction of Lincoln Hall be used to mark the grave. The plot was re-sodded and planted with shrubbery, and on June 16, 1914, Allene Gregory, the ex-regent's daughter, unveiled the memorial to her father. A tablet affixed to the boulder bears the following inscription (adapted from the epitaph on British architect Sir Christopher Wren's tombstone): "If you seek his monument look about you." (Wren: "For those who seek his monument look about you.") It is the only gravesite on campus property.

The burr oak tree that shades John Milton Gregory's grave was donated in 1947 by members of the class of 1897 in celebration of their fiftieth anniversary. Gregory's wife, Professor Louisa C. Allen Gregory, whom he married in 1879, two years after his first wife, Julia Gregory, died, is buried at Mount Hope Cemetery on the south side of the campus. For many years, the university commemorated Founders' Day with a wreath at Gregory's grave, a practice that faded away.

FIGURE 9.7. John Milton Gregory, the U of I's first regent—now called president—is buried in a shady grove between Altgeld Hall and the Henry Administration Building. (Photo by Karyl Wackerlin.)

Mount Hope and Roselawn Cemeteries

For more than two decades the university was in the cemetery business, the unfortunate consequence of a bad case of land lust.

In the earliest decades of the university, Mount Hope Cemetery was far south of the main campus. It was founded in 1856—more than a decade before the Illinois Industrial University opened its doors—and sprawls over thirty-five acres from Pennsylvania Avenue south to Florida Avenue and from Fourth Street east to Maryland Drive.

Its principal connection to the University of Illinois in those early days was as a burial ground for U of I notables. Several university presidents are buried there and at adjacent Roselawn, including Edmund Janes James and David

FIGURE 9.8. Mount Hope-Roselawn Cemetery, on the southern edge of the U of I campus on the Urbana-Champaign city line, was established in 1856, eleven years before Illinois Industrial University, later the U of I, was chartered. Several campus plans show the cemetery paved over in buildings and roads. (Photo by Karyl Wackerlin.)

Kinley, as well as such distinguished faculty members as the naturalist Stephen Alfred Forbes and the agronomist Cyril Hopkins.

But, as the campus advanced inexorably southward, Mount Hope began to appear on the radar and the maps of university planners and as something more than a final resting place. Some viewed Mount Hope as an obstacle, a barrier, to future campus expansion. In a 1912 scheme, Clarence Blackall, the U of I's first campus planner, addressed the problem head-on by simply wiping the cemetery off the map. In place of the cemetery, Blackall's plan showed a semicircular landscaped area crisscrossed by pathways radiating from a monumental structure astride Pennsylvania Avenue. A decade later, Charles Platt, in his first campus plan for the university, also proposed eliminating the cemetery.

Supervising architect James White, the Christopher Wren of the U of I, agreed that the cemetery must go, and in the 1920s he set the wheels in motion to achieve that. In a letter dated January 14, 1924, White suggested to President David Kinley that the university purchase the cemetery and stop the selling of plots. "It is certain that if the sale of lots were discontinued," White explained, "a way would ultimately be found of abolishing the cemetery, though it might take fifty years to do it. By that time I think we will need that area for building purposes and therefore I hope we can make the start to acquire it at an early date."

White patiently laid in wait for an opportunity, and in 1930 the time arrived, thanks to the onset of the Depression. The owners of most of the unsold lots in Roselawn Cemetery—Mount Hope's former western section that had been purchased by an independent cemetery association in 1906—needed money and were willing to sell out to the university for $22,000. White jumped at the chance, the board of trustees approved, and, just like that, the U of I was in the cemetery business.

University officials soon discovered the cemetery business could be unpleasant. In March 1933, for instance, a decision had to be made whether to allow a burial in a plot whose title was in dispute. Provost Albert Harno wisely let the funeral go on, believing, not without reason, "that the University would be criticized if permission to proceed with the burial was not given."

The U of I's cemetery experiment proved to be mercifully short lived. James White died early in 1933—he was buried, ironically, in Mount Hope Cemetery—and his successor, Charles Havens, quickly set about reversing White's cemetery policy. Havens sympathized with White's desire to eliminate "the blockade on the southern expansion of the campus" but didn't think White's scheme to achieve this was practical. With approval from the board of trustees in 1936, Havens began selling off the university-owned lots in Roselawn. It took a long time—the Depression and World War II didn't help—but, finally, in 1947, the university sold the last of its Roselawn plots and was out of the cemetery business for good. Which is not to say that an occasional athletics administrator hasn't looked at the cemetery as a potential north-south pathway to new sports facilities south of Florida and east of Fourth Street.

A less-storied Catholic cemetery, St. Mary's, was established by Rev. Charles Berry. It runs north and south along the railroad just east of South Neil Street and along the western edge of what is now the University Research Park.

Gardens, Woods, and Water

Boneyard Creek

The narrow waterway that runs through Champaign-Urbana and Campustown has a storied past and a fully engineered present. Boneyard Creek (two streams that converge near Scott Park before heading into Campustown) drains an area some seven and a half miles in the two communities.

It eventually merges with other tributaries and feeds into the Wabash River. Fourteen hundred miles from Campustown, water from Boneyard Creek empties into the Gulf

FIGURE 9.9. Kids will be kids. In "Splash the Frosh," a University of Illinois freshman is thrown into Boneyard Creek as part of class rivalry activities. (Image ca. 1910-15. Photo courtesy of the University of Illinois Archives 0005190.)

of Mexico. The creek is visible on the earliest known photo of the campus.

A 1984 bicentennial history of Champaign County reports that the creek draws its name from the piles of bones white settlers found along its banks—near "an abundant spring"—when they moved into central Illinois in the early 1800s. They believed they had found the bones of animals killed by Indians near a favorite camping site along the stream. The white settlers called the stream the Bone Yard Branch and eventually it was known as Boneyard Creek.

Locals and early students swam in and fished the Boneyard, according to Winton Solberg's 1867-94 history of the University of Illinois. The stream's other early name, Silver Creek, never caught on, despite a public-relations push from

FIGURE 9.10. During the 1990s redevelopment of the South Engineering Quad, the murky Boneyard Creek was transformed into a meandering, graceful landscape element in the new space north of Green Street. The new Quad is named after John Bardeen, the U of I professor who won two Nobel Prizes, one for invention of the transistor, the second for solving the puzzle of superconductivity. (Photo by Karyl Wackerlin.)

the university's president, Andrew Draper (1894-1904). In 1893 *The Illini* mourned the (ultimately futile) attempt to formally change the waterway's name. "Our little brooklet is just as beautiful and prattles on just as gaily as if it were the best named brooklet in the world," read an introduction to a poem about the Boneyard's beauty. On the other hand, the *Daily Illini* sponsored a contest in 1918 to create the best "Boneyard Hymn of Hate." Students in the 1910s performed a "Boneyard Baptism" on freshmen, throwing them into the dirty, murky stream.

But the creek maintains some hold on popular culture in the region. There's a Boneyard Arts Festival and a student engineering group called the Boneyard Yacht Club, which formed to build concrete canoes.

The stone arch bridge near Springfield Avenue and Second Street was built in 1863. It carried the horse-car railway that linked the Champaign County Courthouse in downtown Urbana and the Illinois Central Depot in downtown Champaign. The Champaign Park District bought the partially collapsed bridge in the late 1970s, and volunteer union carpenters and bricklayers rebuilt it.

The clear-water creek's depth was first lowered in 1908, and an elaborate plan to improve its flood patterns and aesthetics came in 1949, followed by another ten years later. Legal jurisdiction over the skinny creek—which regularly overwhelmed its channel and repeatedly, extensively, and expensively flooded Campustown businesses and U of I engineering buildings and graduate housing—was complex and often contentious. The result: inertia.

Over decades, governmental agencies and entities wrangling over maintaining and/or fixing the Boneyard included the Saline Branch Drainage District, the Urbana and Champaign Sanitary District, the separate municipalities of Champaign and Urbana, the separate Champaign and Urbana park districts, the Illinois Department of Natural Resources, the U.S. Army Corps of Engineers, the Illinois Environmental Protection Agency, and the "third city," the University of Illinois. This does not include the courts or opposition groups, such as Citizens for Accountability on the Boneyard and Friends of Boneyard Creek.

While efforts to "fix" the Boneyard date to the 1920s, during the national bicentennial year of 1976 Champaign County regional planners chose the Boneyard as a bicentennial community-development project, first focusing on cleanup and beautification issues, then flooding and sanitation. The state Environmental Protection Agency pursued businesses and landowners for illegal storm-drain hookups, some containing raw sewage, dumping directly into the creek.

Finally, the two cities took full jurisdiction of the creek and, in time, two strong characters tackled the Boneyard. They were Champaign Mayor Dannel McCollum (1987-99) and U of I Chancellor Michael Aiken (1993-2001), both of whom aggressively employed their bully pulpits to motivate change and pry money from their respective institutions.

From 1988 to the present day, the two cities and the university committed to and are executing a thirty-year, $52 million series of Boneyard projects, including a fifty-five-foot deep detention basin near Locust and Healey Streets to hold water during major rains and release it gradually downstream; to widen, deepen, and cover the creek from First to Wright Streets; to create a pool of water directly north of Engineering Hall with a porch and overlook as part of the Bardeen Quad; to bury the creek underground in Scott Park, leaving room for overflow above ground, and more. The work is being done, in order, from downstream to upstream in phases. The Urbana portion runs north from Griggs Street to Broadway, where a local restaurateur built a cantilever deck to overlook the cities' only natural body of water. His business: Silvercreek Restaurant.

"It was the biggest single project in the history of the city," Champaign's McCollum said in a 2009 interview. "And there wouldn't be a single tall building on Green Street today if it had not happened."

Illini Grove, a.k.a. The Forestry

Located at the northwest corner of Lincoln and Pennsylvania Avenues, the Forestry—now called Illini Grove—dates almost to the beginning of the university. In 1868 a board of trustees committee called for the campus to establish a "forest plantation" to help test the kinds of trees best suited to Illinois growing conditions. With money the Illinois legislature appropriated in March 1869, the campus purchased several thousand forest tree seedlings, raised them in a nursery, and planted them outdoors in spring 1871.

The board of trustees believed the practical research done in the Forestry would be a boon to Illinois commerce if the timber—tried and tested and then planted across the

FIGURE 9.11. Illini Grove is at the corner of Lincoln and Pennsylvania on the east edge of campus in Urbana. Established in 1871 as a forestry-study area, it now is a campus recreation area with basketball, sand-court volleyball, tennis courts, and cookout and picnicking areas. (Photo by Karyl Wackerlin.)

state—were turned into manufactured products from fence posts to wagons and carriages, houses and railroad cars.

"To bring these useful trees within the bounds of culture and to utilize them, is one of the objects of this industrial institution," the board's Committee on Horticulture wrote in November 1868. "To teach the people of the State how to add these products of the forest to their other crops, and thus add millions of dollars annually to the wealth of the State, to give labor a wider range and a more comprehensive field for its employment, are objects worthy of such an institution."

This same report laid out plans not only for the Forestry but also for an expanded arboretum, a market garden, experimental orchards, and a vineyard. The entire project, including a barn and outbuildings, wagons and harnesses, plant stock, horses, a house for a superintendent and one for a gardener, would cost $22,000. By 1871 the nursery had

177,000 "young trees" for planting elsewhere on campus (including the Forestry) and an astonishing 2,319 apple trees of 1,180 varieties.

At its peak the Forestry contained thirty-seven different varieties of trees arranged in clusters, clumps, and rectangles of identical trees that filled eighteen acres. In its early days the grove was enclosed by a formidably high fence topped with barbed wire and secured by two gates. "They were locked promptly at 7 o'clock every evening, and all the children in the neighborhood, who loved to play under the pine trees, were mortally afraid of being locked in," a Champaign resident recalled.

The fence came down sometime after 1916 when the Forestry ceased being a timber experiment and became instead a "pleasure park" controlled by the campus's Department of Buildings and Grounds. It had become clear that Illinois was not a good candidate for commercial forests, and Professor Thomas J. Burrill (a botanist who twice was acting U of I president) had recommended the timber experiment be ended.

"Now the forest has served a very useful purpose aside from the timber experiment, a purpose not originally contemplated at all; namely a unique, phenomenally interesting, instructive, and enjoyable recreation equipment on the Campus," Burrill said. "The area in its present condition is certainly worth more for its direct interest and benefit than it would possibly have yielded in commercial timber."

By the time it was designated "Illini Grove" in 1950 and converted into a recreation ground and picnic area, the Forestry was about half its original size. The northern half of the grove had been carved up in the 1920s to make room for McKinley Hospital, now McKinley Health Center. Writing to the *Daily Illini* in 1923, a commerce student mourned the impending loss of so much living beauty:

> Trees!—I pause to weep. Are we
> to see them fell our forestry
> To make a place for piles of brick
> and stone?

Many of the trees—so carefully planted in rows—have died or been thinned out, giving the grove an informal look. At the 1950 land transfer from the Department of Forestry to the general university, the parcel also was considered a "land reserve as sites for future major construction."

Illini Grove is now managed by Campus Recreation and has basketball and sand volleyball courts, lighted tennis courts, a log pavilion, grills, and drinking fountains set into remainder trees (oak, hickory, and larch) from an earlier time. Only larches stand tall in a tidy block or stand along Lincoln Avenue like sentries over a forgotten experiment. Close by is a flood-control detention basin.

Since 1991 Illini Grove has been known formally (and rarely) as Seward Staley Illini Grove, named for Staley, longtime physical education/recreation professor and dean of what was at the time the School (College) of Physical Education (1937-61). He was instrumental in the transition from experimental forestry to recreational site.

In 2002 a bronze plaque was fixed to a limestone boulder at the outer edge of Illini Grove to honor Stanley B. Weaver and his late wife, Mary, for their efforts at preserving natural sites and his longtime service as an Illinois state senator. In May 2002 the Illinois General Assembly had passed a resolution honoring the couple and urging the U of I and the Illinois Department of Natural Resources to preserve Illini Grove forever. Weaver died in 2003.

Rock Garden and Lily Pond

Laid out in 1917, the rock garden and lily pond were major features in an ambitious landscape scheme designed to make the then-South Campus "the beauty spot of the University." The creation of floriculture professor Herman B. Dorner, the rock garden sprawled to the east of the Morrow Plots and was built to overcome an irregularity in the landscape. "The general effect of the garden," a *Daily Illini* writer explained in 1918, "is that of a tiny mountain cut in

FIGURE 9.12. The Rock Garden was created in 1917 and abandoned in 1951. This photo, looking northeast, was taken in the Rock Garden's glory years. In the background are the Observatory, the Auditorium, and Smith Memorial Music Hall. (Photo dated ca. 1925. Courtesy of the University of Illinois Archives 0003580.)

two by a meandering stream, which, incidentally, gets its source from an artistic fountain near the top of the hill." In its heyday in the 1920s and 1930s the rock garden was said to have been "the most popular spot on the campus for strollers and picture-takers" and even reportedly enjoyed "a statewide reputation" for its beauty.

As a *Daily Illini* columnist, Helene Foellinger (who much later underwrote a major renovation of the Auditorium)

FIGURE 9.13. Lily Pond in the Rock Garden. (Photo dated ca. 1930. Courtesy of the University of Illinois Archives 0003585.)

urged her fellow students to take their mothers to the rock garden. "Take our word for it—it's a beautiful place," Foellinger wrote.

Situated to the east of the rock garden, the bean-shaped lily pond also was a popular spot for sightseers. Every spring the pond was stocked with hundreds of goldfish that had spent the winter in a nearby greenhouse. The purpose of the fish was not merely to beautify the pond but to prevent the breeding of mosquitoes.

In 1951 Robert S. Chamberlin, chief of the Physical Plant Department, deemed the rock garden to be in a "deplorable condition" and suggested, among other alternatives, that it be eliminated and re-graded as a lawn area, and ultimately it was. The lily pond suffered a similar fate. Narrowly surviving extinction in 1954 thanks to a public "howl," four years later it was filled in and replaced by a lawn, leaving no trace.

Japan House and Arboretum

Japan House arose from the creative mind of U of I Professor Shozo Sato. An expert in the Japanese tea ceremony, Ikebana flower arranging, black-ink calligraphy, and Kabuki theater, Sato hoped to employ art to promote understanding between the East and the West. "I came to see art as the most honest voice of the people," Sato, a native of Osaka who came to the university in 1964, told a reporter. "I wanted to use it to introduce who Japan is."

For thousands of students and visitors each year, Japan House served as an introduction to the culture of Sato's home country. It opened in spring 1976 in a rambling Victorian home at 902 West California Street in Urbana, east of the Krannert Center for the Performing Arts, where Sato produced Kabuki-style Shakespeare and other theater. The house was remodeled to include several authentic Japanese rooms, and a Japanese garden was planted near the entrance. During class hours the rooms were crowded with students taking courses in woodblock printing, tea ceremony, Kabuki theater, and flower arranging.

By 1979 the old house was showing its age, with its foundations sagging and its roof beginning to leak. As a result, Sato and Roger E. Martin, an associate vice chancellor for academic affairs, spearheaded an early—but unsuccessful—effort to raise money for a new Japan House. The project languished for a decade, then received a major boost in 1989 with the completion of the central campus master plan by Sasaki and Associates. In their report the landscape

FIGURE 9.14. The Arboretum and Japan House are part of the College of Fine and Applied Arts. They are both a teaching facility and a space open to the public. Japan House grounds offer Zen gardens, tea ceremonies, and authentic tea rooms and architecture. (Photo by L. Brian Stauffer, University News Bureau.)

architects/planners argued that the house at 902 West California should be razed because its structure and its mechanical/electrical systems had deteriorated beyond repair.

In 1990 university officials began studying possible sites for a new Japan House, but it wasn't until the middle years of the decade that the project really got off the ground. In 1995 a site was selected in the new arboretum being developed south of the President's House, and a lightning fundraising campaign was launched. Within three years, donors contributed close to $650,000—the scheme's anticipated cost—including some $100,000 from members of the Japan Illini Club, an alumni organization.

Architecture Professor Emeritus Jack Baker—a longtime supporter of the project—and the Isaksen-Glerum architectural firm designed the new Japan House as an elegant structure demonstrating "the pure geometry of the rectangle." The

FIGURE 9.15. Aerial image from the northeast of the U of I's three round barns, which were built in 1907-13. The first one cost $3,200. (Image dated 1948. Photo courtesy of the University of Illinois Archives 0003570.)

home's interior—roughly two thousand square feet—boasts a traditional entrance hall, a teaching laboratory, a stage for performances, a kitchen, and formal, semi-formal, and informal rooms. Beautifully situated atop a slight rise and nestled beside a pond, the structure is surrounded by serene Japanese gardens.

On June 19, 1998, the new Japan House was dedicated. "It is an extraordinary idea that an elegant center of Japanese aesthetics should rise from the rich, black soil of a great Midwestern university," President James J. Stukel said at the dedication ceremony that day. "And it is a testament to our continuing commitment to the cultural life of this university, this state and this country."

The latest incarnation of the campus arboretum, including ponds and allées, fills about 160 acres east and south of the intersection of Lincoln and Florida Avenues and sprawls behind the President's House. From its earliest years, the campus laid down extensive gardens that were uprooted and moved successively southward, just as the campus itself moved south, decade after decade.

Starting in the late 1980s, several on- and off-campus units and interest groups created discrete gardens to delight casual visitors and serious gardeners. The Miles C. Hartley Selections Garden, made possible by an alumni gift and dedicated in 1994, led the way to full development of the campus arboretum. Other notable gardens include the Noel Welcome Garden, the Idea Garden (sponsored and maintained by Master Gardeners of Champaign County), and the American Hosta Society National Display Garden.

Agriculture

The Round Barns

Built between 1907 and 1913, the university's three round barns stand on a windswept ridge along St. Mary's Road on what is now the northernmost edge of the South Farms. Designed by dairyman Wilber Fraser and university supervising architect James M. White, the barns—the largest is seventy feet in diameter—were built as part of a twenty-acre demonstration dairy farm.

The agricultural purpose was to create a dairy operation that would produce the most milk per acre at the least cost. Since the barns were built at roughly two-year intervals, each succeeding barn benefitted from improvements in construction and design informed by practical use.

Fraser, university professor of dairy husbandry, was a driving force behind the concept of round barns. Fraser argued that round barns, in contrast with traditional rectangular ones, provided more interior space and were more wind-resistant and cheaper to build. Crucially, they also were stronger. Fraser compared the strength of a round barn to that of a barrel.

"A barrel, properly hooped and headed," he wrote, "is almost indestructible, and much stronger than a box." Round barns made dairy work easier because many cows could be stationed and fed around a central point.

The advocacy of Fraser and others led to proliferation of round barns across the Illinois countryside in the earliest decades of the twentieth century. By the 1920s, however, their popularity was fading, and the era of the round barn was effectively over.

In 1994 the U of I Experimental Dairy Farm Historic District, which includes the three round barns, was listed on the U.S. National Register of Historic Places, where Kell and Bernard also are given design credit.

Morrow Plots

Few cornfields have their own song. Few have caused giant elm trees to be felled. And few have made trustees, planners, and architects site and design multimillion dollar buildings to protect them. The Morrow Plots—a sacred mini-farm—is one.

FIGURE 9.16. Morrow Plots, established in 1876, were the first continuous experimental cornfields at an American college. The experimental plots are still planted today and were designated a National Historic Landmark in 1968. The Other Guys, a campus singing group, immortalized the plots in the witty and perennial audience favorite, "The Morrow Plots Song." (Photo by Karyl Wackerlin.)

The Morrow Plots—shrunk to a bare three-fifths of an acre just south of the Observatory—continue a series of cropping experiments begun in 1876 and claim to be "the first field experimental plots established by a college or university in the United States." The plots are remnants of the campus's much larger on-campus agriculture fields, a living laboratory to test long-term effects of different cropping systems. The Morrow Plots, named for George E. Morrow, the first dean of the College of Agriculture (1878-94), were five acres originally—ten plots, each one-half acre in size.

Professor Manly Miles, considered the first professor of agriculture in the United States (at what is now Michigan State University, founded in 1855), laid out the U of I plots in 1876, and it is that fact and that date—and that the plots have been planted continuously since—that make the Morrow Plots important. In 1903 and 1904 some plots were discontinued and the remaining ones reduced in both number and size.

But their purpose remained: test what happens to soil when corn is planted year after year, or rotated with oats and hay in defined patterns. As time passed and hybrids, pesticides, and commercial fertilizers entered the agricultural scene, the experiments at the Morrow Plots changed, too. (Soybeans were added in 1968.) Good records have been kept only since 1888; 1879 was the most commonly referenced starting date for the plots until the 1960s, when the campus made a believable case that the original plots can be traced back to 1876, thereby making them the first field experimental plots in the United States.

The plots were celebrated in 1968 when their historic landmark status was observed with a dedication ceremony that featured a representative of the U.S. Department of the Interior National Park Service, which grants historic status, and U.S. Rep. William L. Springer (R-Champaign), who represented the campus district in Congress from 1951 to 1973.

U of I President David Dodds Henry (1955–71) praised the meaning of the Morrow Plots at the 1968 ceremony. “The Congressman has reminded us that a hundred years ago agriculture was not a science,” he said. “It was an aggregate of folklore, rumor, and report. Not very many people were really sure of anything about agriculture and what many thought they were sure of was often not so. Out of that condition, because of the research activity represented by the Morrow Plots, came the agricultural science which has had a fantastic impact upon the world and which today is regarded as the salvation of the human race.”

The plots had competition from other universities. The nomination form for the National Register clarifies why the Morrow Plots merited inclusion:

> Although the University of Illinois was the first to establish field experiment plots in the United States, the knowledge gained there in the early years was not widely disseminated. No accurate records of crop yields were kept until after the establishment of the [U of I] Agricultural Experiment Station in 1888. By that time, many colleges had agricultural experiment stations or were conducting informal experiments of a similar kind. Agronomists at Pennsylvania State College were the first to perform field experiments with fertilizers in 1881. The Jordan Plots, however, were destroyed in 1958.
>
> At Sanborn Field, established at the University of Missouri in 1888, similar experiments in crop rotation and soil depletion were performed on a somewhat larger scale; Sanborn Field became a National Historic Landmark in 1965.
>
> Yet the investigations made at the University of Illinois loom large in early agricultural research, especially in the area of prairie soils. Most college texts in agronomy mention the experiments conducted there.

As revered as the plots are now—they are blessed in the spring on Rogation Day, when congregants and choir gather at the plots, and the only recorded vandalism, a twenty-five-foot crop circle carved into the corn, occurred late in the growing season in 2003—their standing was not always so assured.

In 1930 and again in 1940, agriculturalists raised concerns about a double row of elm trees west of the plots and the planned east-side boardwalk on the Quad extended south. The worry was the trees “would in time cause trouble” to the plots by pulling moisture and nutrients away from plant roots, “thus defeating the value of the plots for observation on crops growing under an ideal situation.”

A 1939 memo by Robert S. Chamberlin, the campus landscape chief, outlined this “possible menace” to the Morrow Plots. Interestingly, he suggests that since the Morrow Plots experiments already had been running some sixty years at that point, that the plots had already proved their worth and could be ended. “It would seem that records should certainly be complete enough at this time to make possible a graph of anticipated yields under all conditions,” he said. And, he wrote,

> If the plots are to be retained for predominantly sentimental reasons the use seems out of proportion to the value of the land in the campus plan.” He also said if the elm trees have to go, one line of them can remain on the west because their roots would not encroach into the plots for fifty years. He recommended the plots be enclosed by an evergreen hedge with some small flowering trees. “Not only would this hedge have a strong ornamental value, but it would also serve as a much more impressive enclosure than the existing fence.

This struggle to preserve a small grove of elms on the south campus is ironic; within two decades Dutch elm disease, which reached the United States in 1928 and Chicago in 1960, would wipe out significant portions of the campus landscape. But the Morrow Plots would keep on growing in their tidy, enclosed space, wrapped by hedges and one small gate.

A few decades later, as the opening cohorts of the baby boom surged through the campus, the new Undergraduate Library was built underground, just west of the Morrow Plots and east of the Main Library. Now, it is true that subterranean buildings were popular at the time. And it is also true that going underground permitted an open plaza on top that would not rival the monumental Main Library and would respect the open mall effect of the South Campus. But the 1969 Undergrad—when built underground—also "would not throw shade on the corn."

That line comes from "The Morrow Plots Song," whose lyrics were written in 1971 by a graduate student, Bruce Johnson, for The Other Guys, an a cappella octet of the campus Varsity Men's Glee Club. The tune, Johnson told the *News-Gazette* in a 2009 interview, "was patched together" from other musical numbers, including the Illinois state song and various drinking songs. The song is a crowd favorite and traditionally closes performances of The Other Guys.

Here are two verses of "The Morrow Plots Song," with the chorus in the middle:

> "Well, old Stratford has its bard and old Harvard has its yard
> And Annapolis has midshipmen who tie knots.
> But whatever you compare, there is nothing quite so fair
> As our genuine, number one, homegrown Morrow Plots."
>
> Oh, you can't throw shade on the corn.
> It'll die as sure as you're born.
> No sir, we don't mess around, our library's underground
> Cause you can't throw shade on the corn.
>
> Pasadena's got its roses and the Bible's got old Moses
> And at Michigan they're the champions of the west.
> San Francisco's got its quakes, Minnesota's got its lakes.
> But the Morrow Plots at Illinois are best.

In 1998 the design of yet another building—a red-brick and limestone combined fire station and parking structure—was substantially revised at the urging of crop scientists worried the planned five-level building would have a negative impact on the ongoing experimental work at the Morrow Plots.

According to a report in the November 16, 1998, *News-Gazette*, researchers from four campus departments told officials the building as proposed in 1997 would shade the plots, causing unequal growth; that night lighting would affect growth patterns at the plots; and that the sheer size of the building would generate heat and change air flow on the eastern side of the plots.

The result: reduce the parking structure to four levels and sink the lowest level about five feet below grade, reducing the whole structure by about twenty vertical feet and the number of parking spaces to eight hundred from the eleven hundred originally planned. This new $13.5 million structure was located due west of the Morrow Plots; its lights point downward to protect not only the plots but users of the Observatory worried about light pollution.

Fields and Arenas

Illinois Field

Illini legend George A. Huff, known as "G," peered more than a half-century into the future when he hoped aloud in 1931 that Illinois Field would stay tucked into the northeast corner of University Avenue and Wright Street rather than be moved "while I'm still around here."

Huff died in 1936. But the move south for the baseball portion of Illinois Field—the football field and track were taken out in 1923 and moved to the brand-new Memorial Stadium—didn't happen until the season opener in 1988, and then to a site much farther south and east than proposed some fifty-seven years earlier.

FIGURE 9.17. Illinois Field, where Illini played football, baseball, and track and field, viewed from Drill Hall with the Old Mechanical Building and the Old Armory in the foreground. (Image dated ca. 1892. Courtesy of the University of Illinois Archives 0003584.)

Huff, a chunky third baseman who joined the varsity in 1889, and was Illini football coach (1895-99), baseball coach (1896-1919), and athletic director (1901-35), opposed relocating Illinois Field to the area bounded by First Street, Armory Avenue, Stadium Boulevard, and the railroad tracks just east of Neil Street. That site had been suggested by campus architect James M. White in a study he sent to President David Kinley (1919-30) in late 1921. The construction of both Huff Gymnasium in 1926 (then called the Men's New Gymnasium) and Memorial Stadium (1924) signaled the inexorable—but sluggish—movement south of facilities for intercollegiate athletics.

"The sentiment connected with Illinois Field has tended to hold it in its present location," White said. "But it is certain that when the present wooden bleachers have to be rebuilt, they will not be reconstructed in that location." Sentiment, inertia, and lack of money kept Illinois Field in place, improved, and wrapped in a wonderful iron fence for two more generations.

Illini baseball, as all other U of I intervarsity sports of the 1880s and 1890s, was under the control of the student-managed Athletic Association, which merged the Baseball Association and the Football Association. The earliest games, often pitting teams from civic clubs and nearby colleges, were played at the Champaign County Fairgrounds until the May 15, 1891, contest at the new field, called Athletic Park at the time. The Illini beat Wabash College, 14-10, to cap the ninth annual Field Day, which featured band music, pole vaults, jumps and dashes, three-legged races, and interclass tugs of war from 9:30 A.M. to when the first pitch was thrown at 4 P.M.

President Kinley, who joined the U of I as a faculty member in 1893, later described what he saw his first autumn on campus. "The seating capacity of bleachers located on the north field, I would estimate, ranged from 300 to 500 spectators. The seats rose only about 6 or 8 feet and stretched along the side of the football field. There was a high, wooden fence which ran and east and west across Illinois Field just north of the tree which still stands virtually in the center of the grounds."

By 1897 the student-controlled Illinois Field was both unkempt and considered too small. President Andrew S. Draper (1894-1904) urged the board of trustees to authorize $2,500 to fix this "unsatisfactory situation." They took no action. Then, on June 8, 1898, the faculty members of a group that advised the board on athletics petitioned the board for $4,500 for grading and draining the grounds and to install an ornamental iron fence, a grandstand to seat five hundred, and a new, longer track. Instead, the trustees appropriated $3,000. Within a year Stewart Iron Works of Cincinnati was contracted to build and install a seven-foot-high iron fence with two double gates, each twelve-feet wide—big enough to accommodate carriages, the transportation of the day. The cost was $2,500.

Drainage and a new one-third-mile track, costing $1,000 total, were approved the next year; in 1901 the ball diamond was improved and the fence extended. And so it went . . . year after year: re-grading, re-draining, fence fixing, and building more grandstands, concessions, toilets, and storage.

In 1937 a "new" Illinois Field was shown high on a composite list of proposed new buildings, land purchases, roads, and remodeling and additions to existing buildings planned for the next fourteen years, from July 1, 1937, to June 30, 1951. By then, Illinois Field was for baseball only and its size diminished; when it was a three-sport playing area, it ran north-south from University Avenue to the back end of what is now Kenney Gym on Springfield Avenue, nearly four city blocks. Its east boundary was Burrill Avenue, which was flanked by a neighborhood of two- and two-and-a-half-story houses. (Today this is in the heart of the north engineering campus.)

F. Way Woody, a footballer in 1892, 1893, and 1894, student manager in 1895, and coach until 1916, recalled those earliest days in a 1937 interview.

> All athletic events were held on Illinois Field then enclosed by a wooden fence. The Field had a grandstand with 300 seating capacity. I never saw over a six "riser" while I was at Illinois. Most were four-high. In 1895 the notable year we played Purdue at Lafayette, the bleachers towered to 12 rows. . . .
>
> Students planned and built the Illinois grandstand, bleachers, cinder track, without any subsidy I ever heard of.
>
> The football field, to insure against aggression by the spectators, was surrounded by a barbed wire fence.
>
> Locker room space was in the southeast corner of the old Drill Hall [now Kenney Gym Annex]. No baths were to be had except in wooden wash tubs in which we stood while Slyvanus Anderson, a tall colored boy, dipped a sponge in

> the ice cold water and squeezed same over our perspiring bodies. A large zinc shower was installed in the corner for the fall of 1893. Yes, and we almost had hot water.
>
> The Athletic Association furnished football players with moleskin pants, canvas jackets, sweaters and stockings, but afforded no shoes, shin or shoulder guards, or helmets.

In 1941 the Athletic Association said it intended to turn the nine-hole golf course south of Florida Avenue near Fourth Street into a baseball park and general recreation fields and return Illinois Field for general university use. The board of trustees accepted the offer. And everyone waited. This time, more than four decades.

In the mid-1980s, alumnus Lou Proano pledged $1.5 million as the lead gift to build a new Illini baseball stadium south of Florida Avenue and east of Fourth Street. Venerable Illinois Field, built on the site of the U of I's very first building on University Avenue, was displaced after ninety-five years to make way for the $50 million Beckman Institute for Advanced Science and Technology.

The Fighting Illini baseball team compiled an 852-334-10 (.717) record at old Illinois Field from 1891 to 1986, with only three losing seasons: 1924, 1964, and 1979. The Illini recorded a scorching .879 from 1900 to 1909, followed by .833 from 1910 to 1919.

The football team went 114-38-7 at Illinois Field before the gridders moved to the new Memorial Stadium for one game in 1923, followed by a full season in 1924, memorialized by Harold "Red" Grange's spectacular dedication-game performance.

The Fighting Illini baseball team played the 1987 home season on a field owned by the Urbana Park District, while awaiting the new Proano Field on the old golf course. In the meantime, Lou Proano hit a financial rough patch and lost his naming right. So the new ballpark is called . . . Illinois Field.

The Fighting Illini beat Western Illinois University, 11-10, in the first game played at the new Illinois Field on March 24, 1988. The field has permanent seating for fifteen hundred and lawn seating for an additional thousand. Its outfield fence is wooden.

The ballpark cost $1.32 million at original construction. Since 2008 the surface is artificial FieldTurf covering the infield but not the pitching mound; the turf can drain up to seven inches of rain per hour.

Coach Dan Hartleb (2006–), who led the 2015 Illini baseball team to a record-setting 50-10-1 season, 21-1-0 in the Big Ten, pledged to be instrumental in raising private money to expand permanent seating at Illinois Field, among other improvements.

State Farm Center, née Assembly Hall

Campus officials had long envisioned a single building that could house musical performances, sold-out basketball games, and live theater. As far back as 1939—nearly two decades before the Assembly Hall moved to the drawing board—Athletics Director Wendell Wilson and Charles S. Havens, the powerful director of the physical plant, explored alternatives to George Huff Gymnasium, which seated only forty-five hundred spectators.

A national search for an architect for an "auditorium-gymnasium multi-purpose building" in 1956-57 attracted Harrison & Abramovitz of New York City. The goal: a multi-purpose facility seating eighteen thousand to twenty thousand. Max Abramovitz, a 1929 U of I architecture grad, also designed the near-campus Hillel Center (replaced in 2008) and the Krannert Center for the Performing Arts at the U of I, the United Nations headquarters and Avery Fisher Hall (Lincoln Center) in New York City, and many midtown Manhattan skyscrapers.

The U of I Music Department, as early as 1957, had petitioned the campus to remove "auditorium" from the building's description unless sufficient acoustic capabilities were installed. In response, the construction team hired acoustical engineers Bolt, Beranek & Newman Inc. (now BBN

FIGURE 9.18. The State Farm Center, formerly Assembly Hall, opened in 1963. It is the court for Fighting Illini men's and women's basketball and is also a venue for performance and events, from concerts to commencement, Broadway to monster trucks. A $169.5 million renovation began in 2014 and finished in fall 2016. (Photo by L. Brian Stauffer, University News Bureau)

Technologies of Cambridge, Massachusetts) and installed a synchronous winch system conceived by theater design and technology pioneer George C. Izenour to raise and lower scenery for theater productions.

During construction from May 25, 1959, to March 3, 1963, the public described the building as "a flying saucer," "a giant mushroom," and "an inverted soup bowl." The arena was a four-hundred-foot diameter, 128-foot-tall concrete dome sunk thirty feet into the ground on a thirty-nine-acre site immediately south of Memorial Stadium. The structure is supported not by interior pillars but by an underground tension ring consisting of 614 miles of steel wire.

The university hired a local general contractor, Felmley-Dickerson Company, for about $6.5 million; the total project eventually reached $8 million. Two series of revenue bonds and fees assessed on twenty-five thousand students (student enrollment in 2016 was 44,800) paid for the project; student fees (as well as ticket revenue) continue to pay for building upkeep and events. Construction started May 25, 1959, and—after weathering labor strikes and steel shortages—finished May 3, 1963.

The *News-Gazette*'s Tom Kacich celebrated the fiftieth anniversary of the start of construction in a column in 2009, noting that the local chapter of the American Association of University Professors had predicted the saucer would "stand as some outmoded concept of university life" and that the money spent building it would be better spent on an intramural physical facility and a midsized auditorium for cultural offerings.

The unsupported lip-to-lip bowl design of the Assembly Hall scared some people, but 39,317 visitors filed through the hall during an open house, March 2, 1963. The Illini men's basketball team played its first game in the hall March 4, 1963, beating Northwestern 79-73. (The women's squad didn't play there until 1981, when they vacated the friendlier confines of Huff Hall.)

The Assembly Hall's multipurpose character lends itself to basketball, monster truck shows, the circus, touring Broadway troupes, ice shows, rock and country music performances, home and garden shows—more than one hundred events each year. Its distinctive form is largely unchanged and, with the Quad and the *Alma Mater*, is among the most photographed and well known of campus landmarks.

The Division of Intercollegiate Athletics, which took over managing the Assembly Hall in 2008 from Student Affairs, in 2008-09 explored renovating or replacing the Assembly Hall as a basketball venue. But campus and university leadership was disinclined to even consider razing this icon; Landmarks Illinois, an advocacy group that supports historic preservation, in 2008 put the Assembly Hall on its annual list of the state's most endangered historic places.

A new athletic director, Mike Thomas (2011), moved renovation front and center on the facilities agenda and, at the end of the 2013-14 basketball season, the campus launched a complete gut and rebuild of the interior, adding long-needed air conditioning, a major entrance on the east side, suites and boxes, and pushing out the angle of the windows in the lower bowl to create additional concourse floor space. The suites buildout into the concourses blocks the ability to walk the entire interior circumference of the building. Final touches were added before the 2016-17 basketball season tipped off in November 2016.

Financing for the $170 million project ($250+ million with interest over thirty years) comes from naming rights sold to State Farm Insurance Company ($1.5 million per year for naming and $500,000 per year for sponsorship rights for thirty years for a total of $60 million), an array of private gifts for everything from the west horseshoe drive to restricted hospitality rooms, from the coaches locker room to a premium seating area and a Hall of Fame venue; and $50 per year additional mandatory student fee, which will generate about 17 percent of the cost. Architect is AECOMM, headquartered in Los Angeles.

Sculpture, Structures, and Chimes

The *Alma Mater*

Famous Chicago sculptor Lorado Taft, class of 1879, longed to honor his alma mater, the University of Illinois. As early as 1883 he had fashioned a relief model that was an early prototype of what would become his *Alma Mater*.

Taft never let go: he once called his dream "a vision or hallucination which greets me whenever I approach that

FIGURE 9.19. The bronze *Alma Mater* by prominent sculptor and U of I alumnus Lorado Taft welcomes all to the University of Illinois and is the last stop for photos with graduating students in their caps and gowns. For two years ending in April 2014, *Alma Mater* was extensively restored to her 1920s sheen and integrity by a Forest Park, Illinois, conservator. (Photograph by Larry Kanfer, www.kanfer.com.)

auditorium." In 1916, encouraged by Wall Street broker Roland Conklin, class of 1891, he began work on the *Alma Mater* in earnest.

"I warn you that I do not wish to make any dwarf Alma Mater," the sculptor cautioned Conklin. "It must stand at least twelve feet high."

In June 1922, as the university celebrated its fiftieth commencement, Taft unveiled for exhibit on the Auditorium steps a plaster cast of the *Alma Mater*. The statuary group featured three heroic figures, each about fifteen feet high. The stately woman "Alma Mater"—Taft's depiction of the Greek goddess Athena—dominated the trio, standing in front of a massive throne, her arms outstretched in welcome to students and alumni. Behind her and on either side of the throne were her two children clasping hands: "Learning," shown as the Greek god of wisdom Apollo, on the right, and "Labor," represented as a "young mechanic with an eager intelligent appearance."

Five thousand alumni from the classes of 1923 through 1929 and others contributed to a fund to have the figures cast in bronze. Taft was there on the hot and windy commencement day of June 11, 1929, when the completed *Alma Mater* was dedicated. Total cost was about $25,000, including the casting, granite base, lettering, landscaping, freight, and the like. "I have always had a desire to personify the college which is so dear to my boyhood," Taft confessed in a 1929 letter. "All through life I have retained a romantic love for my Alma Mater and have long been dreaming of this group."

For decades *Alma Mater* was located about twenty feet south of the 1907 Auditorium, whose rear was truncated during its construction for lack of funds. In 1938 an alumnus wrote President Arthur Cutts Willard (1934-46) that the *Alma Mater* would better "perpetuate the spirit of the Illini by being out in the open where all can see and pass under its uplift of arms." Over the years criticisms of the *Alma Mater*'s location hidden behind the Auditorium continued. Finally, in 1962 it was moved to its present site west of the Illini Union, diagonal to the intersection of Green and Wright Streets.

Today, the campus icon is wrapped in basketball jerseys, Illini caps, a gigantic graduation gown, and garlands in periodic celebration. In the Vietnam War era, silent protests were held weekly at her feet, led by the local Quaker community. Graduating students, clad in caps and gowns, and their families line up for photos on and around *Alma Mater*.

The inscriptions read:

(Front)

Alma Mater
To Thy Happy Children of the Future
Those of the Past Send Greetings

(Left/donors)

Given to the University
By the Sculptor
The Alumni Fund
and the Senior Classes of
1923-1924-1925-1926
1927-1928-1929

(Right)

Her Children Arise Up
And Call Her Blessed

On the back of the chair is the seal of the State of Illinois; on the breast of the Alma Mater figure is the simple U of I emblem.

"Alma," as the grouping is called colloquially (she has her own Twitter handle), left campus for two years beginning August 7, 2012, for a major makeover at the hands of Forest Park conservator Andrzej Dajnowski, who took the five-ton sculpture apart, cleaned and repaired her at the Conservation of Sculpture and Objects Studio. The one thousand bolts holding her forty-eight sections together were replaced, and her familiar blue-green patina was taken off with lasers. She now shines with a bronze glow. Private money was used for the renovation: $360,000.

Hallene Gateway

The 1871 portal, an elaborate, carved sandstone entryway from University Hall that was demolished in 1938 to make way for the Illini Union, laid shamefully buried—broken and forgotten—at historic Robert Allerton Park for some three decades.

In the early 1990s, serendipity met desire for a new gateway park or plaza to welcome visitors to the campus, near Illinois Street and Lincoln Avenue, then as now delineated by planners as the campus's easternmost boundary.

FIGURE 9.20. The Hallene Gateway with the university motto, "Learning & Labor." The portal was a design element of University Hall razed to make room for the Illini Union. (Photo by L. Brian Stauffer, University News Bureau.)

Alumni couple Phyllis and Alan Hallene, class of 1951, had already committed to a $1 million gift for a new, as yet undesigned, gateway—a grand entrance to the campus—when U of I architecture professor William Youngman in 1994 casually told campus preservationist David Garner that he had seen tops of columns peeking from the ground near maintenance sheds at Allerton.

Garner found ninety percent of the portal, half-buried and in pieces among a stand of trees, thickets, and raspberry bushes; when he spied an "L" and an "E" from the original "Learning & Labor" inscription on the lintel—the horizontal top portion of the 1871 entryway, also called an "entablature"—he knew he had "hit pay dirt," as he told a local reporter in 1998. "My eyes got really big, and I said, 'This is really good,'" Garner said.

The neoclassical portal was a double set of matched, fifteen-foot Corinthian columns carved of sandstone and linked at the top, where the 1868 motto, "Learning & Labor" was carved. The entire portal had surrounded the Quad entrance to University Hall, also called New Main Hall or the New University Building when it was built in 1871 to replace the old seminary building on University Avenue. John M. Van Osdel, who practiced primarily in Chicago, was the architect; much of his work was done before the Great Fire in 1871, and little remained. He died in 1891 and was an early trustee of the Illinois Industrial University.

A four-verse/stanza ode, "Learning and Labor," was written for the 1873 dedication, which set front and center the university's second motto from 1868. (The first motto was "Onward and Upward.") The fourth verse reads:

> Then to labor and to learning
> Let us consecrate these halls:
> Lo! they come as God's strong angels
> Bringing light and breaking thralls;
> Kindling in us hopes supernal
> Of a glorious coming time,
> When the love and might eternal
> Shall work out God's will sublime.

When University Hall was razed after sixty-five years, several of its architectural elements, including the portal, were salvaged; the portal was stored behind the main Architecture Building and then, lost in memory, was moved about twenty-five miles west to the Allerton properties, where it languished until Youngman stumbled upon it.

It is a story of good intentions gone south. Correspondence between 1945 and 1964 involving the Physical Plant, two deans of fine arts, the Architecture Department, campus planners, and the proposed Education Building shows a gradually changing environment, gentle conflict, and growing disinterest in the portal.

"It is very much our hope therefore to preserve this doorway as a significant architectural fragment and probably the largest item in an outdoor museum to be created in the court yard," wrote FAA Dean Rexford Newcomb to Charles Havens in summer 1945.

"The present arrangement of this material is somewhat of an eyesore, and I believe that if we are to keep it, we should make some arrangement to make it presentable and useful," wrote Charles S. Havens to the dean of the College of Fine and Applied Arts in summer 1945.

The University Hall fragments at one time—maybe—were to be incorporated into the commerce quadrangle or an outdoor museum near the Architecture Building. From 1938 on, they were stored west of the north wing of the Architecture Building along with fragments from Chicago buildings by famed architect Louis Sullivan.

But, wrote Robert Chamberlin, in 1963 the director of the Division of Campus Development, he learned from an architecture professor that "these pieces were never contemplated for use in the proposed 'sculpture garden' west of Krannert Museum and north of the Fine Arts Building." Writing a memo for the record, Chamberlin said the fragments had to be removed, that Havens pledged money to move them to Allerton. "If the fragments need to be moved in the near future, an effort should be made to store them at Allerton Park pending action for their ultimate disposition." Landscape and architecture faculty believed the style and scale of the portal would fit in the Allerton properties better than on campus. So the salvaged portal pieces were trucked to Monticello, probably in spring 1964, and set on wood supports that, over the years, rotted away, setting the stage for the Youngman-Garner discovery thirty years later.

Garner viewed the buried wreckage as found history. The Hallenes were not so sure when they saw the pieces, dirty and incomplete at a campus warehouse. But it was, Alan Hallene said, an act of faith to restore the past. "I would call it a gift from God," he said. "It was something that was destined. Now it's really got the meaning it deserved."

The bits and pieces were cleaned and restored, missing parts were built, and the entire portal was mounted on an open framework wall of red Illinois brick. Prairie grasses, flowers, and bushes now soften the landmark, which is set on a diagonal to the southwest intersection of Illinois and Lincoln. An illuminated fountain splashes and bubbles on

FIGURE 9.21. The Eternal Flame, located between Lincoln Hall and the English Building, was built of Bedford, Indiana, limestone. University legend has it that lovers who kiss beneath the torch's flame will stay together forever. (Photo by Karyl Wackerlin.)

the north side of the nearby Alice Campbell Alumni Center. Curved sidewalks take visitors both through and around the gateway to the north entrance of the alumni center. Nearby are the Spurlock Museum and the Admissions and Records Building, and the east side of the massive Krannert Center for the Performing Arts is visible.

The University Foundation reports that three generations of the Hallene family have attended the U of I, including Mrs. Hallene's parents, Olin and Hazel Welsh. Alan Hallene, a member of the Marching Illini and Acacia, graduated with a bachelor's degree in mechanical engineering and was a Bronze Tablet scholar and salutatorian. He was a longtime president of Montgomery Elevator Company; Phyllis graduated from LAS. Before the Hallene Gateway gift the couple had donated more than $750,000 to campus academic programs, including an endowment for the University Library that made possible creation, rather than purchase, of its ten-millionth volume. The couple was named joint recipients of the Alumni Association's Distinguished Service Award in 2000.

Alan Hallene died in 2004.

The Eternal Flame

Located just northeast of Lincoln Hall, the Quad Bench and Light—also popularly known as the "Eternal Flame" since the early 2000s—was presented to the university by the class of 1912. It cost about $800, roughly $17,000 in today's currency.

The monument consists of a semi-circular bench and a Grecian column, both carved of Indiana Bedford limestone, and was designed by the architecture student Max Alfred Montgomery, class of 1912. The column bears the legend "Class of 1912" and is topped by a glass globe containing an electric light, originally a gas light.

Since at least the 1920s the monument has been described as a "lovers' bench," and campus legend holds that those couples who kiss under its "eternal flame" will remain in love forever.

Altgeld Hall Chimes

H. P. "Pete" Daugherty, class of 1914, is credited as the father of the campus chimes. As a *Daily Illini* editor in spring 1914, Daugherty called on his fellow seniors to inaugurate a "chimes fund."

Hazen S. Capron, cashier of Champaign's First National Bank, made this pie-in-the-sky notion workable by suggesting that all senior classes from 1914 until 1921 contribute $1,000 each to the fund. If the targets were met, Capron said that a set of chimes costing about $10,000 could be installed as early as 1919. "There is nothing that could be heard upon the campus of Illinois which would appeal to the sentiments of the citizens of the state as would 'Illinois Loyalty' rung out on the bells of the chimes," Capron said.

War and rising prices hampered early fundraising efforts, but led by Victor Cullin, class of 1920, the Senior Memorial Committee helped push the chimes fund well past the $10,000 goal by spring 1920. With this money, fifteen bells—composed of 79 percent copper and 21 percent tin—were purchased from the McShane Bell Foundry of Baltimore. The smallest weighed 560 pounds and the largest, three thousand. This last bell was inscribed to honor former President Edmund Janes James (1904-20), "an inspiring leader, an educational statesman."

In fall 1920 the chimes were installed in the tower of the Library (now Altgeld Hall) but it was hoped they eventually would be moved to a "great Campanile" that was planned for the south campus. On October 30, 1920, the chimes were dedicated and the ceremony concluded with the playing of "Illinois Loyalty." "It was a beautiful and inspiring experience when the bells pealed out from the old tower," Dean of Men Thomas Arkle Clark wrote. "Many a one who had listened had a mist before his eyes and felt a choking in his throat. To the young there was the vision of the future and what it holds, and to the old there was the recollection of the past and of the thousands who have gone before."

FIGURE 9.22. University President Edmund J. James next to the Altgeld chimes outside the then-Library before their dedication on Homecoming Weekend, October 30, 1920. (Photo dated ca. October, 1920. University Archives 0002706.)

Not to be outdone, the class of 1922 provided the clock mechanism that strikes the hours in the familiar four-note Westminster chimes melody. To this day, the Altgeld bells are manually rung by manipulating a series of wooden levers; the levers connect to sixty-foot cables through the ceiling of the tower room to pulleys that move clappers that strike the bells. Sue Wood took over as chimes master in 1995, replacing Albert Marien, chimes master for thirty-seven years, but she has been playing the bells since 1971.

A 1990s plan to install additional bells in the Altgeld tower was abandoned in favor of building a new electronically automated bell tower—a campanile—on the south campus. The 185-foot tower is, in part, a gift of Richard McFarland in honor of his late wife, Sally.

Today, a new bell dedicated to chimes master Marien is displayed near the security gates of the Willard Airport terminal.

Diana Fountain

Created by Swedish sculptor Carl Milles, the fifteen-foot-tall Diana Fountain of weathered bronze and marble decorates the west-side plaza entrance of the Illini Union. The verdigris sculpture depicts Diana, the Greek goddess of the hunt, holding a bow and surveying her surroundings from a complex base.

Milles's friends and well-known Chicago architects John Holabird and John Root commissioned the sculptor in 1928 to create the fountain for the Michigan Square Building in Chicago, later the Time-Life Building. The first of three sculptures Milles would create for Holabird and Root, the Diana Fountain was unveiled in its downtown Chicago home November 6, 1930. It remained there, surrounded by shops in an indoor courtyard, until the Time-Life Corporation, which owned the building, decided to move; the building was to be razed.

Samuel A. Lichtmann, an architect and 1921 graduate, heard about the building's planned sale in 1966 and approached Time-Life about donating the fountain to the university. A fellow 1921 graduate and university trustee (1949-67), Frances Best Watkins, called Lichtmann "the right man in the right place at the right time" for his work in securing the donation of the fountain to the university in time for the class's fifty-year reunion.

Members of the class of 1921 raised $50,000 to transport and re-install the fountain, which was valued at $250,000 in 1971. The Diana Fountain was dedicated in her new location October 23, 1971, her first outside living space since she was cast forty years earlier.

Although campus physical plant officials worried about vandalism and maintenance of the fountain, when it was "turned on during the long summer months," wrote Illinois art historian Muriel Scheinman, it gave "a sensation of coolness to the Illini Union's patio."

Milles also created and cast the monumental *Sun Singer* for the Robert Allerton estate near Monticello, which was donated to the university in 1946. Like the Diana Fountain, it was based on an earlier version of a mythical figure, in this case Apollo. Milles lived in the United States for two decades beginning in 1931.

FIGURE 9.23. *The Diana Fountain*, a 1930 bronze by Swedish sculptor Carl Milles, is on a plaza just west of the Illini Union. It was a gift of the class of 1921 that raised $50,000 to bring it to campus in 1971 from Chicago, where it had stood for four decades on Michigan Avenue. Time Incorporated donated the fountain sculpture of the nude female with a bow in her left hand and a startled look on her face. (Photo by Karyl Wackerlin.)

Sources

Chapter 1

Baker, Willis C., and Patricia L. Miller. *A Commemorative History of Champaign County, Illinois: 1833-1983*. Champaign: Illinois Heritage Association, 1984.

Bane, Juliet Lita. *The Story of Isabel Bevier*. Peoria, Ill.: Bennett, 1955. Full text available at https://archive.org/details/storyofisabelbev00bane.

Chapman, M. Perry. *American Places: In Search of the Twenty-First Century Campus*. Westport, Conn.: Praeger, 2006.

Deno, William R. *Body and Soul: Architectural Style at the University of Colorado at Boulder*. Boulder: Publications Service, University of Colorado, 1994.

"ECE Illinois." The Building Campaign for ECE Illinois. Available at www.buildingcampaign.ece.illinois.edu/project-details.

Illinois State Geological Survey. *Guide Leaflet (1958 and 1977-B and 1977-D) Geological Science Field Trip, Champaign-Urbana Area*. Illinois State Geological Survey, 1958, 1977.

Joncas, Richard, David J. Neuman, and Paul V. Turner. *The Campus Guide: Stanford University*. 2nd edition. New York: Princeton Architectural, 2006.

Lewis, Roger K. "Bricks, Mortar, and Vision: A Guide for Campus Planning." *Chronicle of Higher Education* 50, no. 29 (March 26, 2004): B20–B22.

National Center for Supercomputing Applications (NCSA). "About Blue Waters." Available at http://www.ncsa.illinois.edu/enabling/bluewaters.

——. "National Petascale Computing Facility." Available at http://www.ncsa.illinois.edu/about/facilities/npcf.

Scott, John Beldon, and Rodney P. Lehnertz. *The University of Iowa Guide to Campus Architecture*. Iowa City: University of Iowa Press, 2006.

University of Illinois Alumni Association. "Fortnightly News." January 1, 1914.

Wiggers, Raymond. *Geology Underfoot in Illinois*. Missoula, Mont.: Mountain, 1997.

Chapter 2

Board of Trustees of the University of Illinois. *Minutes of the Proceedings*. January 30, 1906.

——. *Reports*. September 8, 1903, 215.

Brichford, Maynard. *Bob Zuppke: The Life and Football Legacy of the Illinois Football Coach*. Jefferson, N.C.: McFarland, 2008.

Champaign News, September 28, 1905.

Daily Illini, November 11, 1909; May 26 and November 14, 1911; January 20, February 29, and December 10, 1912; March 19, 1914.

Ebert, Roger, ed. *An Illini Century*. Urbana: University of Illinois Press, 1967.

Hoffmann, John. *Lincoln Hall at the University of Illinois*. Urbana: University of Illinois Press, 2010.

The Illini, February 4, 1898.

James, Edmund J. *Sixteen Years at the University of Illinois*. Urbana: University of Illinois Press, 1920.

Kruty, Paul. "Nathan Clifford Ricker: Establishing Architecture at the University of Illinois." In *No Boundaries: University of Illinois Vignettes*, edited by Lillian Hoddeson, 3-14. Urbana: University of Illinois Press, 2004.

Moore, Charles. *Daniel Burnham: Architect, Planner of Cities*. Vol. 2. Boston: Houghton Mifflin, 1921.

Nevins, Allan. *Illinois*. New York: Oxford University Press, 1917.

Novak, Alice Edwards. "Reports on Campus Plans." Unpublished manuscript, 2007-2010.

"President James Offers His Resignation." *Alumni Quarterly and Fortnightly Notes of the University of Illinois* 4, no. 1 (October 1, 1918): 1.

Ricker, Nathan Clifford. "A Story of a Life." Unpublished manuscript, 1922. Architecture Department Subject File. University of Illinois Archives, Urbana-Champaign.

Roth, Leland. *A Concise History of American Architecture*. New York: Harper and Row, 1979.

Scott, Frank William, ed. *The Semi-Centennial Alumni Record of the University of Illinois*. Chicago: Lakeside, 1918.

Solberg, Winton U. *The University of Illinois 1867-1894*. Urbana: University of Illinois Press, 1968.

——. *The University of Illinois, 1894-1904*. Urbana: University of Illinois Press, 2000.

Stephens, Carl. *Illini Years: A Picture History*. Urbana: University of Illinois Press, 1950.

Tate, Lex. "UI History 101." *Illinois Alumni* (March/April 1999): 14-17.

Tilton, Leon Deming, and Thomas Edward O'Donnell. *History of the Growth and Development of the Campus of the University of Illinois*. Urbana: University of Illinois Press, 1930.

Urbana Daily Courier, September 8, 1903.

White, James M. Letter to President Edmund J. James, May 16, 1911. Edmund J. James Faculty Correspondence. University of Illinois Archives, Urbana-Champaign.

——. "Our Campus Development." *Alumni Quarterly* (April 1911): 102-14.

Chapter 3

Board of Trustees of the University of Illinois. *Reports*. November 19, 1920; August 1, September 21, October 12, November 9, and December 13, 1921; April 12, May 10, October 20, and December 15, 1922; May 15, 1926; September 27, 1927; June 29, 1928; May 17, 1929; September 18, 1929; June 26, 1931.

Board of Trustees of the University of Illinois. *Transactions of the Board of Trustees: September 20, 1928, to June 19, 1930*, 183. Available at http://uihistories.library.illinois.edu/cgi-bin/rview?REPOSID=8&ID=8020.

Brichford, Maynard. *Bob Zuppke: The Life and Football Legacy of the Illinois Football Coach*. Jefferson, N.C.: McFarland, 2008.

Daily Illini, January 25 and February 22, 1916; September 23 and October 8, 1919; January 16 and 19, February 15, March 23, April 16 and 21, and June 16, 1920; April 5 and 6, and December 9, 13, 18, 20, 21, and 22, 1921; January 14, February 24, March 10, 11, 12, 15, and 21, April 11 and 13, September 17, October 3 and 28, and December 31, 1922; January 6 and 18, April 22, and May 16, 1923; January 20, February 15, and October 18, 1924;

February 7, 1925; March 8, 1927; April 8, 1928; April 18, 1929; April 24, and July 23 and 24, 1930; October 21, 1932; February 28, April 21, and September 15, 1933.

Ebert, Roger, ed. *An Illini Century*. Urbana: University of Illinois Press, 1967.

Hottes, Charles. Oral history interviews, 1963-64. Charles F. Hottes Papers. Record series 15/4/21. University of Illinois Archives, Urbana-Champaign.

Kacich, Tom. *Hot Type*. Champaign, Illinois: Sports Publishing, 2002.

Novak, Alice Edwards. Reports on Campus Plans. Unpublished manuscript, 2007-2010.

Platt, Charles Adams. Letter to James M. White, April 30, 1926. Physical Plant Director's Office Subject File. University of Illinois Archives, Urbana-Champaign.

——. Letter to James M. White, November 14, 1927. Physical Plant Director's Office Subject File. University of Illinois Archives, Urbana-Champaign.

——. Letter to James M. White, March 20, 1928. Physical Plant Director's Office Subject File. University of Illinois Archives, Urbana-Champaign.

Roth, Leland. *A Concise History of American Architecture*. New York: Harper and Row, 1979.

Scott, Frank William. Letter to Thomas Arkle Clark, October 5, 1930. Dean of Men General Correspondence. University of Illinois Archives, Urbana-Champaign.

——, ed. *The Semi-Centennial Alumni Record of the University of Illinois*. Chicago: Lakeside, 1918.

Stephens, Carl. *Illini Years: A Picture History of the University of Illinois*. Urbana: University of Illinois Press, 1950.

Tilton, Leon Deming, and Thomas Edward O'Donnell. *History of the Growth and Development of the Campus of the University of Illinois*. Urbana: University of Illinois Press, 1930.

Urbana Daily Courier, September 22, 1919; February 18, March 8, and April 24 and 29, 1922.

Vitale, Ferruccio. Letter to Charles Adams Platt, March 9, 1928. Physical Plant Director's Office Subject File. University of Illinois Archives, Urbana-Champaign.

White, James M. Letter to David Kinley, December 18, 1919. Physical Plant Director's Office Subject File. University of Illinois Archives, Urbana-Champaign.

——. Letter to David Kinley, July 5, 1921. Physical Plant Director's Office Subject File. University of Illinois Archives, Urbana-Champaign.

——. Letter to David Kinley, February 23, 1922. Physical Plant Director's Office Subject File. University of Illinois Archives, Urbana-Champaign.

——. Letter to David Kinley, September 20, 1922. Physical Plant Director's Office Subject File. University of Illinois Archives, Urbana-Champaign.

——. Letter to David Kinley, October 18, 1922. Physical Plant Director's Office Subject File. University of Illinois Archives, Urbana-Champaign.

——. Letter to David Kinley, May 11, 1923. Physical Plant Director's Office Subject File. University of Illinois Archives, Urbana-Champaign.

——. Letter to David Kinley, October 5, 1926. Physical Plant Director's Office Subject File. University of Illinois Archives, Urbana-Champaign.

——. Letter to David Kinley, May 26, 1928. Physical Plant Director's Office Subject File. University of Illinois Archives, Urbana-Champaign.

——. Letter to Edmund J. James, November 6, 1919. Physical Plant Director's Office Subject File. University of Illinois Archives, Urbana-Champaign.

——. Letter to Edmund J. James, November 22, 1919. Physical Plant Director's Office Subject File. University of Illinois Archives, Urbana-Champaign.

——. Letter to Edmund J. James, February 9, 1920. Physical Plant Director's Office Subject File. University of Illinois Archives, Urbana-Champaign.

——. Letter to Edmund J. James, March 8, 1920. Physical Plant Director's Office Subject File. University of Illinois Archives, Urbana-Champaign.

——. Letter to Edmund J. James, March 30, 1920. Physical Plant Director's Office Subject File. University of Illinois Archives, Urbana-Champaign.

——. Letter to Edmund J. James, April 30, 1920. Physical Plant Director's Office Subject File. University of Illinois Archives, Urbana-Champaign.

——. Letter to Edmund J. James, January 4, 1922. Physical Plant Director's Office Subject File. University of Illinois Archives, Urbana-Champaign.

——. "Report of the Supervising Architect and Superintendent of Business Operations for the Period July 1928–July 1930." Physical Plant Director's Office Subject File. University of Illinois Archives, Urbana-Champaign.

——. "Report of the Supervising Architect and Superintendent of Business Operations for the Period July 1930–July 1931." Physical Plant Director's Office Subject File. University of Illinois Archives, Urbana-Champaign.

Chapter 4

Board of Trustees of the University of Illinois. Report, Meeting of the Executive Committee, July 21, 1938. Available at http://archives.library.illinois.edu/erec/University%20Archives/0101802/02_volume_sections/1938-1940/02_meeting_1938-07-15.pdf.

——. Reports. February 16, 1933; May 22, 1934; April 20 and October 25, 1935; June 29, July 10, and November 21, 1936; January 29, November 10, and December 3, 1937; March 18, May 14, and June 9, 1938; November 27, 1942; April 8 and June 22, 1944; February 24, 1945; May 29, June 15, October 21, and December 28, 1946; March 27, 1947; October 21, 1948; January 12, October 26, and November 24, 1950; September 19, 1951; July 16, 1952; January 21 and July 25, 1953.

Brichford, Maynard. *Bob Zuppke: The Life and Football Legacy of the Illinois Football Coach*. Jefferson, N.C.: McFarland, 2008.

Briggs, Cecil. Letter to George Stoddard, August 20, 1950. George Stoddard General Correspondence. University of Illinois Archives, Urbana-Champaign.

——. "Preliminary Report-Proposed Program." January 4, 1950. George Stoddard General Correspondence. University of Illinois Archives, Urbana-Champaign.

The Building Program at the University of Illinois during the Eight Years, 1934-1942. Urbana: University of Illinois, 1942.

Cheney, Howard. Letter to George Stoddard, January 14, 1947. George Stoddard General Correspondence. University of Illinois Archives, Urbana-Champaign.

——. Letter to George Stoddard, February 3, 1947. George Stoddard General Correspondence. University of Illinois Archives, Urbana-Champaign.

Daily Illini, February 7, 9, and 17, 1933; May 23, October 24, and November 4, 1934; May 24, 1935; August 1 and 7, September 27, and November 12, 1936; February 28, April 22, May 15, June 30, July 14, August 7, and December 4, 1937; January 20, 22, 23, and 25, February 12, March 4 and 12, May 19 and 26, June 3, 7, 8, 13, 15, 16, 23, and 27, July 9, August 7, September 9, September 25, October 18, and December 16 and 30, 1938; January 1 and November 19, 1939; March 5, 1940; February 8 and 12, 1941; October 18 and October 21, 1942; July 11, 1943; June 22, 1944; September 29, October 12, and November 8, 1945; April 6, May 10 and May 30, July 3 and July 30, September 19, and October 23, 1946; February 2, June 15, and July 31, 1947; January 28 and 30, August 10, and October 27, 1948; March 24, April 7, August 5, and September 20 and 28, 1949; October 9, 1951; January 20 and 21, 1953; February 9, 1965.

Davis, Frank. Letter to Arthur Willard, October 9, 1934. Physical Plant Director's Office Subject File. University of Illinois Archives, Urbana-Champaign.

——. Letter to Arthur Willard, October 20, 1934. Physical Plant Director's Office Subject File. University of Illinois Archives, Urbana-Champaign.

——. Letter to Arthur Willard, December 12, 1934. Physical Plant Director's Office Subject File. University of Illinois Archives, Urbana-Champaign.

Ebert, Roger, ed. *An Illini Century*. Urbana: University of Illinois Press, 1967.

Franch, John. "The University of Illinois Goes to War." Unpublished manuscript, 2007. Commissioned by University of Illinois Archives' Student Life and Culture Archival Program.

Harno, Albert. Letter to Arthur Willard, February 3, 1943. Arthur Willard General Correspondence. University of Illinois Archives, Urbana-Champaign.

Havens, Charles. "Annual Report of the Office of the Supervising Architect, 1932-1933." Physical Plant Director's Office Subject File. University of Illinois Archives, Urbana-Champaign.

———. "Annual Report of the Physical Plant Department, 1933-1934." Physical Plant Director's Office Subject File. University of Illinois Archives, Urbana-Champaign.

———. Letter to Arthur Willard, November 5, 1934. Physical Plant Director's Office Subject File. University of Illinois Archives, Urbana-Champaign.

———. Letter to Arthur Willard, February 17, 1941. Physical Plant Director's Office Subject File. University of Illinois Archives, Urbana-Champaign.

———. Letter to Arthur Willard, June 26, 1942. Physical Plant Director's Office Subject File. University of Illinois Archives, Urbana-Champaign.

———. Letter to Arthur Willard, April 19, 1945. Physical Plant Director's Office Subject File. University of Illinois Archives, Urbana-Champaign.

———. Letter to Arthur Willard, May 1, 1946. Physical Plant Director's Office Subject File. University of Illinois Archives, Urbana-Champaign.

———. Letter to George Stoddard, October 13, 1946. Physical Plant Director's Office Subject File. University of Illinois Archives, Urbana-Champaign.

Hill, Chance. Letter to George Stoddard, January 16, 1947. George Stoddard General Correspondence. University of Illinois Archives, Urbana-Champaign.

Horner, George. Letter to George Stoddard, May 6, 1947. George Stoddard General Correspondence. University of Illinois Archives, Urbana-Champaign.

Kacich, Tom. *Hot Type*. Champaign, Illinois: Sports Publishing, 2002.

Leuchtenburg, William Edward. *Franklin D. Roosevelt and the New Deal*. New York: Harper and Row, 1963.

McElvaine, Robert. *The Great Depression*. New York: Times Books, 1984.

Newcomb, Rexford. Letter to Charles Havens, March 13, 1945. Physical Plant Director's Office Subject File. University of Illinois Archives, Urbana-Champaign.

Novak, Alice Edwards. "Reports on Campus Plans." Unpublished manuscript, 2007-2010.

Richardson, Ambrose. Oral history interview. February 1-3, 1990. Chicago Architects Oral History Project. Ryerson and Burnham Libraries, Art Institute of Chicago.

Ross, Betsy. Oral history interview. August 30, 1967. Betsy Ross Papers. Record series 2/9/22. University of Illinois Archives, Urbana-Champaign.

Roth, Leland. *A Concise History of American Architecture*. New York: Harper and Row, 1979.

Saarinen, Eliel. Letter to George Stoddard, August 1, 1947. George Stoddard General Correspondence. University of Illinois Archives, Urbana-Champaign.

Schaffer, Otto. Letter to Arthur Willard, December 20, 1940. Arthur Willard General Correspondence. University of Illinois Archives, Urbana-Champaign.

Stephens, Carl. *Illini Years: A Picture History of the University of Illinois*. Urbana: University of Illinois Press, 1950.

Stoddard, George. Letter to Cecil Briggs, December 30, 1949. Building Program Committee Subject File. University of Illinois Archives, Urbana-Champaign.

———. Letter to Charles Havens, May 12, 1947. George Stoddard General Correspondence. University of Illinois Archives, Urbana-Champaign.

——. Letter to Eliel Saarinen, October 3, 1947. George Stoddard General Correspondence. University of Illinois Archives, Urbana-Champaign.

——. Letter to Howard Cheney, May 12, 1947. George Stoddard General Correspondence. University of Illinois Archives, Urbana-Champaign.

——. Letter to Howard Cheney, March 9, 1949. George Stoddard General Correspondence. University of Illinois Archives, Urbana-Champaign.

——. Letter to Lloyd Morey, June 12, 1951. George Stoddard General Correspondence. University of Illinois Archives, Urbana-Champaign.

Stouffer, Ernest. Letter to Arthur Willard, May 26, 1941. Arthur Willard General Correspondence. University of Illinois Archives, Urbana-Champaign.

Tilton, Leon Deming, and Thomas Edward O'Donnell. *History of the Growth and Development of the Campus of the University of Illinois*. Urbana: University of Illinois Press, 1930.

Urbana Daily Courier, February 6, 1933.

Watkins, T. H. *Righteous Pilgrim: The Life and Times of Harold L. Ickes, 1874-1952*. New York: Holt, 1990.

White, James. Letter to David Kinley, July 5, 1929. Physical Plant Director's Office Subject File. University of Illinois Archives, Urbana-Champaign.

——. Letter to Harry Chase, February 10, 1932. Physical Plant Director's Office Subject File. University of Illinois Archives, Urbana-Champaign.

Willard, Arthur. Letter to Charles Havens, July 27, 1938. Physical Plant Director's Office Subject File. University of Illinois Archives, Urbana-Champaign.

Chapter 5

Bareither, Harlan. "Some Thoughts about Planning at U of Illinois." June 5, 2005. Lex Tate Papers. Privately held.

Board of Trustees of the University of Illinois. *Reports*. July 25, 1953; November 18, 1959; July 27, 1966; September 16, 1970; September 15, 1976; July 19 and September 20, 1978; November 15, 1979; July 16, 1981; January 14, May 20, and October 21, 1982; January 20 and June 16, 1983; September 20, 1984.

Brichford, Maynard. "Brief History of the University." 1970, revised 1983. Posted September 26, 2012, by Chris Prom. Available at http://archives.library.illinois.edu/blog/brief-history-of-the-university.

Chamberlin, Robert. "Comments on Campus Landscape Evaluation Report by Mr. Hideo Sasaki." Undated (ca. 1960). Physical Plant Director's Office Subject File. University of Illinois Archives, Urbana-Champaign.

——. Letter to Hideo Sasaki, January 18, 1960. Physical Plant Director's Office Subject File. University of Illinois Archives, Urbana-Champaign.

——. Letter to Hideo Sasaki, February 15, 1960. Physical Plant Director's Office Subject File. University of Illinois Archives, Urbana-Champaign.

——. Letter to Hideo Sasaki, April 22, 1960. Physical Plant Director's Office Subject File. University of Illinois Archives, Urbana-Champaign.

——. Letter to Hideo Sasaki, November 21, 1960. Physical Plant Director's Office Subject File. University of Illinois Archives, Urbana-Champaign.

——. Letter to Hideo Sasaki, January 3, 1961. Physical Plant Director's Office Subject File. University of Illinois Archives, Urbana-Champaign.

——. Letter to Hideo Sasaki, June 10, 1963. Physical Plant Director's Office Subject File. University of Illinois Archives, Urbana-Champaign.

——. Letter to C. D. Thomas, February 10, 1967. Physical Plant Director's Office Subject File. University of Illinois Archives, Urbana-Champaign.

Chicago Sun-Times, December 25, 1960.

Courier (Urbana, Ill.), September 26, 1972; September 15, 1976; January 6, March 27, May 12 and 27, and June 24 and 29, 1977; March 2 and 19, and June 1, 1978; March 8, 1979.

Daily Illini, July 21, 1949; August 18, 1950; March 12, May 8, and October 23, 1953; May 15, July 16 and 22, and October 14, 1954; January 6, May 17, July 6, and September 22, 1955; January 25, February 7, 9, and 22, March 29, April 12, and August 1, 1956; January 18, March 15, June 1, July 18 and 25, September 11, October 18, and November 22, 26, and 27, 1957; February 18, March 1, April 22, 23, and 25, June 16, July 31, September 24, October 29, November 18 and 22, and December 16, 1958; July 9, September 19 and 26, and November 11 and 25, 1959; January 6 and 15, March 23, April 21, May 3, July 14, August 1, September 20 and 24, and December 1, 1960; January 7 and 10, and July 6, 1961; March 21 and 29, April 11, May 5, October 17, and December 7, 1962; January 9, 1963; February 9 and April 1, 1965; May 6, June 20, and September 15, 1966; August 1, 1967; October 2, 1968; February 7 and 8, and August 1, 1969; April 11, June 22, August 1, September 17, and October 20, 1970; January 6, February 17, April 14, May 27, July 23, September 16, October 7, and November 18, 1971; January 21, March 21, and September 26, 1972; March 27, July 3, July 19, and August 22, 1973; April 5, May 15, and July 24, 1974; November 6, 1976; July 21 and September 3, 1977; November 16 and 29, 1979.

Division of Planning and Construction, University of Illinois. *Provisional Long-Range Campus Planning Report 1971-1980*. 1970. Campus Master Plan Reports. University of Illinois Archives, Urbana-Champaign.

Ebert, Roger, ed. *An Illini Century*. Urbana: University of Illinois Press, 1967.

Gibson, Harold. "The Story of the Universities Bond Issue." November 12, 1960. David Henry Subject File. University of Illinois Archives, Urbana-Champaign.

Golla, Marie. *The Corbally Years: An Overview*. Urbana: University of Illinois Foundation, ca. 1980.

Havens, Charles. Letter to Ambrose Richardson, June 29, 1956. Physical Plant Director's Office Subject File. University of Illinois Archives, Urbana-Champaign.

———. Letter to David Henry, June 7, 1957. David Henry General Correspondence. University of Illinois Archives, Urbana-Champaign.

———. Letter to David Henry, December 12, 1963. David Henry General Correspondence. University of Illinois Archives, Urbana-Champaign.

———. Letter to David Henry, December 19, 1963. David Henry General Correspondence. University of Illinois Archives, Urbana-Champaign.

———. Letter to David Henry, November 16, 1964. David Henry General Correspondence. University of Illinois Archives, Urbana-Champaign.

———. Letter to David Henry, October 18, 1965. David Henry General Correspondence. University of Illinois Archives, Urbana-Champaign.

———. Letter to David Henry, June 7, 1971. John Corbally General Correspondence. University of Illinois Archives, Urbana-Champaign.

———. Letter to George Stoddard, July 13, 1953. Physical Plant Director's Office Subject File. University of Illinois Archives, Urbana-Champaign.

———. Letter to J. V. Edsall, March 15, 1955. Physical Plant Director's Office Subject File. University of Illinois Archives, Urbana-Champaign.

———. Letter to Lyle Lanier, March 15, 1962. David Henry General Correspondence. University of Illinois Archives, Urbana-Champaign.

———. Letter to Lyle Lanier, March 18, 1964. David Henry General Correspondence. University of Illinois Archives, Urbana-Champaign.

Henry, David. Letter to Alan Laing and Nathan Newmark, June 26, 1959. David Henry General Correspondence. University of Illinois Archives, Urbana-Champaign.

———. Letter to Alan Laing, December 22, 1960. David Henry General Correspondence. University of Illinois Archives, Urbana-Champaign.

——. Letter to Allen Weller, June 8, 1960. David Henry General Correspondence. University of Illinois Archives, Urbana-Champaign.

——. Letter to A. Richard Williams, December 1, 1960. David Henry General Correspondence. University of Illinois Archives, Urbana-Champaign.

——. Letter to Charles Havens, May 1, 1959. David Henry General Correspondence. University of Illinois Archives, Urbana-Champaign.

——. Letter to Charles Havens, November 30, 1960. David Henry General Correspondence. University of Illinois Archives, Urbana-Champaign.

——. Letter to Charles Havens, June 29, 1962. David Henry General Correspondence. University of Illinois Archives, Urbana-Champaign.

——. Letter to Charles Havens, June 29, 1963. David Henry General Correspondence. University of Illinois Archives, Urbana-Champaign.

——. *Memoirs*. 1983. David Henry Papers. University of Illinois Archives, Urbana-Champaign.

——. *Recollections in Tranquility*. 1991. David Henry Papers. University of Illinois Archives, Urbana-Champaign.

Howard, Robert P. *Mostly Good and Competent Men: Illinois Governors 1818 to 1988*. Springfield, Illinois: *Illinois Issues* and Illinois State Historical Society, 1988.

Ikenberry, Stanley. Oral history interview. October 16, 2008. Lex Tate Papers. Privately held.

Illinois Alumni News, March 1962, November 1962, September 1976, July 1977, April 1982.

Kenney, David. *A Political Passage: The Career of Stratton of Illinois*. Carbondale: Southern Illinois University Press, 1990.

Lanier, Lyle. Letter to David Henry, January 23, 1962. David Henry General Correspondence. University of Illinois Archives, Urbana-Champaign.

——. Letter to David Henry, December 27, 1963. David Henry General Correspondence. University of Illinois Archives, Urbana-Champaign.

——. Letter to David Henry, August 10, 1964. David Henry General Correspondence. University of Illinois Archives, Urbana-Champaign.

News-Gazette (Champaign, Ill.), August 15 and 17, 1976; May 15 and July 3, 1977; September 23, 1979; June 12, 1994.

Novak, Alice Edwards. "Reports on Campus Plans." Unpublished manuscript, 2007-2010.

Parker, Norman. Letter to David Henry, June 22, 1956. David Henry General Correspondence. University of Illinois Archives, Urbana-Champaign.

——. Letter to David Henry, May 23, 1958. David Henry General Correspondence. University of Illinois Archives, Urbana-Champaign.

Richardson, Ambrose. Letter to Charles Havens, September 18, 1959. Physical Plant Director's Office Subject File. University of Illinois Archives, Urbana-Champaign.

——. Oral history interview. February 1-3, 1990. Chicago Architects Oral History Project. Ryerson and Burnham Libraries, The Art Institute of Chicago.

——. *University of Illinois Ten Year Development Plan 1959-1969*. 1960. Campus Master Plan Reports. University of Illinois Archives, Urbana-Champaign.

Rosen, George. *Decision-Making Chicago-Style: The Genesis of a University of Illinois Campus*. Urbana: University of Illinois Press, 1980.

Roth, Leland. *A Concise History of American Architecture*. New York: Harper and Row, 1979.

Sasaki, Hideo. Letter to Robert Chamberlin, November 3, 1959. Physical Plant Director's Office Subject File. University of Illinois Archives, Urbana-Champaign.

——. Letter to Robert Chamberlin, May 19, 1961. Physical Plant Director's Office Subject File. University of Illinois Archives, Urbana-Champaign.

——. Letter to Robert Chamberlin, June 19, 1961. Physical Plant Director's Office Subject File. University of Illinois Archives, Urbana-Champaign.

——. Letter to Robert Chamberlin, October 5, 1965. Physical Plant Director's Office Subject File. University of Illinois Archives, Urbana-Champaign.

Severns, John. Oral history interview. July 19, 2006. Lex Tate Papers. Privately held.

Stoddard, George. Letter to Charles Havens, July 17, 1953. Physical Plant Director's Office Subject File. University of Illinois Archives, Urbana-Champaign.

Stouffer, Ernest. Letter to Charles Havens, October 10, 1961. Physical Plant Director's Office Subject File. University of Illinois Archives, Urbana-Champaign.

——. Letter to George Stoddard, July 18, 1952. Physical Plant Director's Office Subject File. University of Illinois Archives, Urbana-Champaign.

Tate, Lex. "The Ikenberry Years: A Fond Farewell." *Illinois Quarterly* (March/April 1995): 18-23.

Weller, Allen. Letter to Charles Havens, April 15, 1959. Physical Plant Director's Office Subject File. University of Illinois Archives, Urbana-Champaign.

——. Letter to David Henry, September 19, 1956. David Henry General Correspondence. University of Illinois Archives, Urbana-Champaign.

——. Letter to David Henry, May 25, 1960. David Henry General Correspondence. University of Illinois Archives, Urbana-Champaign.

Williams, A. Richard. "History of the Education Building 1960-63." University of Illinois Archives, Urbana-Champaign.

Chapter 6

Brown, Theodore. *Bridging Divides: The Origin of the Beckman Institute at Illinois*. Champaign, Illinois: University of Illinois Press, 2009.

Chapman, M. Perry. Oral history interview. March 20, 2006. Lex Tate Papers. Privately held.

Dawson, Stuart O. Oral History Series interview transcript, Cultural Landscape Foundation Pioneers of American Landscape Design, June 8-10 and July 9, 2009.

Dawson, Stuart, and Hibbard, Joseph. Oral history interview. March 19-20, 2006. Lex Tate Papers. Privately held.

Ikenberry, Stanley O. Oral history interview. October 16, 2008. Lex Tate Papers. Privately held.

Kehe, Roland. Oral history interview, 2009, and emails, 2015-16. Lex Tate Papers. Privately held.

News-Gazette (Champaign, Ill.), September 6, 2010.

Ryan, George H. "Fiscal Year 2000 Budget State of the State Address of the 91st General Assembly." Press release. February 17, 1999. Available at http://www3.illinois.gov/PressReleases/ShowPressRelease.cfm?SubjectID=3&RecNum=189.

University of Illinois. "At the Crossroads: The State, the University and Tomorrow's Technology." February 22, 2000.

——. *Master Plan Update, March 2007: Executive Summary*. Available at https://www.uocpres.uillinois.edu/UserFiles/Servers/Server_7758/file/UIUC/reports/UIUCmpu_execsum.pdf.

——. *North Campus Master Plan Executive Summary*. Watertown, Mass.: Sasaki Associates Inc., April 10, 1986. Available at https://www.ideals.illinois.edu/bitstream/handle/2142/27886/universityofillinoi00univ.pdf?sequence=1.

Chapter 7

Chase, Harry W. Letter to James M. White, March 27, 1931. Physical Plant Director's Office Subject File. University of Illinois Archives, Urbana-Champaign.

Clark, Thomas Arkle. "How the Students Are Fed," *Alumni Quarterly* 9 (April 1915), 86-94.

Courier (Urbana, Ill.), May 22, 1905; October 18, 1905; September 14, 1907; October 1, 1908; July 27, 1909; May 2, 1914; January 17, 1916; March 1, 1966.

Daily Illini, November 28, 1918; September 23, 1919; January 22, 1920; September 21 and December 22, 1923; November 27, 1924; February 14, 1925; March 17 and June 3, 1926; July 1, and October 18 and 27, 1928; September 15, 1929; September 14, and October 10 and 11, 1930; September 11, 1936; June 6, 1937; April 11 and November 17, 1939; October 19, 1940; September 14,

1941; September 11, 1945; August 1, 1957; September 25, 1963; May 15 and 29, and August 1, 1964; February 24 and October 14, 1965; April 20, and November 12 and 18, 1966; November 21, 1969; February 12 and August 11, 1972; November 13, 1974; May 6 and August 17, 2010.

Daly, Patrick J. *A Campus Ministry*. [Urbana], 2001.

Franch, John. "The University of Illinois Goes to War." Unpublished manuscript, 2007. Commissioned by University of Illinois Archives Student Life and Culture Archival Program.

Frederick, Charles R. Letter to Arthur Willard, August 15, 1938. Arthur Willard General Correspondence. University of Illinois Archives, Urbana-Champaign.

Goldstein, Jacob. Letter to Lena Wolkow, October 28, 1929. Jacob Goldstein Papers. University of Illinois Archives, Urbana-Champaign.

Hallett, Timothy. Interview with Lex Tate, October 28, 2008.

Havens, Charles. Letter to Arthur Willard, October 17, 1936. Physical Plant Director's Office Subject File. University of Illinois Archives, Urbana-Champaign.

Illinois Alumni News, April 1938, 15.

Illinois Association of State Officials. *Report of the Organization and First Meeting of the Illinois Association of State Officials, Held at Springfield, February 1 and April 8, 1903*. Pontiac: Illinois State Reformatory Printing Trade-School, 1903.

Illio 82 (1982): 46-47.

Inside Illinois, February 7, 2008, 2.

Kamerer, Jack. Email communication and phone interviews by Lex Tate. November 11 and 14, 2009; October 13, 2012; spring 2013.

Milkent, Craig, "A Guide to Preservation Planning for the Greek System," Master's project, University of Illinois at Urbana-Champaign, 1983.

News-Gazette (Champaign, Ill.), February 19, 1997; August 23, 2009; March 24, 2011; January 26, 2014; February 2 and March 22, 2015.

Peters, Scott J. *The Promise of Association*. Champaign: Crouse, 1997.

Potter, Frances A., "Those Early Days," *Alumni Quarterly and Fortnightly Notes of the University of Illinois* 1 (October 15, 1915): 23-28.

Scott, Frank William, ed. *The Semi-Centennial Alumni Record of the University of Illinois*. Chicago: Lakeside, 1918.

Sifferd, Calvin S. "History of Housing Owned and Operated by the University of Illinois in Its First Hundred Years." Unpublished manuscript, 1967.

Solberg, Winton U. "The Catholic Presence at the University of Illinois." *Catholic Historical Review* 76 (October 1990): 765-812.

——. "The Early Years of the Jewish Presence at the University of Illinois." *Religion and American Culture* 2 (Summer 1992): 215-45.

——. *The University of Illinois 1867-1894*. Urbana: University of Illinois Press, 1968.

——. *The University of Illinois, 1894-1904*. Urbana: University of Illinois Press, 2000.

Spurlock, Albert. Oral history. Interview with Ellen Swain, January 21, 2001. Student Life and Culture Archives, University of Illinois.

Tilton, Leon Deming, and Thomas Edward O'Donnell. *History of the Growth and Development of the Campus of the University of Illinois*. Urbana: University of Illinois Press, 1930.

Turner, Fred. Letter to Arthur Willard, May 18, 1942. Dean of Men General Correspondence. University of Illinois Archives, Urbana-Champaign.

Wesley Illini World, February 1926, 2.

Wesley News, December 1959, 1.

Willard, Arthur. Letter to Charles J. Jenkins, April 5, 1937. Arthur Willard General Correspondence. University of Illinois Archives, Urbana-Champaign.

University of Illinois. *Alumni Quarterly of the University of Illinois* 8 (1914). Available at https://archive.org/details/illinoisalumnine91915univ.

Chapter 8

ACES Library, Information and Alumni Center. See http://uihistories.library.illinois.edu/cgi-bin/cview?SITEID=1&ID=4.

"All Gifts and Memorials." Available at http://uihistories.library.illinois.edu/cgi-bin/cview?SITEID=1&ID=292.

"Alumni Center Closer to Reality on Urbana-Champaign Campus." *Investing in Illinois*, University of Illinois Foundation newsletter, Fall 2002.

"Alum Thomas Siebel Commits $32 Million for New Computer Science Center." *Investing in Illinois*, University of Illinois Foundation newsletter, Spring 2000.

American National Business Hall of Fame. Laureates: Richard D. Irwin. See http://anbhf.org/laureates/richard-d-irwin.

"Arnold Beckman—Scientist, Inventor, Philanthropist—Dies at 104." *Investing in Illinois*, University of Illinois Foundation newsletter, Summer 2004.

"Atkins Tennis Center Trains Children, Teens Next to Former Illini NCAA Tennis Champs." *Good Sports* (Champaign, Ill.), Spring 2009.

"A Work of Art." *News-Gazette* (Champaign, Ill.), January 12, 2015.

Beckman Coulter. "Our Heritage—Arnold O. Beckman, 1900-2004." See https://www.beckmancoulter.com/wsrportal/wsrportal.portal?_nfpb=true&_windowLabel=UCM_RENDERER&_urlType=render&wlpUCM_RENDERER_path=%252Fwsr%252Fcompany%252Fabout-us%252Four-history%252Farnold-o-beckman%252Findex.htm.

"Billionaire Shares His Philosophy for Giving." *News-Gazette* (Champaign, Ill.), April 4, 2014.

Blackall, C. H. Letter to A. C. Willard, March 2, 1938. University of Illinois Archives, Urbana-Champaign.

———. Letter to Edmund James, March 17, 1908. University of Illinois Archives, Urbana-Champaign.

———. Letter to James M. White, January 29, 1923. University of Illinois Archives, Urbana-Champaign.

Bohlin Cywinski Jackson. See http://bcj.com.

Brichford, Maynard. *Bob Zuppke: The Life and Legend of the Illinois Coach*. Jefferson, N.C.: McFarland, 2009.

Business Development. A newsletter of the University of Illinois College of Business. September 21, 2000.

"Campbell Hall for Public Telecommunication and Richmond Journalism Teaching Studio and Swanson Center." Available at http://uihistories.library.illinois.edu/cgi-bin/cview?SITEID=1&ID=49.

"Campbells' Latest Gift Commitment to Create Chair in Law, Help Fund Aiken Chair, Matthews Scholars Program." *Investing in Illinois*, University of Illinois Foundation newsletter, Winter 2002.

"Career Filled with Interest; Rose Rapidly." *Daily Illini*, December 8, 1926.

"Champaign Couple Endows TV Teaching Studio at UI." *News-Gazette* (Champaign, Ill.), September 13, 1996.

"Champaign Family Funds Broadcast Teaching Studio on U of I Campus." Press release. University of Illinois Foundation, September 13, 1996.

"Chicago Publisher Richard D. Irwin's $1.5 Million-Plus Gift to Support Varsity Football Coaching and Training Headquarters at the University of Illinois at Urbana-Champaign." News release. University of Illinois Foundation, May 9, 1986.

Cochran, John D. Letter to B. A. Nugent, September 28, 1990. Stanley O. Ikenberry General Correspondence File, record series 2/14/1, box 252, folder: SO 1990-1. University of Illinois Archives.

"College of Business Announces Fellowship Winners." News release. University of Illinois at Urbana-Champaign College of Business, May 22, 2003.

"Commerce West / Wohler's Hall." Available at http://uihistories.library.illinois.edu/cgi-bin/cview?SITEID=1&ID=278.

"Couple's $1.5 Million Gift Will Name Reception Gallery in New Alumni Center." *Investing in Illinois*, University of Illinois Foundation newsletter, Fall 2003.

Courier (Urbana, Ill.), April 17, 1918.

Daily Illini, April 17, 1918; April 14, November 5, and December 4, 1938; September 14 and November 5, 1940; November 4 and March 30, 1941; September 23, 1958; November 11, 1960; May 24, 1961; February 20, 1964; September 19, 1968; April 12, June 25, and February 13, 1969; July 13, 1971; October 8, 1972; September 14, 1982; October 1, 2007.

"Decades after Bad Break, Ex-Gymnast Commits to Scholarships for U of I Gymnastics Team." *Investing in Illinois*, University of Illinois Foundation newsletter, Summer 2005.

"The Dedication of Foellinger Auditorium." Booklet published by the University of Illinois Foundation, April 26, 1985.

Farmer's Weekly Review, May 27, 1982.

"Fiftieth Anniversary." Booklet published by U of I Foundation, 1985.

Franch, John. "Illinois Homecoming: A Century of Spirit," *Illinois Alumni* 23, no. 1 (Fall 2010): 22-29.

"Funks Gift Challenge for UI Center." *News-Gazette* (Champaign, Ill.), December 3, 1986.

"Gift from L.A. Couple to Build WILL Broadcasting Facility." *Investing in Illinois*, University of Illinois Foundation newsletter, Mid-Winter 1994.

Golfweek. September 6, 2008.

"Historical Preservation Capital Programs." Appendix 26, U of I Facilities and Services Preservation Index. Available at http://www.fs.illinois.edu/services/capital-programs/historic-preservation/appendices.

"History of Foellinger Auditorium." Available at http://www.registrar.illinois.edu/foellinger-history.

Huse, Kevin. Library architect, undated correspondence with Lex Tate.

Illini Week, April 25, 1985 and October 30, 1986.

Illinois Alumni. Magazine of the University of Illinois Alumni Association, November/December 2006; Summer 2013.

Illinois Alumni News. December 1982; November 1985.

"In Memoriam: Albert Wohlers." College of Business News, November 13, 2014. Available at https://business.illinois.edu/news/college/2014/11/in-memoriam-albert-wohlers.

"Innovative Siebel Center for Computer Science Opens on Campus." *Investing in Illinois*, University of Illinois Foundation newsletter, Summer 2004.

Investing in Illinois. University of Illinois Foundation newsletter, Mid-Winter 1994; Spring 1998; Fall 2000 (dedication of Wohlers Hall photo); Fall 2002; Winter 2004.

"Investiture of Jennifer K. Robbenolt as the Alice Curtis Campbell Professor of Law." February 12, 2016. Available at https://www.law.illinois.edu/events/3093.

"Irwin Family Foundation's $1.5 Million Gift Will Create Academic Center for Student Athletes at U of I." *Investing in Illinois*, University of Illinois Foundation newsletter, Winter 1996.

"Irwin Foundation Honored for Gift for Indoor Football Facility at U of I." *Investing in Illinois*, University of Illinois Foundation newsletter, Fall 1999.

"Jewel of the ACES Campus." A publication of the College of ACES commemorating dedication of the ACES Library, Information and Alumni Center, October 4, 2001.

"Krannert Art Museum." *Explore CU*. Available at http://explorecu.org/items/show/195.

Krannert Art Museum, University of Illinois at Urbana-Champaign. See http://kam.illinois.edu.

Krannert Center for the Performing Arts, University of Illinois at Urbana-Champaign. See https://krannertcenter.com.

La Grassa, John Paul, and Denise La Grassa. "Memorial Stadium: True Illini Spirit." Documentary. WILL-TV, 2008.

"Landmarks of the Next Century." *Community Concierge*, Spring 2010.

Mason, Robert L. *History of Cannon County, Tennessee*. Memphis: Memphis State University Press, 1982.

"Million Estate Distributed by M'Kinley Will." *Chicago Daily Tribune*, December 21, 1926.

"M'Kinley a Hero in Love Tragedy." *New York Times*, December 12, 1926.

"New Alumni Center Opens to Public, Open for Business." *Investing in Illinois*, University of Illinois Foundation newsletter, Summer 2006.

News-Gazette (Champaign, Ill.), November 7, 1962; August 24, 1981; April 27, 1985; September 9 and 11, 1992; October 23, 2010; July 19, 2015.

"Officials Break Ground for Library." *News-Gazette* (Champaign, Ill.), October 10, 1998.

"100 Million Gift Commitment from Alumnus Thomas Siebel Jumpstarts `Brilliant Futures' Campaign." Press release. Office of the Chancellor at the University of Illinois at Urbana-Champaign, June 1, 2007.

"100 Years of Exploring the World." *Community Concierge*, Summer 2011, 6-7, 15.

On Our Watch. University of Illinois Office of the Chancellor newsletter, vol. 1, no. 1.

"Peoria Family Donates $1 Million to U of I Ag School." *Peoria Journal Star*, December 8, 1992.

"Philanthropist Gave Millions to UI." *News-Gazette* (Champaign, Ill.), April 20, 2011.

"Philanthropist, Publisher R. D. Irwin." *Chicago Tribune*, November 28, 1989.

Raphaelson, Samson. *Story of the Stadium*. Urbana: University of Illinois, 1922.

"Rediscovering Smith Hall." *Sonorities: The News Magazine of the University of Illinois School of Music*, Winter 2014.

"Richmond Gift Endows U of I Hoops Head Coach Position." *Investing in Illinois*, University of Illinois Foundation newsletter, Fall 1999.

"Richmonds Recognized for Their Generosity at UIF Annual Meeting." *Investing in Illinois*, University of Illinois Foundation newsletter, Winter 1995.

Save the Auditorium Committee study. Undated (circa 1979).

"Senator M'Kinley, of Illinois, Dead after Long Illness." *Washington Post*, December 8, 1926.

"Seven Major Gifts to Benefit Urbana-Champaign Campus of University of Illinois." News release. University of Illinois Foundation, October 18, 2013.

Smith, Thomas L. Letter to Captain Edward Bailey, August 4, 1913.

Snips Magazine, March, 1985.

Stephens, Carl. "History, 1943-47." Unpublished manuscript. Carl Stephens Manuscript, record series 26/1/21.

———. *The University of Illinois—A History, 1867-1947*. Carl Stephens Manuscript, record series 26/1/21.

"Student Life at Illinois." University of Illinois Library Archives, 1910-1919.

"Swanlund Influence Expands across U-C Campus." *Investing in Illinois*, University of Illinois Foundation newsletter, Mid-Winter 1994.

"Tina Weedon Smith Memorial Building/Smith Hall." Available at http://uihistories.library.illinois.edu/cgi-bin/cview?SITEID=1&ID=232.

"Trustees Approve Presidential Search Committee." News release. University of Illinois Office of University Relations, March 6, 2014. Available at http://uofi.uillinois.edu/emailer/newsletter/49260.html.

"Trustees OK Final Design of Beckman Institute." University of Illinois faculty-staff newspaper, ca. spring 1986.

"Ubben Gifts to Athletics at UIUC Establish Basketball Complex, Scholarships." *Investing in Illinois*, University of Illinois Foundation newsletter, Fall 2000.

"UI and Foundation Receive $140 Million in Private Gifts during Past Year." *Inside Illinois*, University of Illinois Foundation newsletter, October 7, 1999.

"UI Benefactors Tim and Sharon Ubben Add Name to SFC Donor Recognition Wall with $2 Million Gift." University of Illinois Division on Intercollegiate Athletics, January 22, 2014. Available at http://www.fightingillini.com/news/2014/1/22/

UI_Benefactors_Tim_and_Sharon_Ubben_Add_Name_to_SFC_Donor_Recognition_Wall_with_2_Million_Gift.aspx.

"UI Gets $2.5 Million Gift for Construction of Tennis Facility." *News-Gazette* (Champaign, Ill.), November 13, 1987.

"UI Graduate Is a Self-Made Man." *News-Gazette* (Champaign, Ill.), November 30, 2011.

"U of I Brilliant Futures Campaign Eclipses Its $2.25 Billion Goal 4 Months Early." News release. University of Illinois Foundation, September 23, 2011.

"U of I Honors Los Angeles Couple at 'Construction Celebration' of Campbell Hall." *Investing in Illinois*, University of Illinois Foundation newsletter, Winter 1996.

"U of I Honors Los Angeles Couple at 'Construction Celebration' of Campbell Hall." Press release. University of Illinois Foundation, October 3, 1996.

"University Dedicates New Broadcast Facilities for WILL AM-FM-TV, Student Journalism Instruction." *Investing in Illinois*, University of Illinois Foundation newsletter, Fall 1999.

"University Dedicates New Library, Alumni Center for College of ACES." *Investing in Illinois*, University of Illinois Foundation newsletter, Spring 2002.

University of Illinois Alumni Association. *Alumni Quarterly*, April 1907.

University of Illinois at Urbana-Champaign. *Chancellor's Advisor for Architecture and Master Planning 2013-14: Year End Report.*

University of Illinois Board of Trustees. *Minutes*, June 2 and 23, 1905; March 13 and 14, 1906; January 12, 1924; July 26, September 18, and November 22, 1968; April 12, 1978.

University of Illinois College of Agricultural, Consumer and Environmental Sciences. See http://aces.illinois.edu.

University of Illinois Division of Intercollegiate Athletics. "Atkins Tennis Center." Available at http://fightingillini.com/sports/2015/6/27/tennis_facilities.aspx.

University of Illinois Division of Intercollegiate Athletics. See http://fightingillini.com.

University of Illinois Foundation. "Fun Facts about Harker Hall." Available at http://www.uif.uillinois.edu/aboutuif/overview/harkerhall.php.

"University of Illinois History of Achievement." Booklet published by the U of I Foundation at the kickoff of the 1991 Campaign Illinois.

"University of Illinois: Virtual Campus Tour; Harker Hall." Available at http://uihistories.library.illinois.edu/virtualtour/maincampus/harkerhall.

Weller, Allen S. *100 Years of Architecture at the University of Illinois*. Urbana: University of Illinois Press, 1968.

"Woodrow Wilson Awards Dinner Honors Thomas M. Siebel and Condoleeza Rice." Press release. University of Illinois Foundation, May 27, 2010.

Chapter 9

Alumni News. December 1969; November 1971.

Alumni Quarterly and Fortnightly Notes of the University of Illinois, January 15, 1916, 177-78.

Baselt, F. D., and J. F. Moeller. *Cemeteries of Champaign County,Illinois: A Location Guide with Plat Maps*. Champaign, Ill.: Baselt and Moeller, 1984.

Board of Trustees of the University of Illinois. *Reports*. September 24, 1938;

Board of Trustees of the University of Illinois. *Proceedings*, November 18, 1868; March 7, 1871; March 8, 1872; March 10 and 14, 1891; September 21, 1897; June 7 and 8, 1898; April 18, 1900; June 7, 1903; September 27, 1905; March 12, 1907; February 8, 1916; December 5, 1940; May 15, 1941; October 21, 1941; January 8, 1948; February 16, 1950; March 12, 1957; June 23, 1959.

"Buried Treasure Will Serve as Focus for New East Entrance to Campus." *Investing in Illinois*, University of Illinois Foundation newsletter, Late Spring 1995.

Chamberlin, R. S. Letter to Allen S. Weller, December 2, 1963. Physical Plant Director's Office Subject File. University of Illinois Archives, Urbana-Champaign.

——. Letter to Allen S. Weller, December 10, 1963. Physical Plant Director's Office Subject File. University of Illinois Archives, Urbana-Champaign.

"Circular Thinking: Round Barns in America." Voice of America News, January 7, 2008.

Courier (Urbana, Ill.), May 28, 1903; August 21, 1903; September 18, 1954; May 11, 1969.

Daily Illini, February 18, March 3, May 6, and November 23, 1909; May 9, 22, and 28, 1912; January 15, April 12, and October 15, 1916; March 21, 1918; February 18, 1919; May 16, 1920; October 31 and November 9, 1922; January 3, April 15, May 12, June 27, and August 1, 1923; February 6, April 23, November 22 and 23, and December 23, 1924; January 10, 1925; November 12, 1926; June 3, 1928; February 9 and 14, and June 28, 1930; April 12 and December 13, 1931; May 6, 1932; September 1934; July 21, November 22, 1935; June 23, July 16, and September 25, 1938; January 17 and 18, 1939; March 5, 1940; February 8 and March 18, 1941; January 20, 1961; March 8 and 9, 1957; February 9, 1965; May 6, 1966; October 3, 2003; March 8, 2013; July 3, 2014; October 12, 2016.

Fighting Illini/Division of Intercollegiate Athletics Fighting Illini Facilities. "State Farm Center." See http://fightingillini.com/sports/2015/3/24/statefarmcenter.aspx.

Frances Best Watkins Papers, University of Illinois Archives.

Fraser, Wilber. "Economy of the Round Dairy Barn." University of Illinois Agricultural Experiment Station *Bulletin* 143 (February 1910).

——. "The Round Barn," University of Illinois Agricultural Experiment Station *Bulletin* 230 (September 1918); *LifeTimes*, November 1995.

Fujiwara, John. "Documentation of the University of Illinois Assembly Hall," 1963. University of Illinois Archives.

Hallene Gateway Plaza Dedication Program, October 8, 1998. University of Illinois Foundation.

Hallene Gateway Portal Project Profile. WJE Engineers, Architects, Materials Scientists; undated, ca. 1995.

Havens, Charles S. Letter to Arthur Willard, February 12, 1937. Physical Plant Director's Office Subject File. University of Illinois Archives, Urbana-Champaign.

——. Letter to Arthur Willard, May 8, 1937. Physical Plant Director's Office Subject File. University of Illinois Archives, Urbana-Champaign.

——. Letter to Arthur Willard, June 20, 1938. Physical Plant Director's Office Subject File. University of Illinois Archives, Urbana-Champaign.

——. Letter to Arthur Willard, July 13, 1938. Physical Plant Director's Office Subject File. University of Illinois Archives, Urbana-Champaign.

——. Letter to Arthur Willard, January 13, 1939. Physical Plant Director's Office Subject File. University of Illinois Archives, Urbana-Champaign.

——. Letter to Arthur C. Willard, June 20, 1939, March 20, 1940, Physical Plant Department Subject File, University of Illinois Archives.

——. Letter to Arthur Willard, November 28, 1940. Physical Plant Director's Office Subject File. University of Illinois Archives, Urbana-Champaign.

——. Letter to Arthur Willard, February 6, 1945. Physical Plant Director's Office Subject File. University of Illinois Archives, Urbana-Champaign.

——. Letter to Howard L. Cheney, August 31, 1938. Physical Plant Director's Office Subject File. University of Illinois Archives, Urbana-Champaign.

——. Letter to Rexford Newcomb, July 21, 1945. Physical Plant Director's Office Subject File. University of Illinois Archives, Urbana-Champaign.

——. Memo to College of Agriculture Dean L. B. Howard and Professor N. A. Parker, April 14, 1958. Physical Plant Director's Office Subject File. University of Illinois Archives, Urbana-Champaign.

——. Memo to R. S. Chamberlin, December 9, 1963. Physical Plant Director's Office Subject File. University of Illinois Archives, Urbana-Champaign.

Henry, David D. Remarks at ceremony dedicating Morrow Plots as a National Historic Landmark, September 12, 1968.

"History of Japan House." UIUC College of Fine and Applied Arts on the U of I. See http://japanhouse.art.uiuc.edu/information/history.

The Illini, May 16, 1891; November 22, 1893.

Illinois Alumni, June 26, 1929; June 1963; December 1969; November 1971; July/August 2000; March/April 2010; Summer 2011; Spring 2014.

Illinois Engineer, October 1960.

Illinois Quarterly, September 1989.

"In Probate: In the Matter of the Estate of George W. Davidson, Deceased." Filed October 4, 1915, Champaign County Court.

Inside Illinois, December 4, 1997.

Investing in Illinois. University of Illinois Foundation newsletter, Winter 2004.

James, Edmund Janes. "A Center for Helpful Associations." *Alumni Quarterly and Fortnightly Notes of the University of Illinois*, January 15, 1916, 177-78.

Jamieson, Bridget. Memo from Campus Communication Council to U of I listserv on *Alma Mater* refurbishing update, March 4, 2013.

Kinley, David. Letter James White to January 14, 1924. David Kinley General Correspondence. University of Illinois Archives, Urbana-Champaign.

———. Letter to James White, May 31, 1930. David Kinley General Correspondence. University of Illinois Archives, Urbana-Champaign.

———. Letter to James White, November 29, 1930. David Kinley General Correspondence. University of Illinois Archives, Urbana-Champaign.

Kroner, Fred. *"A Saucer Coming to Rest": A Half Century of the Assembly Hall*. With Melissa Merli. Champaign, Ill.: News-Gazette, 2013.

Liden, Elisabeth, *Between Water and Heaven*. Stockholm, Sweden: Almqvist and Wiksell International, 1986.

"Life and Death on the Prairie: A Tour of Mount Hope Cemetery." Brochure. Preservation and Conservation Association and the Champaign Theater Company, undated, ca. 2007.

Lock, John. Communications Associate, Fighting Illini-Division of Intercollegiate Athletics, e-mail to Lex Tate, August 10, 2011.

"Max Abramovitz." *Chicago Tribune*, April 2, 2008.

"Morrow Plots." Reference Folder, University of Illinois Archives; "Morrow Plots Song," by Bruce Johnson, The Other Guys, 1971.

"The Morrow Plots: A Symbol of Hope." U of I College of Agriculture Special Publication 16, January 1969.

Muriel Scheinman Papers, University of Illinois Archives.

News Gazette (Champaign, Ill.), March 9, 1957; January 9, 1963; December 4, 1966; September 13, 1968; January 28, 1973; June 15, 1978; March 14, 1982; July 1, 1988; September 3, 1995; November 16, 1998; June 9, 2000; April 12 and 20, May 3 and 20, July 15, and October 20, 2009; February 17, May 6, and September 18, 2012; January 9, March 7, April 30, and June 8, 2013; February 23, March 14, April 1, 9, and 10, May 14, June 14, and July 14, 2014.

New York Times, September 15, 2004.

Pantagraph (Bloomington, Ill.), November 27, 2006.

Perspectives on Campus Planning. Issue 25 (2010). Dober Lidsky Mathey, Creating Campus Solutions, Belmont, Massachusetts.

"Portal from UI's Past a Part of New Gateway." *News-Gazette* (Champaign, IL), October 9, 1998.

"Programme of Dedicatory Exercises of the New University Building, Wednesday, December 10, 1873." University of Illinois Archives. See http://uihistories.library.illinois.edu/REPOSITORYCACHE/84/IvDLW1FJtNkdG3Of35J9z2A42r4yfolcvVC-n2beE3sq31AAmDQ9UPB80M9FUz3gjW99l0R96qP0VDzvm-wwZtXWeRn4Gik6N4frEhQh6Z082_30658.pdf.

Rhode, C. S., and W. A. Foster. "Building and Remodeling Dairy Barns." University of Illinois College of Agriculture *Circular* 478 (October 1937).

Ross, Betsy. Oral history interview. August 30, 1967. Betsy Ross Papers. University of Illinois Archives, Urbana-Champaign.

Roth, Leland. *A Concise History of American Architecture*. New York: Harper and Row, 1979.

"Round Dairy Barns." National Register of Historic Places Inventory—Nomination Form, 1990.

Scheinman, Muriel. *A Guide to Art at the University of Illinois: Urbana-Champaign, Robert Allerton Park and Chicago*. Urbana: University of Illinois Press, 1995.

Skvarla, Melvyn. Interview. Campus Historic Preservation Officer, U of I Facilities and Services, July 22, 2011.

Solberg, Winton U. *The University of Illinois, 1867-1894: An Intellectual and Cultural History*, Urbana: University of Illinois Press, 1968.

Spencer, Nelson S. Letter to Board of Trustees, 1908.

Stephens, Carl. *Illini Years: A Picture History of the University of Illinois*. Urbana: University of Illinois Press, 1950.

Stouffer, Ernest L. Letter to Arthur Willard, May 1, 1946. Arthur Willard General Correspondence. University of Illinois Archives, Urbana-Champaign.

——. Letter to R. S. Chamberlin, October 22, 1951. Physical Plant Director's Office Subject File. University of Illinois Archives, Urbana-Champaign.

Tapales, Athena. Memo to Vice Chancellor for Student Affairs Stanley R. Levy, May 2, 1990.

Tate, Lex. Personal and phone interviews with Champaign Mayor Dan McCollum, April–May 2009.

Tate, Loren. *News-Gazette* (Champaign, Ill.) sports columnist, e-mail to Lex Tate, June 28, 2011.

Ten Years: Illini Union. Urbana: University of Illinois at Urbana-Champaign, 1951.

University of Illinois Campus Tours. See http://illinois.edu/about/tours.html.

University of Illinois Foundation newsletter 8 (Late Spring 1995).

Viravec, Andrea. *The Plotting of the University's History*. Preservation and Conservation Association cemetery file, undated.

"A Walk in the Past." Champaign County Historical Museum newsletter, Fall 2007.

Watson, Frances B. Letter from Watson and Memorial Committee Chairman Rodney E. Spangler to President David D. Henry, July 30, 1969.

——. Letter to President David D. Henry, November 25, 1969.

——. Meeting notes, class of 1921 Memorial Committee meeting, May 3, 1969.

Weiss, Andrew. Champaign Parks Planner/Landscape Architect e-mail, August 11, 2015.

"Welcome Change." *Illinois Alumni*, July/August 1998.

Weller, Allen S. Letter to Granville S. Keith. December 5, 1963. University of Illinois Archives, Urbana-Champaign.

White, James. Letter to David Kinley, January 8, 1924. Physical Plant Director's Office Subject File. University of Illinois Archives, Urbana-Champaign.

——. Letter to David Kinley, May 24, 1930. Physical Plant Director's Office Subject File. University of Illinois Archives, Urbana-Champaign.

Willard, Arthur. Letter to Avery Brundage, September 29, 1937. Arthur Willard General Correspondence. University of Illinois Archives, Urbana-Champaign.

——. Letter to Charles Havens, July 27, 1938. Arthur Willard General Correspondence. University of Illinois Archives, Urbana-Champaign.

——. Letter to D. R. Kennicott dated Nov. 21, 1938. Arthur Willard General Correspondence. University of Illinois Archives, Urbana-Champaign.

Woody, F. Way. "Recollections of University of Illinois Early Athletic History," August 10, 1937, University of Illinois Archives.

Index

Page numbers in italic reference images.

LEX TATE is an adjunct lecturer in journalism and advertising at the University of Illinois at Urbana-Champaign, and served as associate director of the University of Illinois Office for University Relations.

JOHN FRANCH is the author of *Robber Baron: The Life of Charles Tyson Yerkes.*

The University of Illinois Press
is a founding member of the
Association of American University Presses.

Text designed by Jennifer S. Holzner
Composed in 10.75/15.25 Georgia
by Jennifer S. Holzner
at the University of Illinois Press
Cover designed by Jennifer S. Holzner
Cover photo by L. Brian Stauffer. University of Illinois News Bureau
Manufactured by Bang Printing

University of Illinois Press
1325 South Oak Street
Champaign, IL 61820-6903
www.press.uillinois.edu